Reader's Guide
to
SAMUEL COLERIDGE

Reader's Guide
to
SAMUEL COLERIDGE

John T. Nichol

CENTRUM PRESS
NEW DELHI-110002 (INDIA)

CENTRUM PRESS
H.O.: 4360/4, Ansari Road, Daryaganj,
New Delhi-110 002 (India)
Ph.: 23278000, 23261597

B.O.: No. 1015, Ist Main Road, BSK IIIrd Stage
IIIrd Phase, IIIrd Block,
Bangalore - 560 085 (India)
Tel.: 080-41723429
Visit us at: www.centrumpress.com

Reader's Guide to Samuel Coleridge

First Edition, 2009

ISBN 978-93-80106-62-5

PRINTED IN INDIA

Printed at Salasar Imaging Systems, Delhi-110035 (India)

Contents

Preface

Samuel Taylor Coleridge, English lyrical poet, critic, and philosopher, whose *Lyrical Ballads*,(1798) written with William Wordsworth, started the English Romantic movement. Samuel Taylor Coleridge was born in Ottery St Mary, Devonshire, as the youngest son of the vicar of Ottery St Mary. After his father's death Coleridge was sent away to Christ's Hospital School in London. He also studied at Jesus College. In Cambridge Coleridge met the radical, future poet laureate Robert Southey. He moved with Southey to Bristol to establish a community, but the plan failed.

In 1795 he married the sister of Southey's fiancée Sara Fricker, whom he did not really love. Inclined to investigate the complexities of the human condition, both poetically and philosophically, Coleridge has tried to resolve the extremes of human existence through a synthesis of both western and oriental visions through which the universe ultimately emerges as an organic cosmos rhythmically unfolding through an intricate web of influxes, echoes and correspondences.

Coleridge's collection *Poems On Various Subjects* was published in 1796, and in 1797 appeared *Poems*. In the same year he began the publication of a short-lived liberal political periodical *The Watchman*. He started a close friendship with Dorothy and William Wordsworth, one of the most fruitful creative relationships in English literature. From it resulted *Lyrical Ballads,* which opened with Coleridge's "Rime of the Ancient Mariner" and ended with Wordsworth's "Tintern Abbey". These poems set a new style by using everyday language and fresh ways of looking at nature.

Author

Chapter 1

Introduction

Samuel Taylor Coleridge was an English poet, critic and philosopher who was, along with his friend William Wordsworth, one of the founders of the Romantic Movement in England and one of the Lake Poets. He was born on 21 October 1772 in the rural town of Ottery St Mary, Devonshire. He was the youngest of ten children, and his father, the Reverend John Coleridge, was a well respected vicar. Coleridge suffered from constant ridicule by his older brother Frank, partially due to jealousy, as Samuel was often praised and favoured by his parents.

He is probably best known for his poems *The Rime of the Ancient Mariner* and *Kubla Khan*, as well as his major prose work *Biographia Literaria*. To escape this abuse, he frequently sought refuge at a local library, which led him to discover his passion for poetry.

In one of a series of biographical letters written to Thomas Poole, Coleridge wrote:

"At six years old I remember to have read *Belisarius*, *Robinson Crusoe*, and *Philip Quarll* - and then I found the *Arabian Nights' Entertainments* - one tale of which (the tale of a man who was compelled to seek for a pure virgin) made so deep an impression on me (I had read it in the evening while my mother was mending stockings) that I was haunted by spectres whenever I was in the dark - and I distinctly remember the anxious and fearful eagerness with which I used to watch the window in which the books lay - and whenever the sun lay upon them, I would seize it, carry it by the wall, and bask, and read."

After the death of his father in 1781, contrary to his desires, he was sent to Christ's Hospital. The school was originally founded in the 16th century in Greyfriars, London and Hertford. It is now a boarding school in West Sussex. The school was notorious for its unwelcoming atmosphere and strict regimen under the Rev. James Bowyer, many years head master of the grammar school, which fostered thoughts of guilt and depression in young Samuel's maturing mind.

However, Coleridge seems to have appreciated his teacher, as he wrote in detailed recollections of his schooldays in *Biographia Literaria*:

"I enjoyed the inestimable advantage of a very sensible, though at the same time, a very severe master...At the same time that we were studying the Greek Tragic Poets, he made us read Shakspeare and Milton as lessons: and they were the lessons too, which required most time and trouble to bring up, so as to escape his censure. I learnt from him, that Poetry, even that of the loftiest, and, seemingly, that of the wildest odes, had a logic of its own, as severe as that of science; and more difficult, because more subtle, more complex, and dependent on more, and more fugitive causes....

In our own English compositions (at least for the last three years of our school education) he showed no mercy to phrase, metaphor, or image, unsupported by a sound sense, or where the same sense might have been conveyed with equal force and dignity in plainer words... In fancy I can almost hear him now, exclaiming *Harp? Harp? Lyre? Pen and ink, boy, you mean! Muse, boy, Muse? your Nurse's daughter, you mean! Pierian spring? Oh aye! the cloister-pump, I suppose!...* Be this as it may, there was one custom of our master's, which I cannot pass over in silence, because I think it ... worthy of imitation. He would often permit our theme exercises,... to accumulate, till each lad had four or five to be looked over. Then placing the whole number abreast on his desk, he would ask the writer, why this or that sentence might not have found as appropriate a place under this or that other thesis: and if no satisfying answer could be returned, and two faults of the same kind were found in one exercise, the irrevocable verdict followed, the exercise was torn up, and another on the same subject to be produced, in addition to the tasks of the day."

Throughout life, Coleridge idealized his father as pious and innocent, while his relationship with his mother was more problematic. His childhood was characterized by attention seeking, which has been linked to his dependent personality as an adult. He was rarely allowed to return home during the school term, and this distance from his family at such a turbulent time proved emotionally damaging. He later wrote of his loneliness at school in the poem *Frost at Midnight*: "With unclosed lids, already had I dreamt/Of my sweet birthplace"

From 1791 until 1794, Coleridge attended Jesus College, Cambridge. In 1792, he won the Browne Gold Medal for an ode that he wrote on the slave trade. In November 1793, he left the college and enlisted in the Royal Dragoons, perhaps because of debt or because the girl that he loved, Mary Evans, had rejected him. Afterwards, he was rumored to have had a bout with severe depression. His brothers arranged for his discharge a few months later (ironically because of supposed homosexuality) and he was readmitted to Jesus College, though he would never receive a degree from Cambridge.

Pantisocracy and marriage

At the university, he was introduced to political and theological ideas then considered radical, including those of the poet Robert Southey. Coleridge joined Southey in a plan, soon abandoned, to found a utopian commune-like society, called pantisocracy, in the wilderness of Pennsylvania. In 1795, the two friends married sisters Sara and Edith Fricker, but Coleridge's marriage proved unhappy. He grew to detest his wife, whom he only married because of social constraints. He eventually divorced her. In 1795, Coleridge met poet William Wordsworth and his sister Dorothy. They became immediate friends.

Around 1796, Coleridge started taking Laudanum as a pain-reliever. His suffering, caused by many ailments, including toothache and facial neuralgia, is mentioned in his own notebook as well as that of Dorothy Wordsworth. There was no stigma associated with taking opium at the time, but also little understanding of the dangers of addiction.

The years 1797 and 1798, during which he lived in what is know known as Coleridge Cottage, in Nether Stowey, Somerset, were among the most fruitful of Coleridge's life. (Wordsworth, having visited him and being enchanted by the surroundings, rented Alfoxton Park, a little over three miles [5 km] away.) Besides the *Rime of The Ancient Mariner*, he composed the symbolic poem *Kubla Khan*, written—Coleridge himself claimed—as a result of an opium dream, in "a kind of a reverie"; and the first part of the narrative poem *Christabel*. The writing of *Kubla Khan*, written about the Asian emperor Kublai Khan, was said to have been interrupted by the arrival of a "Person from Porlock"—an event that has been embellished upon in such varied contexts as science fiction and Nabokov's *Lolita*. During this period, he also produced his much-praised "conversation" poems *This Lime-Tree Bower My Prison, Frost at Midnight,* and *The Nightingale.*

A statue of the Ancient Mariner at Watchet Harbour, Somerset, England, unveiled in September 2003 as a tribute to Samuel Taylor Coleridge.

Ah ! well a-day ! what evil looks
Had I from old and young !
Instead of the cross, the Albatross
About my neck was hung.

In 1798, Coleridge and Wordsworth published a joint volume of poetry, *Lyrical Ballads,* which proved to be the starting point for the English romantic movement. Though the productive Wordsworth contributed more poems, Coleridge's first version of *The Rime of the Ancient Mariner* was the longest poem and drew more immediate attention than anything else in the volume.

In the spring of 1798, Coleridge temporarily took over for Rev. Joshua Toulmin at Taunton's Mary Street Unitarian Chapel while Rev. Toulmin grieved over the drowning death of his daughter Jane. Poetically commenting on Toulmin's strength, Coleridge wrote in a 1798 letter to John Prior Estlin,

I walked into Taunton (eleven miles) and back again, and

performed the divine services for Dr. Toulmin. I suppose you must have heard that his daughter, (Jane, on 15 April 1798) in a melancholy derangement, suffered herself to be swallowed up by the tide on the sea-coast between Sidmouth and Bere (sic. Beer). These events cut cruelly into the hearts of old men: but the good Dr. Toulmin bears it like the true practical Christian, - there is indeed a tear in his eye, but that eye is lifted up to the Heavenly Father.

In the autumn of 1798, Coleridge and Wordsworth left for a stay in Germany; Coleridge soon went his own way and spent much of his time in university towns. During this period, he became interested in German philosophy, especially the transcendental idealism of Immanuel Kant, and in the literary criticism of the 18th century dramatist Gotthold Lessing. Coleridge studied German and, after his return to England, translated the dramatic trilogy *Wallenstein* by the German Classical poet Friedrich Schiller into English.

In 1799, Coleridge and Wordsworth stayed at Thomas Hutchinson's farm on the Tees at Sockburn, near Darlington. There both of them fell in love, Coleridge with Sara Hutchinson ('Asra'), and Wordsworth with her sister Mary, whom he married in 1802.

It was at Sockburn that Coleridge wrote his ballad-poem *Love,* addressed to Sara. The knight mentioned is the mailed figure on the Conyers tomb in ruined Sockburn church. The figure has a wyvern at his feet, a reference to the Sockburn worm slain by Sir John Conyers (and a possible source for Lewis Carroll's Jabberwock). The worm was supposedly buried under the rock in the nearby pasture; this was the 'greystone' of Coleridge's first draft, later transformed into a 'mount'. The poem was a direct inspiration for John Keats' famous poem *La Belle Dame Sans Merci.*

Coleridge's greatest intellectual debts were first to William Godwin's *Political Justice,* especially during his Pantisocratic period, and to David Hartley's *Observations on Man,* which is the source of the psychology which is found in *Frost at Midnight.* Hartley argued that one becomes aware of sensory events as impressions, and that "ideas" are derived by noticing similarities and differences between impressions and then by naming them. Connections resulting from the coincidence of impressions create linkages, so that the occurrence of one impression triggers those links and calls up the memory of those ideas with which it is associated.

Coleridge was critical of the literary taste of his contemporaries, and a literary conservative insofar as he was afraid that the lack of taste in the ever growing masses of literate people would mean a continued desecration of literature itself.

In 1800, he returned to England and shortly thereafter settled with his family and friends at Keswick in the Lake District of Cumberland to be near Grasmere, where Wordsworth had moved. Soon, however, he was beset by marital problems, illnesses, increased opium dependency, tensions with Wordsworth, and a lack of confidence in his poetic powers, all of which fueled the composition of *Dejection: An Ode* and an intensification of his philosophical studies.

Growing dependency on opium

In 1804, he traveled to Sicily and Malta, working for a time as Acting Public Secretary of Malta under the Commissioner, Alexander Ball. He gave this up and returned to England in 1806. Dorothy Wordsworth was shocked at his condition upon his return. From 1807 to 1808, Coleridge returned to Malta and then traveled in Sicily and Italy, in the hope that leaving Britain's damp climate would improve his health and thus enable him to reduce his consumption of opium. Thomas de Quincey alleges in his *Recollections of the Lakes and the Lake Poets* that it was during this period that Coleridge became a full-blown opium addict, using the drug as a substitute for the lost vigour and creativity of his youth. It has been suggested, however, that this reflects de Quincey's own experiences more than Coleridge's.

His opium addiction (he was using as much as two quarts of laudanum a week) now began to take over his life: he separated from his wife in 1808, quarreled with Wordsworth in 1810, lost part of his annuity in 1811, and put himself under the care of Dr. Daniel in 1814.

In 1809, Coleridge instigated his second attempt to become a newspaper publisher with the publication of the journal entitled *The Friend*. It was a weekly publication that, in Coleridge's typically ambitious style, was written, edited, and published almost entirely single-handedly. Given that Coleridge tended to be highly disorganized and had no head for business meant that the publication was doomed from the start. Coleridge financed the journal by selling over five hundred subscriptions, over two dozen of which were sold to members of Parliament. *The Friend* was an eclectic publication that drew upon every corner of Coleridge's remarkably diverse knowledge of law, philosophy, morals, politics, history, and literary criticism. Although it was often turgid, rambling, and inaccessible to most readers, it ran for 25 issues and was republished in book form a number of times. Years after its initial publication, *The Friend* became a highly influential work and its effect was felt on writers and philosophers from J.S. Mill to Emerson.

Between 1810 and 1820, this "giant among dwarfs", as he was often considered by his contemporaries, gave a series of lectures in London and Bristol – those on Shakespeare renewed interest in the playwright as a model for contemporary writers. Much of Coleridge's reputation as a literary critic is founded on the lectures that he undertook in the winter of 1810-11 which were sponsored by the Philosophical Institution and given at Scot's Corporation Hall off Fetter Lane, Fleet Street. These lectures were heralded in the prospectus as "A Course of Lectures on Shakespeare and Milton, in Illustration of the Principles of Poetry."

Coleridge's ill-health, opium-addiction problems, and somewhat unstable personality meant that all his lectures were plagued with problems of delays and a general irregularity of quality from one lecture to the next. Furthermore, Coleridge's mind was extremely dynamic and his personality was spasmodic. As a result of these factors, Coleridge often failed to prepare anything but the loosest set of notes for his lectures and regularly entered into extremely long digressions which his audiences found difficult to follow. However, it was the lecture on *Hamlet* given on 2 January 1812 that was considered the best and has influenced *Hamlet* studies ever since. Before Coleridge, *Hamlet* was often denigrated and belittled by critics from Voltaire to Dr. Johnson. Coleridge rescued *Hamlet* and his thoughts on the play are often still published as supplements to the text.

In August 1814, Coleridge was approached by Lord Byron's publisher, John Murray, about the possibility of translating Goethe's infamous occult classic *Faust* (1808). Coleridge was regarded by many as the greatest living writer on the demonic and he accepted the commission, only to abandon work on it after six weeks. Until recently, scholars have accepted that Coleridge never returned to the project, despite Goethe's own belief in the 1820s that Coleridge had in fact completed a long translation of the work. In September 2007, Oxford University Press sparked a heated scholarly controversy by publishing an English translation of Goethe's work which purported to be Coleridge's long-lost masterpiece. The text in question first appeared anonymously in 1821.

In 1817, Coleridge, with his addiction worsening, his spirits depressed, and his family alienated, took residence in the home of the physician James Gillman, first at South Grove and later at the nearby 3 The Grove, Highgate, London, England. He remained there for the rest of his life, and the house became a place of literary pilgrimage of writers including Carlyle and Emerson. In Gillman's home, he finished his major prose work, the *Biographia Literaria* (1815), a volume composed of 23 chapters of autobiographical notes and dissertations on various subjects, including some incisive literary theory and criticism.

He composed much poetry here and had many inspirations — a few of them from opium overdose. Perhaps because he conceived such grand projects, he had difficulty carrying them through to completion, and he berated himself for his "indolence". It is unclear whether his growing use of opium (and the brandy in which it was dissolved) was a symptom or a cause of his growing depression.

He published other writings while he was living at the

Gillman home, notably *Sibylline Leaves* (1820), *Aids to Reflection* (1823), and *Church and State* (1826). He died of a lung disorder including some heart failure from the opium that he was taking in Highgate on 25 July 1834.

Where Coleridge first developed his opium habit is an issue of some scholarly dispute but it clearly dates from a fairly youthful period in his life. Coleridge's own explanation is clearly laid out in a letter to Joseph Cottle. The explanation may, in fact, be the truth as Coleridge remembered it, but as with much of what Coleridge says, it should be taken with a grain of salt.

However, as good as this story is, everyone who has dealt with the issue of addiction knows, any statement by a victim of addiction concerning their drug use should not be taken at face value. Whatever Coleridge said about his use of opium during the time of this painful illness, most scholars agree that he had resorted to the use of Laudanum (the tincture form of opium) before this date, particularly during times of nervousness and stress. Because Laudanum was widely available and widely used as an analgesic as well as a general sedative, many people were given the drug for all sorts of medical and nervous complaints.

Coleridge was probably given the drug numerous times in his youth during several bouts of rheumatic illness. These small medicinal dosages seldom led to full-blown addiction but for Coleridge, who experienced the painful return of the symptoms many times in his life, it surely introduced him to the use of the drug much earlier than his story to Cottle admits. Regardless of when and where Coleridge's opium addiction began, it is clear that the more reliant on the drug he became, the more his work suffered, the less he was able to focus and concentrate, and the more strained his relations became. In fact, it is arguable that any analysis of Coleridge's life must be done against the constant background of opium usage.

But as important as the issue of opium is in Coleridge's life, it is never a straightforward issue because he often hid it from public and familial view and at other times he exaggerated its importance to his work. In the 1816 publication of this major 'opium' poems Coleridge purposely drew a connection between his creative work and his opium usage. Desperate for some financial success with his poetry, Coleridge intentionally attempted to portray himself as a dreamy-opium eater because he, perhaps rightly, believed that it would draw a morbid fascination to his work. Opium played an interesting role in the public image of Romantic literature. There was, for a long time, a kind of cult glamorization of the drug and a morose allure to stories of its usage for respectable members of the bourgeoisie who were titillated by such taboo subjects. It was with this in mind that Coleridge generated an image of himself as dreamy poet who created drug induced fantasies.

This dreamy image of himself began even before he was widely known to have been addicted to opium. In one of a series of biographical letters written to his friend Thomas Poole Coleridge painted this picture of himself, a picture that would always endure.

This slothful image was one that endured even with some of Coleridge's close friends and may have been consciously created by Coleridge in the earlier part of his career in order to draw attention away from his addiction. It was only later, as pointed out above, that Coleridge perceived an advantage to drawing attention not to himself as simply a slothful scholar but a dreamy opium eater. However, again one must treat the idea that Coleridge's most famous poems were actually rooted in his opium usage with a degree of scepticism. The most popular story that connects Coleridge's work with his opium usage was created by Coleridge in his well known story of the creation of Kubla Khan. Coleridge wrote:

"The author continued for about 3 hours in a profound sleep, at least of the external senses, during which time he has the most vivid confidence, that he could not have composed less than from two or three hundred lines ... On waking he appeared to himself to have a distinct recollection of the whole and taking up his pen, ink, and paper, instantly and eagerly wrote the lines that are here preserved. At this moment he was unfortunately called out by a person on business from Porlock, & and detained by him above an hour, and on his return to his room found, to his no small surprise and mortification, that though he still retained some vague and dim recollection of the general purport of the vision, yet, with the exception of some eight or ten scattered lines and images, all the rest had passed away like the images on the surfaces of a stream into which a stone has been cast, but alas! without the after restoration of the later!."

The sleep of this story, which is endless repeated, is implied to be a sleep of opium. Much speculation has surrounded this story concerning the identity of the stranger from Porlock,(Person from Porlock) or indeed whether it is not, in fact, a complete fabrication. Coleridge had the long standing habit of changing, or even fabricating, the dates of certain poems in order to create a more interesting, one might say romantic, story around his creative acts. These fabrications, along with the long and complicated story surrounding his various acts of plagiarism, can in large part be put down to the effects of opium, for if truth is the first casualty of war, then it is also the first casualty of addiction. To understand Coleridge it is important not to see him as simply a weak, slothful, man who lied, plagiarized, and abandoned his wife and children. Rather, his behaviour closely corresponds to the kind of difficulties that arise from typical morphine abuse and addiction. Coleridge, in his lucid moments, understood these problems with which he struggled better than most. In an 1814 letter to his friend John Morgan, Coleridge wrote about his difficulties.

"In exact proportion, as I loved any person or persons more than others, & would have sacrificed my life to them, were they sure to be the most barbarously mistreated by silence, absence, or breach of promise. What Crime is there scarcely which has not been included in or followed from the one guilt of taking opium? Not to speak of ingratitude to my maker for the wasted Talents; of ingratitude to so many friends who have loved me I know not why; of barbarous neglect of my family ... I have in this one dirty business of Laudanum an hundred times deceived, tricked, nay, actually & consciously LIED. – And yet all these vices are so opposite to my nature, that but for the free-agency-annihilating Poison, I verily believe that I should have suffered myself to be cut in pieces rather than have committed any one of them."

Unfortunately, as much as Coleridge had some grasp of his addictions and its results, as well as an unusually sharp sense of how this addiction might be treated, many of his closest friends and peers did not understand. The people who might have served him best, like Southey and Wordsworth, were far too willing to maintain his image as slothful and selfish; this despite the professional help that he constantly bestowed upon them. Men like Robert Southey, naturally conservative in outlook were not forward looking enough to comprehend the possibility of Coleridge's addiction being a largely physical dependence, despite the fact that Coleridge himself, as well as a growing number of professionals like his friend Gillman, were aware of the physical aspect of drug reliance.

On more than one occasion Coleridge pointed to the fact that physical restraint might eventually lead to a cure, and on several occasions under the treatment of Dr. Gillman, he was led thus to the edge of freedom from the drug on which he had formed such a dependence. Southey wrote from the position of moral indignation and explicitly denied the physical aspect of the drug issue. Southey wrote to Cottle:

"...while acknowledging the guilt of the habit, he impute it still to morbid bodily causes, whereas ... every person who has witnessed his habits, knows that for ... infinitely the greater part – inclination and indulgence are the motives. It seems dreadful to say this ... but it is so and I know it to be so, from my own observation and that of all with whom he has lived ... This, Cottle, is an insanity of that species which none but the Soul's physician can cure."

Coleridge in Highgate

In April of 1816 Coleridge's friend and physician, Joseph Adams, put him in touch with a Highgate doctor named James Gillman with the intention of placing Coleridge in his fulltime care and effect a cure to his addiction problems. Although

Gillman initially had no intention of taking this stranger into his household, he was so charmed by the poet on their first meeting that he agreed to take him in and attempt a cure.

Coleridge spent most of the rest of his life in the Gillman house with only brief periods away. James Gillman was ahead of his time as a physician of addiction and although he was never able to entirely stop Coleridge's intake of opium, he managed to bring it under greater control for many years. It is surely to Gillman's treatment and friendship that we owe much of Coleridge's later prose works, particularly his Biographia Literaria, Lay Sermons, and Opus Maximum.

Coleridge virtually became a member of the Gillman family and even accompanied them on annual vacations. On a number of occasions when Coleridge was away from the Gillman household and fell back into excessive opium use. Each time Gillman managed to step in and return Coleridge to his home and to controlled, less harmful opium dosages. The pharmacy where the poet obtained his prescribed supply (and sometimes, an illicit addition to it) still exists in the High Street, though moved a few dozen yards from the original premises.

Gillman later became one of the great champions of Coleridge's reputation and commonly defended his friend in polite society and in print with one of the earliest biographies of Coleridge. Coleridge's reputation was somewhat restored during his years at Highgate and in his lucid periods he became a kind of elder-statesman of the literary establishment and was visited by many of the period's most important writers and thinkers. Despite Gillman's care, however, Coleridge was overcome with respiratory problems and enlargement of the heart typical of prolonged opium usage. Coleridge died at the relatively young age of 62.

Poetry

Coleridge is probably best known for his long poems, *The Rime of the Ancient Mariner* and *Christabel*. Even those who have never read the *Rime* have come under its influence: its words have given the English language the metaphor of an albatross around one's neck, the quotation of "water, water everywhere, ne any drop to drink (almost always rendered as "but not a drop to drink")", and the phrase "a sadder and a wiser man (again, usually rendered as "sadder but wiser man")". *Christabel* is known for its musical rhythm, language, and its Gothic tale.

Kubla Khan, or, *A Vision in a Dream, A Fragment*, although shorter, is also widely known. Both *Kubla Khan* and *Christabel* have an additional "romantic" aura because they were never finished. Stopford Brooke characterised both poems as having no rival due to their "exquisite metrical movement" and "imaginative phrasing."

Coleridge's shorter, meditative "conversation poems," however, proved to be the most influential of his work. These include both quiet poems like *This Lime-Tree Bower My Prison* and *Frost at Midnight* and also strongly emotional poems like *Dejection* and *The Pains of Sleep*. Wordsworth immediately adopted the model of these poems, and used it to compose several of his major poems. Via Wordsworth, the conversation poem became a standard vehicle for English poetic expression, and perhaps the most common approach among modern poets. *The Eolian Harp*, Speaking symbolically in terms of harp and breeze, Coleridge's implication is that each being is but a single part of the world-soul or over-spirit that emanates from the One. It is interesting to note that Coleridge for the moment feels he has ventured too far, for he then retracts "these shapings of the unregenerate mind," and concludes the poem vowing to forsake "vain philosophy's aye-babbling spring."

It is important to understand that despite not enjoying the name recognition or popular acclaim that Wordsworth or Shelley have had, Coleridge is one of the most important figures in English poetry. His poems directly and deeply influenced all the major poets of the age. He was known by his contemporaries as a meticulous craftsman who was more rigorous in his careful reworking of his poems than any other poet, and Southey and Wordsworth were dependent on his professional advice. His influence on Wordsworth is particularly important because many critics have credited

Coleridge with the very idea of "Conversational Poetry". The idea of utilizing common, everyday language to express profound poetic images and ideas for which Wordsworth became so famous may have originated almost entirely in Coleridge's mind. It is difficult to imagine Wordsworth's great poems, *The Excursion* or *The Prelude,* ever having been written without the direct influence of Coleridge's originality.

And as important as Coleridge was to poetry as a poet, he was equally important to poetry as a critic. Coleridge's philosophy of poetry, which he developed over many years, has been deeply influential in the field of literary criticism. This influence can be seen in such critics as A.O.Lovejoy and I.A. Richards.

Coleridge and the influence of the Gothic

Gothic novels like Polidori's *The Vampire,* Walpole's *The Castle of Otranto,* Mrs Radcliffe's *The Mysteries of Udolpho* and *The Italian,* and Matthew Lewis's *The Monk* were the best-sellers of the end of the eighteenth century, and thrilled many young women (who were often strictly forbidden to read them). Jane Austen satirised the style mercilessly in *Northanger Abbey.*

Coleridge wrote reviews of Mrs Radcliffe's books and *The Mad Monk,* among others. He comments in his reviews:

"Situations of torment, and images of naked horror, are easily conceived; and a writer in whose works they abound, deserves our gratitude almost equally with him who should drag us by way of sport through a military hospital, or force us to sit at the dissecting-table of a natural philosopher. To trace the nice boundaries, beyond which terror and sympathy are deserted by the pleasurable emotions, - to reach those limits, yet never to pass them, hic labour, hic opus est." and:

"The horrible and the preternatural have usually seized on the popular taste, at the rise and decline of literature. Most powerful stimulants, they can never be required except by the torpor of an unawakened, or the languor of an exhausted, appetite... We trust, however, that satiety will banish what good sense should have prevented; and that, wearied with fiends, incomprehensible characters, with shrieks, murders, and subterraneous dungeons, the public will learn, by the multitude of the manufacturers, with how little expense of thought or imagination this species of composition is manufactured."

However, Coleridge used these elements in poems such as *The Rime of the Ancient Mariner* (1798), *Christabel* and *Kubla Khan* (published in 1816, but known in manuscript form before then) and certainly influenced other poets and writers of the time. Poems like this both drew inspiration from and helped to inflame the craze for Gothic romance.

Mary Shelley, who knew Coleridge well, mentions *The Rime of the Ancient Mariner* twice directly in *Frankenstein,* and some of the descriptions in the novel echo it indirectly. Although William Godwin, her father, disagreed with Coleridge on some important issues, he respected his opinions and Coleridge often visited the Godwins. Mary Shelley later recalled hiding behind the sofa and hearing his voice chanting *The Rime of the Ancient Mariner.*

Chapter 2

His Conversation Poems

Samuel Taylor Coleridge, to those who know him well, exists in three modes, as Philosopher, Poet, Friend. If the truth were told, we should all be obliged to admit that the Philosopher escapes us. We hear his voice and enter the room where he is speaking, only to see his retreating figure down some dim corridor. 'Aids to Reflection,' 'Table Talk,' and other echoes of his speach yield merely a confused murmur, baffling, and the more exasperating because the tones are in themselves melodious....

It is the opinion of many that Coleridge as Poet is almost equally an evanescent shadow; and though the many are in this quite mistaken, they have some excuse for thinking thus, because his fulfilment falls far short of his promise. But they fail to appreciate how very great, after all, the fulfilment is. The causes of this injustice to Coleridge the Poet are the splendor of the three poems of his which everybody knows and admires, and also the habit of regarding him as a mere satellite of Wordsworth, or at least as Wordsworth's weaker brother.

Those who are so dazzled by 'The Rime of the Ancient Mariner,' 'Kubla Khan,' and 'Cristabel.' that all the rest of Coleridge's poetry seems to them colorless, are invited to reopen his book, but first to read J. Dykes Campbell's Life of him [*or that by Richard Holmes*] or the collection of his wonderful letters edited by the late Ernest Hartley Coleridge, his grandson; and I wish to direct the attention of those from whom he is obscured by the greater glory of Wordsworth to a group of poems which can be compared only to the 'Lines composed a few miles above Tintern Abbey.' These are his Poems of Friendship. They cannot be even vaguely understood unless the reader knows what persons Coleridge has in mind. They are, for the most part, poems in which reference is made with fine particularity to certain places. They were composed as the expression of feelings which were occasioned by quite definite events.

Between the lines, when we know their meaning, we catch glimpses of those delightful people who formed the golden inner circle of his friends in the days of his young manhood: Charles Lamb, his oldest and dearest, Mary Lamb, practical Tom Poole, William and Dorothy Wordsworth in their days of clearest vision and warmest enthusiasm, and in the later pieces Mrs. Wordsworth and Sarah Hutchinson her young sister.

They may all be termed, as Coleridge himself names one or two of them, Conversation Poems, for even when they are soliloquies the sociable man who wrote them could not even think without supposing a listener. They require and reward considerable knowledge of his life and especially the life of his heart.

This is not so certainly the case with his three famous Mystery Poems, in which the spellbound reader sees visions and hears music which float in from a magic realm and float out again into unfathomable space. Their perfection is not of this world nor founded on history or circumstance. No knowledge of their origin or mechanism can increase their beauty or enrich their charm. To attempt to account for them, to write footnotes about them, if it were hoped thereby to make them more powerful in their effect upon the imagination, would be ridiculous and pedantic, however fruitful of knowledge and interest the exercise might be.

While the Philosopher has wandered away into a vague limbo of unfinished projects and the Poet of 'Cristabel' and its companion stars can only gaze in mute wonder upon the constellation he fixed in the heavens, the Poet of the Friendly Pieces lingers among us and can be questioned. We owe it to him and to ourselves to appreciate them. It is unfair to his genius that he should be represented in most anthologies of English verse only by the Mystery Poems, and that those who read the Poems of Friendship should so generally be ignorant of their meaning. .

It is unfair to ourselves that we should refuse the companionship of the most open-hearted of men, a generous spirit, willing to reveal to us the riches of his mind, a man whom all can understand and no one can help loving. There is not so much kindness, humour, wisdom, and frankness offered to most of us in the ordinary intercourse of life that we can afford to decline the outstretched hand of Coleridge.

Poetry draws mankind together, breaks down barriers, relieves loneliness, shows us ourselves in others and others in ourselves. It is the friendly art. It ignores time and space. National, racial, and secular differences fall at its touch, which is the touch of kinship, and when we feel this we laugh shamefacedly at our pretensions, timidities, and reserves. Everything in antiquity is antiquated except its art and especially its poetry. That is scarcely less fresh than when it fell first from living lips. The religion of the ancients is to us superstition, their science childishness, but their poetry is as valid and vital as our own. We appropriate it, and it unites us with our fathers.

'One precious, tender-hearted scroll
Of pure Simonides'

shines through the mist more brightly than the Nicomachean Ethics or the Constitution of Athens. What is most enduring in the Old Testament is the humanity revealed here and there in veins of poetry, not only as psalms and prophecies but gleaming out from the historical books. It is the nature of all great poetry to open and bring together the hearts of men. And few poets have so generously given themselves out to us as Coleridge. The gift is rare and wonderful because he was a very good man, even more than because of his marvellous mind. When I say he was good, I mean that he was loving. However many other kinds of goodness there may be, this is the indispensable element....

The Poems of Friendship make yet another claim on our

attention: they are among the supreme examples of a peculiar kind of poetry. Others not unlike them, though not surpassing them, are Ovid's 'Cum subit illius tristissima noctis imago,' and several of the Canti of Leopardi. Some passages in Cowper's 'Task' resemble them in tone. Poignancy of feeling, intimacy of address, and ease of expression are even more perfectly blended in Coleridge's poems than in any of these.

The compositions which I denominate Poems of Friendship or Conversation Poems are 'The Eolian Harp,' 'Reflections on having left a Place of Retirement,' 'This Lime-Tree Bower my Prison,' 'Frost at Midnight,' 'Fears in Solitude,' 'The Nightingale,' 'Dejection,' and 'To William Wordsworth' (sometimes printed 'To a Gentleman'). The list is not complete; there are shorter pieces which might be added; but these are the most substantial and, I think, the best. The qualities common to all the eight are qualities of style no less than of subject.

Wordsworth is clearly more entitled than Coleridge to be considered the leader in creating and also in expounding a new kind of poetry.... Until he met Wordsworth, which was probably in 1795, Coleridge wrote in the manner which had been fashionable since the death of Milton, employing without hesitation all those poetic licences which constituted what he later termed 'Gaudyverse,' in contempt.... If one reads Coleridge's early poems in chronological order, one will perceive that Gaudyverse persists till about the middle of 1795, and then quickly yields to the natural style which Wordsworth was practising.

'The Eolian Harp,' composed on Aug. 20, 1795, in the short period when Coleridge was happy in his approaching marriage, sounds many a note of the *dolce stil nuovo,* and is moreover in substance his first important and at the same time characteristic poem. The influence of Wordsworth, whose early works he had read, is to be seen in small details, such as a bold and faithful reference to the scents 'snatched from yon beanfield.' The natural happiness of Coleridge, which was to break forth from him in spite of sorrow through all his darkened later years, flows like a sunlit river in this poem. In two magnificent passages he anticipates by nearly three years the grand climax of the 'Lines composed a few miles above Tintern Abbey,' singing:

'O! the one Life within us and abroad,
Which meets all motion and becomes its soul,
A light in sound, a sound-like power in light,
Rhythm in all thought, and joyance every where—
...
And what if all of animated nature
Be but organic Harps diversely framed,
That tremble into thought, as o'er them sweeps
Plastic and vast, one intellectual breeze,
At once the Soul of each, and God of all.'

Here is the Philosopher at his best, but he steps down from the intellectual throne at the bidding of love; and out of consideration for Sarah's religious scruples, and in obedience to his own deep humility, apologizes for

'These shapings of the unregenerate mind.'

It is to be noted also that the blank verse is more fluent and easy than Milton's, or any that had been written since Milton, moving with a gentle yet sufficiently strong rhythm, and almost free from the suggeston of the heroic couplet, a suggestion which is *felt* in nearly all 18th-century unrhymed verse, as of something recently lost and not quite forgotten. The cadences are long and beautiful, binding line to line and sentence to sentence in a way that the constant use of couplets and stanzas had made rare since Milton's time.

A few weeks later Coleridge wrote 'Reflections on having left a Place of Retirement.' The poem begins with a quiet description of the surrounding scene and, after a superb flight of imagination, brings the mind back to the starting-point, a pleasing device which we may call the 'return.' The imagination, in the second poem, seeks not, as in the first, a metaphysical, but an ethical height. The poet is tormented in the midst of his happiness by the thought of those who live in wretchedness or who die in the war, and asks himself:

'Was it right
While my unnumbered brethren toiled and bled,

That I should dream away the entrusted hours
On rose-leaf beds, pampering the coward heart
With feelings all to delicate for use?'

The problem is not stated in abstract, but in concrete terms. In fact, the only abstract passages in the Conversation Poems are the two quoted above, from 'The Eolian Harp'; and in general it is noticeable that Coleridge, whose talk was misty and whose prose writings are often like a cloud, luminous but impossible to see through, is one of the simplest and most familiar of poets. He, the subtlest metaphysician in England, was, as a poet, content to express elementary and universal feelings in the plainest terms.

On July 2, 1797, Coleridge, with Dorothy Wordsworth sitting beside him, drove from Racedown in Dorset to Nether Stowey in Somerset, and for about two weeks the small cottage behind Tom Poole's hospitable mansion sheltered William and Dorothy and perhaps Basil Montague's little boy, whom they were educating, besides Coleridge and Mrs. Coleridge and Hartley the baby and Nanny their maid. To fill up the measure, Charles Lamb joined them on the 7th and stayed a week. Coleridge, writing to Southey, says:

'The second day after Wordsworth came to me, dear Sara accidentally emptied a skillet of boiling milk on my foot, which confined me during the whole time of C. Lamb's stay, and still prevents me from all walks longer than a furlong. While Wordsworth, his sister, and Charles Lamb were out one evening, sitting in the arbour of T. Poole's garden, which communicates with mine, I composed these lines, with which I am pleased.'

He encloses the poem 'This Lime-Tree Bower my Prison,' in which he refers tenderly to his guests as 'my Sister and my Friends.' It begins:

'Well, they are gone, and here must I remain,
This lime-tree bower my prison! I have lost
Beauties and feelings such as would have been
Most sweet to my remembrance even when age
Had dimmed mine eyes to blindness!'

In imagination he follows them as they 'wander in

gladness along the hill-top edge,' and thinks with special satisfaction of the pleasure granted to his gentle-hearted Charles, who had been long 'in the great City pent,' an expression which he uses again in 'Frost at Midnight' and which Wordsworth later adopted, both of them echoing a line of Milton. The idea of storing up happy memories for some wintry season of the heart, an idea expanded by Wordsworth in 'Tintern Abbey,' and again in 'I wandered lonely as a Cloud,' occurs in the lines quoted above; and Wordsworth's famous brave remark,

> *'Nature never did betray*
> *The heart that loved her,'*
> *is also anticipated in this poem when Coleridge declares,*
> *'Henceforth I shall know*
> *That Nature ne'er deserts the wise and pure,'*

the wise and pure, we may be certain, being in their eyes those who love Nature. In this third Conversation Poem Coleridge has risen above the level attained in the former two; Gaudyverse is gone entirely, and unaffected simplicity, the perfection of tranquil ease, reigns without a rival. No better example, even in Wordsworth's own verse, could be found to illustrate the theory set forth three years later in the Preface to 'Lyrical Ballads.' The beauty and truth of the poem and the picture it gives of Coleridge's yearning heart of love do not depend upon the fact that it was an illustrious trio whom he followed in imagination as they roved 'upon smooth Quantock's airy ridge'; it is a clear boon to us that they happened to be no less than Charles Lamb and Dorothy and William Wordsworth. The significant thing is Coleridge's unselfish delight in the joys of others. Happiness of this kind is an inexhaustible treasure to which all have access.

'Frost at Midnight,' composed in February, 1798, also dates from that most blessed time, when he was living in concord with his wife, under the wide-branching protection of strong Thomas Poole, with William and Dorothy near and poetry pouring unto him from the heaven's height. It is the musing of a father beside the cradle of his child, and the passage is well known in which he foretells that Hartley shall

'wander like a breeze
By lakes and sandy shores, beneath the crags
Of ancient mountain.'

The chief beauty of the poem, however, is in its 'return,' which is the best example of the peculiar kind of blank verse Coleridge had evolved, as natural-seeming as prose, but as exquisitely artistic as the most complicated sonnet:

'Therefore all seasons shall be sweet to thee,
Whether the summer clothe the general earth
With greenness, or the redbreast sit and sing
Betwixt the tufts of snow on the bare branch
Of mossy apple-tree, while the nigh thatch
Smokes in the sun-thaw; whether the eave-drops fall
Heard only in the trances of the blast,
Or if the secret ministry of frost
Shall hang them up in silent icicles,
Quietly shining to the quiet Moon.'

'Fears in Solitude,' written in April 1798, 'during the alarm of an invasion,' is the longest of the Conversation Poems. It begins characteristically in a low key, with a quiet description of the poet's surroundings. He is reposing, happy and tranquil, in a green dell, above which sings a skylark in the clouds. Then quite suddenly his conscience cries out, when he thinks, as in 'Reflections on having left a Place of Retirement,' of the dangers and sufferings of others.

From self-tormenting he passes into an indictment of his countrymen for going lightly to war and for having 'borne to distant tribes' slavery, suffering, and vice. In words of terrible sincerity he charges society and his age with hardness and frivolity. 'We have loved,' he cries, 'to swell the war-whoop, passionate for war.' To read of war has become 'the best amusement for our morning meal.' We have turned the forms of holy religion into blasphemy, until 'the owlet Atheism,

Sailing on obscene wings athwart the noon,
Drops his blue-fringèd lids, and holds them close,
And hooting at the glorious sun in Heaven,
Cries out "Where is it?" '

Down to the 129th line the strain of passionate pacificism

continues. It is the confession of a tender-hearted, conscience-stricken man, to whom has been revealed a region above partisan and national views. We feel that if the passage had been declaimed to an army before battle, the men would have broken ranks in horror of their own designs. Quite unexpectedly, however, the tone changes at this point, and he bursts into a tirade against the French, calling upon Englishmen to stand forth and 'repel an impious foe.' The violence of the transition is disconcerting. But anon, with a thrust in each direction, at the over-sanguine English friends of the Revolution and at its unreasonable foes, he sings a glorious pæan to 'dear Britain,' his 'native Isle.'

Then comes a sweet 'return': he bids farewell to the soft and silent spot where he has been reclining; he thinks with joy of his beloved Stowey and his friend Poole and the lowly cottage where his babe and his babe's mother dwell in peace. It was like Coleridge to see both sides of the problem raised by the war, by all war, and to express both with equal poignancy. Extreme as are the limits to which his imagination carries him, his eloquence is vitiated by no sentimentalism or self-delusion.

The dilemma is fairly stated; the distress is genuine. Were it not for the exquisite frame in which the fears and questionings are set, were it not for the sweet opening and the refreshing 'return,' the pain excited by this poem would outweigh our pleasure in the aptness of its figures and the melody of its verse. But the frame saves the picture, as the profound psychological truth of the picture justifies the beauty of the frame. Coleridge was unaware how successful he had been, for in a note in one of his manuscript copies of this superb work of art he says: 'The above is perhaps not Poetry, but rather a sort of middle thing between Poetry and Oratory, *sermioni propriora*. Some parts are, I am conscious, too tame even for animated prose.' These words must have been dictated by humility rather than critical judgment....

In the same productive month, April 1789, he wrote 'The Nightingale,' which he himself terms a Conversation Poem, though it is neither more nor less conversational than the others of this kind. It was printed five months later in 'Lyrical Ballads.' Hazlitt, in his account of a visit he made that spring to Nether Stowey, tells of a walk he took with William and Dorothy and Coleridge: 'Returning that same evening, I got into a metaphysical argument with Wordsworth, while Coleridge was explaining the different notes of the nightingale to his sister, in which we neither of us succeeded in making ourselves perfectly clear and intelligible.' In Dorothy's Alfoxden journal are brief mentions of many a walk by moon or star light with 'dear Col.' The friendship had ripened fast. 'My Friend, and thou, our Sister' are addressed in the poem.

Thus far we have seen Coleridge in his day of strength. If he has written of sorrow, it has been sorrow for suffering mankind; if he has written of sin, it has been the sin of his country. He has been too manly to invent reasons for self-pity. But he is wretched without the companionship of loving friends. In Germany, when separated from the Wordsworths, he sends a wistful call across the frozen wastes of the Lüneburg Heath:

'William, my head and my heart, dear William and dear Dorothea!
You have all in each other; but I am lonely and want you!'

And when he ran away from them in Scotland, perhaps to escape their anxious care of his health, he was soon in distress and crying out:

'To be beloved is all I need,
And whom I love I love indeed.'

Prior to his return from Germany, in the summer of 1799, he had not become a slave to opium, though the habit of taking it had been formed. In the next three years the vice [sic] grew fixed, his will decayed, he produced less, and fell into depths of remorse.... he was unhappy with his wife; and ... the woman for whom Coleridge felt most affection was Sarah Hutchinson. There was something innocent and childlike in all his sympathies and likings and lovings. He never permanently alienated a friend; he never quite broke the tie between himself and his wife; he could, it seems, love without selfishness and be loved without jealousy....

In the winter of 1801-1802, the two causes of Coleridge's unhappiness, opium and domestic discord, worked havoc with him and brought him to despair. The wings of poesy were broken, as he realized full well. Meanwhile Wordsworth was in high poetic activity, healthy, forward-looking, and happy. On April 4, 1802, when William and Dorothy were on a visit to Keswick, and could judge for themselves of his misery, he composed, in part at least, the poem 'Dejection,' which is a confession of his own failure, and one of the saddest of all human utterances.

But it is a glorious thing, too, for as the stricken runner sinks in the race he lifts up his head and cheers the friend ... and this generosity is itself a triumph. On Oct. 4, Wordsworth's wedding day and the seventh anniversary of Coleridge's marriage, the poem was printed in the 'Morning Post.' It is an ode in form only; in contents it is a conversation. It is not an address to Dejection, but to [Sara Hutchinson]. As printed in the newspaper, it purports to be directed to some one named Edmund; in Coleridge's editions of his collected works this name is changed to Lady;... In this sublime and heartrending poem Coleridge gives expression to an experience of double consciousness.

His sense-perceptions are vivid and in part agreeable; his inner state is faint, blurred, and unhappy. He sees, but cannot feel. The power of feeling has been paralysed by chemically induced excitements of his brain. The seeing power, less dependent upon bodily health, stands aloof, individual, critical, and very mournful.

By 'seeing' he means perceiving and judging; by 'feeling' he means that which impels to action. He suffers, but the pain is dull, and he wishes it were keen, for so he should awake from lethargy and recover unity at least. But nothing from outside can restore him. The sources of the soul's life are within....

Coleridge never faltered in his conviction that spirit was independent of matter. His unhappy experience deepened his faith in the existence of God, and of his own soul as something detachable from his 'body that did him grievous wrong.' Yet he had once been a disciple of David Hartley and had, it seems, made a convert of Wordsworth, whose persistence in a semi-materialistic philosophy now alarmed him. In every other respect he venerates him and humbles himself before him. Wordsworth, pure in heart, that is to say, still a child of Nature, and free, has not lost his birthright of joy, which is the life-breath of poetry. But Oh! groans Coleridge, I have lost my gift of song, for each affliction

'Suspends what Nature gave me at my birth,
My shaping spirit of Imagination.'

His own race prematurely ended, he passes the torch to the survivor [*some editions of the poem were addressed to 'William'*]:

'Dear William, friend devoutest of my choice,
Thus mayst thou ever, evermore rejoice.'

Another awful day of remorse and humiliating comparison was approaching. In April, 1804, Coleridge left England for Sicily and Malta, where he sank very low in what had now become an incurable disease, though he subsequently at various times made heroic stands against it, through religious hope, the marvellous energy of an originally strong and joyous nature, and the devotion of one friend after another. While he was distant from his staunch supporters, Poole and Wordsworth, his creative powers, through the exercise of which he might have preserved some degree of self-respect, more nearly failed than at any period of his life.

He came back to England in August, 1806, so ashamed that for months he avoided his family and his friends.... in January, 1807, he visited them [Wordsworths] at a farmhouse, on Sir George Beaumont's estate, in which they had been living for several months. Here, one long winter night, Wordsworth began reading to him from the manuscript of 'The Prelude,' that poem dedicated to him, in which the Growth of a Poet's Mind is narrated.

What subject could have been more interesting or more painful to him? On the night when Wordsworth's deep voice ceased declaiming the firm pentameters, his brother poet, roused from lethargy, composed in response his lines 'To William Wordsworth.' Lingering in his ear was the graceful tribute which recalled the glory of his youth, so few years past and yet so completely gone:

'Thou in bewitching words, with happy heart,
Didst chaunt the vision of that Ancient Man,
The bright-eyed Mariner, and rueful woes
Didst utter of the Lady Cristabel.'

Coleridge's reply, touching for the gratitude, reverence, and humbleness which it expresses, is remarkable too for the lightning flashes in which it shows us the course of Wordsworth's life and of his own, and summarizes 'The Prelude.' ... The childlike candor of a beautiful spirit shines in the following lines, in which unconquered goodness and imperishable art unite:

'Ah! as I listened with a heart forlorn
The pulses of my being beat anew:
And even as Life returns upon the drowned,
Life's joys rekindling roused a throng of pains—
Keen pangs of Love, awakening as a babe,
Turbulent, with an outcry in the heart:
And fears self-willed, that shunned the eye of Hope;
And Hope that scarce would know itself from Fear;
Sense of past Youth, and Manhood come in vain,
And Genius given, and Knowledge won in vain.'

In the divine economy and equilibrium of the world all things have their uses and every disturbed balance is restored. Genius is *not* given in vain, goodness is never wasted, love comes at last into its own. The misfortunes, nay, even the faults of Coleridge, which were so grievous to him, can be seen now as a purifying discipline. I do not wish to preach a sermon in defence of weakness; but in all justice, not to say charity, let us ask ourselves whether the frailty of this great and essentially good man did not enhance his virtues and make him more lovable. He suffered burning remorse for wasted gifts and opportunities, but never whined about the futility of life. He trifled with his own sensations, but was no sentimentalist. He wandered, athirst and weak, in sandy places, but saw on the horizon a 'shady city of palm trees,' and pointed the way thither.

THE LIFE OF SAMUEL TAYLOR COLERIDGE

This is a clear, splendid biography, whose 407 pages of detailed labour Coleridge has long deserved—perhaps even a little more. But if this biography sometimes minimises the complexities of the Coleridgean philosophy only now emerging in all its untidy splendour, it does manage to do what no other has yet achieved: to paint the picture, warts and all, without either apologies or accusations. Ashton has written an admirable, unsqueemish biography that everyone will be glad to read; Coleridgeans will be relieved to read it.

The task could hardly have been easy. The irresolution, dishonesty and over-dependence that mark all aspects of Coleridge's life might be managed on their own; but united with the generosity and perspicuity for which he is fabled, those ignoble traits demand an elaborate psychological explanation that cannot but be moral, too. Why should a man with such an ebullient intellect, always churning even in the most dire circumstances, a man of such acute self-consciousness and possessed of such insight into human nature, have lived so unwisely, so unhappily?

The question baffled Coleridge's upright nephew, John Taylor, who observed with palpable chagrin: "Nothing can be finer than the principles he lays down in morals and religion; the wonder, the painful wonder is that a man who can think and feel as he does ... should have acted and still act as he has done and does". But it was the opium addiction and unusual domestic arrangements that troubled John Taylor and a whole generation of Victorian readers—moral deficiencies which biographers could not but condemn in language equal to the offence, among them J. D. Campbell (1894) and later E. K. Chambers (1938).

There was of course an alternative, less hostile approach that emphasised the achievement regardless of the circumstances—exemplified by F. J. A. Hort in one of the finest single essays on Coleridge ever published (in Cambridge Essays, 1856)—though few followed it. Today's generation of readers, unruffled by such an untidy life, nevertheless still take offence—not at the drugs and separation, but at the procrastination of so many projected works, the incompleteness of major projects, the white lies in the Biographia, the "strain of dishonesty" as Ashton gently calls it. This, though, is a lover's complaint, not a public prosecutor's.

Painting the good and the bad (and the ugly) in such an even-handed, confident manner, Ashton writes a very satisfying, clearly post-Fruman biography. For philosophical perspicuity it does not always match W. J. Bate's much shorter intellectual life, but then even Bate's magisterial treatment of Coleridge's mind occasionally slips into a reverence that would better be avoided or qualified, especially considering Fruman's hostile, but unavoidable, biography of sins.

Many of the charges against Coleridge (plagiarism, incoherence) have been settled by the new edition of the works as well as in arguments offered by critics like John Beer and Thomas McFarland, largely in the context of intellectual history. Here we have the response in the context of biography. The wonder is, Ashton excuses nothing and still Coleridge comes off well.

Nowhere is this more evident than in the admirable portrait of the young radical Coleridge courting persecution recklessly (though briefly) and the respectful depiction of the older sage of Highgate grown conservative and Anglican (almost). This is clearly the work of an historian who prefers facts to polemics. The same drive delivered, in addition to biographies of *George Eliot* (1983) and *G. H. Lewes* (1991), several indispensable works on the German presence in British culture including *Little Germany* (1986), *The German Idea* (1980) and a valuable Cambridge thesis (1975), well worth the trouble to obtain.

Readers will be satisfied, too, with the generous and insightful commentaries on each of the major poems and all the published prose (with the unexpected exception of the 1814 Bristol essay, *On the Principles of Genial Criticism*). There are excellent discussions of "Dejection" and "Kubla Khan" and a convincing redemption of that very fine later poem, "Work without Hope". Some old stories are told with fresh insight:

in the Lyrical Ballads episode Ashton highlights the very different poetic sensibilities of Wordsworth and Coleridge and ably emphasises their very delicate relationship, and the Biographia's discussion of the imagination gets an admirably short and shrewd retelling.

Indeed, there is something compellingly solid in the way Ashton summarises Coleridge's various philosophical positions, often with a precisiòn Coleridge himself failed to attain. Thus, for example, the philosophical lectures of 1818-19, in which he wished to overcome the dualism which had dominated philosophy through the ages ... The problem was to avoid succumbing to the counter-attractions of monism, which seemed to lead inevitably, as with Spinoza and Schelling, to pantheism ... The answer was to describe a mutual relationship of opposites and their reconciliation, by Reason in the speculative sphere, by Imagination in the aesthetic, and by religious faith in the spiritual. There is something tidy in this scheme which honours Coleridge's intentions, though hardly his practice. Soon after the Biographia, reason, imagination and spirituelle Anschauung appear in such close company any one might be taken for the other. In some of the Tennemann marginalia, they seem deliberately confused.

True, having assembled all the facts, this biographer, too, occasionally grows impatient with the indolence that could not but tarnish so many aspects of Coleridge's life and production, on one or two occasions even pitying him in words Lamb once disapproved of ("Poor Coleridge"). No reader of Coleridge can resist either complaint indefinitely. But for the most part—and this is the glory of the work—the errors, poor judgement and frustrations of Coleridge's life stand unexaggerated and unexcused beside the wealth of his poetry, critical insight and provocative philosophy, not to mention his generosity and vociferous endurance, for which is deservedly remembered. He was persistently careless with his poetry, publishing badly ordered collections with lame or inappropriate prefaces, yet endured the calumny of critics with a measure of dignity that sometimes approached noble suffering.

Between Malta and Highgate he drove himself to despair with worry, unrequited love and opium, yet wrote the first English exploration of idealist ethics in The Friend, and offered the finest Shakespeare criticism since Johnson in his London lectures. He foolishly expected far more from Wordsworth than any person could give (as Poole suspected when Coleridge left Nether Stowey for the Lakes) and was inevitable devastated by the rupture of 1810, yet afterwards he was courteous when Wordsworth remained aloof and still treated the latter's poetry to astute and fair analysis in the Biographia. He could not find time or determination to help plan the university education of his own sons, but he energetically spent himself on behalf of James and Henry Gillman. The picture that emerges is one of Coleridge laboriously overcoming adverse, sometimes nearly devastating circumstances of his own creation.

There is a strong sense in this biography that Ashton is aware of the paradox. And to her credit it does not go unanswered. Of course, fixing blame to any of Coleridge's unwise decisions is not part of the solution: as we are aptly reminded in the words of Virginia Woolf (another whose relentless self-consciousness drove to distraction), Coleridge pre-empts the disapproval of the critic since he already "despises his own hypocrisy ... is humiliated by his own humiliation". The solution involves rather a less partisan account of how Coleridge could act so often against his own interest and yet bequeath a body of texts which every generation since has turned to for instruction and inspiration, perhaps never more so than today.

Ashton gives no direct answer (who could?); those looking for a psychological key will put this book down with disappointment. But they will find plenty of clues. Thus, for example, the Wedgwood annuity of 1798 which Coleridge took "to mean no less than that he should enlighten mankind on every subject of inquiry." No wonder, says Ashton, that he "so embroiled himself as to render himself incapable of repaying the Wedgwoods' generosity on a smaller, more reasonable scale by work with which they and everyone else would have been perfectly satisfied. But we have the easy wisdom of hindsight". The paralysing catholicity of Coleridge's vision has often been noticed, but rarely with as much sensitivity, even sympathy, as here. He wished not only to include everything in his philosophy, intellectually, but to do everything he ought to, morally.

And just as the universality of his philosophical programme decreed that he would never finish it, so the stinging sense of duty decreed that he would never adequately fulfil his moral obligations. Indeed, the only time Coleridge ever did do his duty was in marrying Sara Fricker—which won him a distempered wife, a peaceless home and three loveable and always somehow distant children: that parish duty which Lamb said he ought to have done without. Duty more often stunned than roused him. For a mind so self-reflexive as his, it is hardly surprising that an observation upon his own paralysis should become one of the greatest tenets of his thought, woven into the Ancient Mariner and repeated at every important juncture since: that there is no causal relationship between the intellect and the will.

When Basil Willey came to this subject in his biography (1972), he began by quoting Carlyle: "A man's religion is the chief fact with regard to him." It was unquestionably true of Coleridge, though even that thoughtful book presents mostly the publicly religious Coleridge, the Christian apologist who moved a later, less reckless generation than his own to piety and orthodoxy.

That very Anglican figure is here, too, in greater and more perceptive detail than ever before. Some of the most valuable pages of Ashton's book are in the last quarter, and include a unexpected endorsement of Aids to Reflection ("... it has a surprising freshness and clarity much of the time,") and a summary of Church and State that manages to do justice to Coleridge's tangled political agenda ("At one point ... Coleridge sounds almost radical ...",). Rightly, the liberal side of Coleridge's later thought is emphasised. Nevertheless, in all this the privately religious man remains a shadow, the vicissitudes of his own spirituality obscure amid the various public religious endorsements made throughout his long career.

This is too bad, since the only way to make some sense of the paradox at the heart of Coleridge's life is by reference to the spiritual experience he sought to achieve and explain. For only in religion did Coleridge find a satisfactory account for the abyss between the intellect and the will, and the means of redeeming both. He clung to a notion of redemption throughout his life not, as did so many Christians of his day, out of an emotional or social need alone, but because it was a solution demanded by both morality and philosophy. On the one or two occasions when this biography minimises Coleridge's achievement, it is in relation to this difficult question of his sometimes enigmatic religious commitment.

The Unitarianism of his youth is slightly underplayed, with only a little commentary on the 1795 lectures on revealed religion. The unsteady Trinitarianism which Coleridge found himself espousing with increasing frequency (especially to brother George) is termed "orthodox" and "Anglican" perhaps a little sooner than it deserves. And there is only passing reference to one of Coleridge's greatest contributions to textual interpretation: his long engagement with the higher criticism of Eichhorn and his largely successful bid to fashion a modern hermeneutic for an increasingly scientific audience (still use today). *Confessions of An Inquiring Spirit* (written 1824 and published posthumously in 1840), in which Coleridge crystallises his long ruminations on the subject, is a more important text than this biography suggests: like *Aids to Reflection* (written the following year), it aimed to satisfy the objections of that growing group of doubting believers.

Behind this public, often desperate outcry against atheism lay the privately-pursued goal of a kind of a summa theological for the modern world, the magnum opus, which would establish an epistemological account for knowledge of God. Coleridge needed this as much to reassure himself of his own spiritual experience (often more sought after than achieved) as to recall a generation of wavering Christians from the death trap of scientific materialism. Like Carlyle, he saw with a kind of oppressive clarity the dire social and ideological consequences of a purely materialist philosophy and sought to address the epistemological arguments than made it so appealing. But at its heart the plea was not simply for a return to established religion. Coleridge knew one could act morally without relying upon orthodox forms of belief: he agreed that much with Kantian ethics. And yet the sense that every human achievement which did not partake of God partook of death weighed on him throughout his life. It drove him to the most audacious plan of all: to reconcile all he had gleaned from contemporary science and German metaphysics with the notion of a transcendent God.

Ashton may have reason to downplay both the effort and the achievement in this regard. How much, in fact, did Coleridge produce on the intended reconciliation apart from thirty years of scattered notes and that fragment of fragments, the long unknown and still unpublished *Opus Maximum*? Perhaps a critic's judgement is best suspended for the moment (though there is more promising material in the marginalia than anyone seems to let on).

Francois Maurois said the biographer can implicitly pass some kind of moral judgement upon his or her subject, but ought never express it. Ashton agrees, and her even-handed treatment of Coleridge is what ultimately makes this biography a worthy and in many respects unprecedented telling of a most tangled life. And if the historian's mask hides any judgement, it is a kind of surprised wonder at the breadth of Coleridge's achievement in spite himself: that a man who so often and so unwillingly acted against his own and others' interests, yet managed to exert such a powerful and positive influence upon his own and later generations. This is what makes credible the poignant, sympathetic words of Wordsworth with which this biography concludes: "... S.T.C. is the only wonderful man I ever knew."

Chapter 3

His 'Poetic Faith' and Scientific Hoax

This chapter explores the relation between romanticism and science fiction by examining the development of scientific and futuristic hoaxes in the early nineteenth century. Although these hoaxes are arguably early works of science fiction, the main interest involves the specific manipulations of genre and media that each hoax engages in. The effort is to theorize hoaxing in terms of recent genre theory, which emphasizes the situational aspects of genre; and to do so in a manner that helps explain the inception of science fiction in the early nineteenth century.

My theory of hoaxing derives from Samuel Taylor Coleridge's use of the supernatural in poetry, with special attention to "The Rime of the Ancient Mariner." Coleridge's interest in the supernatural is principally directed towards the way that the creative or active aspects of reading are often not recognized by readers; with the interest of the imagination involving the retrospective recognition of these active or creative aspects. This attention to the psychology of reading provides a rationale for hoaxing that characterizes Poe's development of the hoax into a sort of literary gesture that he deploys throughout his writing, but that tends to occur with greater frequency in those tales that anticipate science fiction.

Poe emphasizes the disclosure of the hoax as a strategy to provoke a reader. Such provocation has a range of effects that are relevant to science fiction. For example, the investment of belief that occurs in a successful hoax may indicate a shift in the collective sense of what is possible. This type of effect not only underscores the speculative dimension of science fiction, it also draws attention to the ways that representations contribute to and rely on a reading public's view of the world. Another type of effect produced by the disclosure of a hoax involves defamiliarization; or what Darko Suvin terms "cognitive estrangement" in reference to science fiction. I am especially interested in the way that familiar patterns, habits, or conventions that inform reading—and that characterize genres—are brought into sharp relief when a hoax is recognized or pointed out.

In order to establish a theoretical basis for discussing hoaxing, I will first outline a number of broad intersections between hoaxes, science fiction, and recent genre theory. I will then look to several examples of scientific and futuristic hoaxes of early and mid-nineteenth century America. While I am interested in a number of Poe's tales, I will focus on two hoaxes perpetrated by the *New York Sun*: the "Great Astronomical Discoveries" or what is usually referred to as the "Great Moon Hoax" of August 1835 and "The Balloon Hoax" of April 1844. Poe does not perpetrate the first hoax, but he discusses it at length several times. The exploitation of the daily newspaper, especially in the case of "Great Astronomical Discoveries," is of special interest because it affords an acute analysis of the way that hoaxes appropriate or co-opt existing genres or media, and I am particularly interested in thinking about genre in terms social and historical contexts.

Following the analyses of these two hoaxes, in order to explain Poe's use of the hoax, I turn to an extended exploration of Coleridge's use of the supernatural in poetry, with specific reference to "The Rime of the Ancient Mariner."

Attention to the role of hoax in the early formation of science fiction as a genre is helpful because it emphasizes aspects of recent genre theory that point out the insufficiency of using form as an exclusive or even fundamental aspect of genre. Aviva Freedman and Peter Medway provide a succinct introduction to recent genre theory in "Locating Genre Studies: Antecedents and Prospects," in *Genre and the New Rhetoric*. The basic tendency of this research has been to identify non-literary genres in places as banal as the tax office (form reports) or as exotic as personal ads. The needs of speech communities give rise to the development of conventions or practices of speech or writing.

These conventions may serve as a sort of shorthand or as a necessary process in the life of a community (or the lack thereof). The move away from an exclusively formalist account of genre draws attention to the ways in which formal aspects of genres, such as lineation in poetry or abbreviations in personal ads, function within the historical relations between writers and readers, in the situations and occasions that give rise to texts or speeches. As Carolyn R. Miller notes, in "Genre as Social Action," genre study is valuable "not because it might permit the creation of some kind of taxonomy, but because it emphasizes [...] social and historical aspects of rhetoric".

The impact of recent genre theory on the study of science fiction is merely one of emphasis. As Paul Alkon notes, theorists of science fiction like Samuel Delany and Darko Suvin tend to emphasize "the interaction of readers and texts rather than... theme and technique as the primary elements of genre. At one level, this emphasis involves questions that attend to the social, literary, and other historical contexts of the genre. Why does science fiction develop in the nineteenth century? What roles does it perform within nineteenth century society? These sorts of questions find a range of answers, from the obvious, such as the rapid technological change that occurs in this period, to the more complex, such as the growing hegemony of a scientific world-view and the role of different media and genre in the consolidation of this worldview.

On another level, this emphasis requires a careful consideration of what readers are being asked to entertain as possible and the way that readers respond to texts. For example, why do stories about journeying to the moon suddenly adopt the form of the hoax? And why does it suddenly seem believable? My immediate task then is to consider the general relation between hoax and genre. Can hoaxes be considered genres proper? How do we think of their sudden incursions into other genres? The situational aspects of a hoax are almost singular. A hoax exploits existing genres, and the ways that these genres have established an audience and a set of expectations or even conventions. A hoax involves deception at some level. Often such deception pertains to a claim regarding fact so that an event is thought to have occurred when it did not.

To trick and to hoax are almost identical endeavors, but the scale of the hoax is grander—it is a practical joke played at the expense of the public. Perhaps most importantly, a hoax almost inevitably takes advantage of an existing condition of trust in order to perpetrate its deception. It is a doppelganger parading as an already familiar confidant. In this sense, as we will see, even at a formal level the hoax co-opts another genre in order to exploit readers' expectations.

If genre is considered in terms of social action and rhetorical situation, as recent genre theory argues it must be, hoax is difficult to understand as a genre unto itself. Hoaxes depend on an element of surprise that precludes any commonality of situation or audience.

It is for this reason that the hoax is inextricable from genre theory, bound up with any genre as its opposite—revealing the context of the rhetorical situation. A hoax is always an occasion. Whatever else we might understand hoaxes to do, it seems sensible to acknowledge that they may perform important roles in genre reformation by drawing attention to (or making visible) aspects of the context of a genre: the extent to which an audience is predetermining what they read; the types of claims that are implicit in a genre; or the way that a genre constructs or arranges shared beliefs about the world.

The relation between hoaxes and science fiction can be treated generally with some success. While science fiction does not pretend that its subject matter will occur—and it certainly doesn't insist that it has occurred—it does rely upon, or at least experiment with, a reader's acceptance of the possibility of the subject matter. In general, it is this emphasis that distinguishes science fiction from fantasy. As Carl Malmgren argues in *Worlds Apart: Narratology of Science Fiction*, science fiction emerges in the early nineteenth century precisely because of a growing consensus regarding how the world is understood. This consensus finds its origins in the Enlightenment. It involves assumptions about the progressive development of science and technology; the efficacy of this science and technology with regard to invention and discovery; and a notion of change that projects a future that will be different from the present (Malmgren 2-5). Malmgren argues that "the appearance of modern SF is predicated upon the establishment of the scientific episteme as the definitive and hegemonic way of envisioning and explaining the human condition and humanity's place in the larger universe".

The proliferation of scientific hoaxes in the nineteenth century directly intersect with and exploit the consolidation of this world view, as well as various media and genres that are involved in establishing the scientific episteme. Early examples of scientific hoaxes include Charles Redheffer's perpetual motion machine (1812) and John Cleves Symmes' claims regarding a hollow Earth (1818). Later examples range from the more banal petrification hoaxes of the middle and late century to the remarkable Piltdown Hoax of 1912. Hoaxes are not merely exploitive. At a simplistic level, they resemble science fiction by realizing the futuristic promise of the genre.

Whereas science fiction projects a possible future, hoaxes pretend that such a future is already happening. In this sense, scientific hoaxes signal the immediacy of the imagined future. At a less simplistic level, hoaxes rely on and reveal a shift in the public's sense of what is possible. As Edgar Allan Poe observes regarding the success of the 1835 "Great Astronomical Discoveries," in his 1846 portrait of Richard Adams Locke in *Godey's Lady's Book*: not "one person in ten discredited it, and (strangest point of all!) the doubters were chiefly those who doubted without being able to say why—the ignorant, those uninformed in astronomy". Poe notes a professor of mathematics who "told me seriously that he had no doubt of the truth of the whole affair".

If science fiction experiments with and explores the possible, hoaxes exploit actual shifts in what is believed to be possible. This belief may pertain to a "discovered" fact or to the mode of discovery itself. For example, as Stephen Jay Gould argues, the Piltdown hoax depended for its success on the early 20th century assumption that the brain was the distinguishing feature of human superiority, and that the large human cranium must have evolved prior to other changes in the body. As such, the discovery of a human cranium with an ape's jaw corresponded to prevailing theory.

In part, the Piltdown hoax can be attributed to the correspondence between the apparent facts of the discovery and the way that the prevailing theory conceived of such facts as possible. The way that a hoax reveals shifts in what is believed to be possible may also pertain to the mode of dissemination itself. For example, both "Great Astronomical Discoveries" and the "Balloon Hoax" exploit several media, from scientific journals to the newspaper proper. The public's belief in the veracity of these sources and the desire for the immediate revelation of discoveries or news of other events that is the basis of the penny newspaper's daily appearance work in concert to create these hoaxes. In this sense, the deception involved in a hoax is not its principal interest.

Even if the hoax is revealed, something else is disclosed. At one level, the belief cannot be removed, because it indicates an acceptance of a possibility. At another level, the manufactured basis of the consent, which belongs to the media or the genre proper, is also recognized. These supplemental recognitions, accompanying the revelation of a hoax, are at the basis of Poe's tendency to conjoin science fiction and hoaxing. They also help explain what Poe means when he says that "we are indebted to the genius of Mr. Locke for one of the most important steps ever yet taken in the pathway of human progress".

In late August of 1835 The *New York Sun* ran a series of articles (August 25, 26, 27, 28, 29, and 31) that purported to be extracts reprinted from a supplement to The Edinburgh Journal of Science, dictated by Sir John Herschel and written by Dr. Andrew Grant, reporting on Sir John Herschel's astronomical observations at the Cape of Good Hope:

GREAT ASTRONOMICAL DISCOVERIES
Lately Made
By Sir John Herschel, L.L., D.F.R.S., &c
At the Cape of Good Hope
(From The Supplement to the Edinburgh Journal of Science)
(14)

The first article details the conception, transportation, and construction of the telescope employed by the expedition. The telescope, which used an objective mirror twenty-four feet in diameter, was based upon a new principle involving the "transfusion of artificial light through the focal object of vision" (Locke 14). The rest of the first article details various astronomical discoveries made by way of this new telescope, including the discovery of "a countless number of new stars and nebulae" (Locke 21). The extract published on August 26 details Herschel's initial observations of the moon. The combination of the size of the telescope and the novel principle of transfusing artificial light through the focal object of vision provided such extreme magnification that Herschel was confident he would be able to study "the entomology of the moon" (Locke 17).

The initial observations discover objects of geological and then botanical interest, definitively establishing the existence of life on the lunar surface. Plants are soon surpassed by the observation of various fauna, including creatures that resemble bison, single horned goats, and birds. The August 27 installment continues the lunar observations but yields little new. Attention is focused on seas and volcanoes, although something resembling a bipedal beaver is seen. On August 28, they identify bat-winged hominids resembling orang-outangs. These creatures are "evidently engaged in conversation," and Herschel names them Vespertilio-homo or man-bat (Locke 37, 38).

The August 29 extract furthers their discoveries by identifying architectural structures including what appears to be a temple. The final installment on August 31 continues these observations, adding the discovery of a higher order of man-bat. The editor of the *New York Sun* concludes the series by noting that the original Supplement includes forty pages of mathematical and scientific notes and illustrations that have been omitted because the cost of reproducing them is prohibitive.

The series of articles were a hoax, of course, and the *New York Sun* admitted it on September 16. The *New York Herald* identified Richard Adams Locke as the author of the articles. There was no supplement to the Edinburgh Journal of Science. Indeed, there was no Edinburgh Journal of Science. Furthermore, the amanuensis, Dr. Andrew Grant, was a fabrication as well. As Poe details in his 1846 portrait of Locke, and as David Evans shows in two articles in *Sky and Telescope* in 1981, much of Locke's science is "gobbledygook" (Evans 198).

The story was not entirely fabricated. Sir John Herschel was at the Cape of Good Hope at the time, having traveled there in November of 1833 to survey the southern hemisphere using two telescopes: "an 18-inch speculum-metal reflector" and "a 7-inch equatorial refractor" (Evans 196). Interestingly, Poe notes that Harpers had issued an American edition of Sir John Herschel's *Treatise on Astronomy* in 1834 (Poe, Literati, R.A. Locke 127). This treatise, which inspired Poe's "The Unparalleled Adventure of One Hans Pfaall," probably established both the credibility of Herschel as an authority on astronomy, as well as the general plausibility of the telescope as an instrument for the dramatic progressive acquisition of certain types of knowledge for the New York audience. In fact, in order to establish the credibility of the large-scale telescope used by Sir John Herschel, Locke accurately notes the extraordinarily high magnification powers of 6000 made possible by the telescope of Herschel's father, Sir William Herschel.

As Evans points out, Sir John Herschel's actual results from the Cape were probably as important as the ones contrived by Locke—albeit, not as sensationalistic.

Poe's own turn came on Saturday, April 13, 1844 when the *New York Sun* issued an "Extra page," a broadside printed on one side, that announced and provided a detailed account of a transatlantic crossing by a balloon, the "flying machine," "Victoria." The Extra was announced in a postscript in the morning edition of the Sun:

BY EXPRESS

Astounding intelligence by private express from Charleston via Norfolk!—The Atlantic ocean crossed in three days!!—Arrival at Sullivan's Island of a steering balloon invented by Mr. Monck Mason!! (quoted in Beaver 368)

Monck Mason was famous for his flight in the balloon Nassau from Vauxhall Gardens, London to Weilberg, Germany, on November 7, 1836. The Extra created an immediate sensation. According to Poe's own account, a large crowd gathered in the square surrounding the *New York Sun*, waiting for the Extra, and when it appeared at two in the afternoon, it sold out immediately at premium prices. The account consists of an introductory section and a journal kept by Monk Mason, to which Mr. Ainsworth added a daily postscript.

The introduction details the invention of the balloon by Mason, who adapted an Archimedian screw for the purpose of propelling a dirigible balloon filled with more than 40000 cubic feet of coal gas. The flight departed from North Wales on the morning of April 6 with the intention of crossing the English Channel. Once aloft, however, the "steel rod connecting the spring with the propeller was suddenly jerked out of place" and while they struggled to fix it, a current of wind from the east bore them out across the Atlantic at approximately 50 to 60 miles per hour. The crew, consisting of eight in total, decided to make the best of the wind and to attempt an Atlantic crossing. They succeed when they sight the coast of South Carolina on the afternoon of April 9. The Extra concludes by noting that the MS, from which the Extra was compiled, was dispatched from Charleston.

Neither of these hoaxes is strikingly original as a story per se: that is, as a topic that had been written about. As Michael J Crowe has shown in *The Extraterrestial Life Debate 1750-1900: The idea of a plurality of worlds from Kant to Lowell*, Richard Adams Locke's "Great Astronomical Discoveries" needs to be situated within the debate over the plurality of worlds; a debate that intensified in the early nineteenth century. While Locke contrives Sir John Herschel's scientific report on his astronomical work, there are precedents, especially in Germany, of serious scientific papers purporting to have discovered evidence of life and indeed civilization on the lunar surface.

For example, Franz von Paula Gruithuisen issued a number of papers along these lines regarding his work in Germany, including "Discovery of Many Distinct Traces of Lunar Inhabitants, Especially of One of Their Colossal Buildings" in 1824 (Crowe 202, 203). Furthermore, the discovery of life on the moon is an old story that was told repeatedly in numerous guises from Ariosto's *Orlando Furioso* in 1532 forward. J.O. Bailey provides a brief survey of moon stories from Lucian's *Icaromenippus* in which Menippus uses wings to fly to the moon in order to ascertain the true shape of the Earth; to Ariosto's 1532 *Orlando Furioso*; to the post-Copernican works of Galileo and Johann Kepler; to Bishop Francis Godwin's *The Man in the Moone* (written in 1638, this book is the first moon story to be written in English) and Bishop John Wilkins *A Discourse Concerning a New World* (1640); including Cyrano de Bergerac's more whimsical and fantasic *Voyages to the Moon and the Sun* (1659 and 1687) and Gabriel Daniel's *A Voyage to the World*. Locke's principal innovation on the moon story consists in the use of the telescope.

Similarly, Poe's "Balloon Hoax" appears in the context of speculation and serious planning for attempts at crossing the Atlantic by balloon; and it is indebted to a number of accounts of actual balloon trips, especially Monck Mason's *Account of the Late Aeronautical Expedition from London to Weilburg, accomplished by Robert Hollond, Esq., and Charles Green, Aeronaut* which was published in London in 1836 and New York in 1837 (Mabbott 1063, 1064). While Poe's narration of a transatlantic balloon flight is original, the mode of the narration and the idea of such a flight is very much current.

The hoaxes succeeded to different extents. Both were successful, but Locke's "Great Astronomical Discoveries" appears to have been radically successful. It boosted the circulation of the *New York Sun* to more than 19,000 readers, which made it the largest circulation of any English daily, and excited such a great degree of speculation and interest that Benjamin Day issued a reprint in the form of a pamphlet that sold more than 60,000 copies. The Balloon Hoax is less successful as a hoax per se. Although the Extra of the *New York Sun* that carried it sold out and created quite a stir, it was reprinted in several Sunday papers, including the *Sunday Times* and the *Mercury*, with humorous asides.

The Monday *New York Sun* carried a retraction noting that the mail had not brought confirmation of the balloon's arrival and that, therefore, "we are inclined to believe that the intelligence is erroneous" (quoted in Mabbott 1067). The hoax was based on the claim that private express would precede the mail from Charleston by several hours. This window of opportunity provided the rationale for an Extra. However, once the mail arrived, there was no way to perpetuate the hoax. In addition, as both the Sunday edition of the Mercury indicated, the *New York Sun* was still remembered for "Great Astronomical Discoveries": "By Express / Astounding Intelligence from the Man in the / Moon" (Quoted in Mabbott 1067).

However, Poe did not seem to care much. He was delighted to have the piece published and to witness the initial stir. The immediate success of the hoax is all the more remarkable because, as Beaver notes, it managed to divert attention "from the raging controversy over the admission of Texas into the Union". I will consider Poe's ambivalence later in terms of his literary appropriation of the hoax as a figure.

"The Balloon Hoax" is important for different reasons than Locke's "Great Astronomical Discoveries." Even as it is less successful, its verisimilitude to probable fact is acute. When the first transatlantic balloon flight did occur in July of 1919, its return flight took seventy-five hours, which is exactly Poe's estimation (Mabbott 1088, n 30). As Hervey Allan notes in *Israfel*, Poe's hoax is simply an anticipation of the news (quoted in Mabbott 1088). It accurately represents an event that hasn't occurred. While verisimilitude is obviously an integral part of any hoax, what is involved in such verisimilitude is quite complex because it is not merely a matter of factual accuracy or rational probability. Verisimilitude depends upon what a reader expects as much as it depends upon what would actually be the case.

In this sense, the issue of verisimilitude underscores what I take to be the salient point of hoaxes—one that is often difficult to recognize when we look back on them. Whatever allows us to fall for a hoax is inextricable from the cultural and historical context in which we read. It should be noted that aspects of this context may seem banal in retrospect, but they are anything but banal in the moment that they are realized. A successful hoax marks the moment that the willingness to suspend disbelief shifts to abandonment and the investment in belief. In this sense, hoaxes offer watermarks for our sense of what is possible.

The differing successes of these hoaxes indicate a willingness on the part of the New York audience to accept specific features of them as true or at least possible. In the case of "Great Astronomical Discoveries," these features may range from the use of the telescope, specifically the technological innovation that allowed for greater magnification; to the belief in the possibility of life on other worlds; to a willingness to accept the authority or at least the veracity of the different media and genres that Locke exploited. The genre of the scientific report, published in a scientific journal; the extract of the report, simplified for the lay-person; the daily newspaper, broadcasting recent developments and events as quickly as possible; all contribute to the success of Locke's hoax.

Poe's hoax exploits ballooning accounts such as Mason's, which was published in New York in 1837. He also relies on recent articles on innovation in ballooning technology, such as an article entitled "Another Aerial Machine" that appeared in *Alexander's Express Messenger* on February 21 of 1844. This article described Mason's model balloon that was on exhibition in London (Mabbott 1065). Poe is also utilizing the form of the journal as a means to include both an immediate narration and the pretense of the written account itself.

I will discuss the use of journal and letters later in terms of the nested narrative of Mary Shelley's *Frankenstein* and the reading psychology. of Coleridge's "The Rime of the Ancient Mariner." In a general sense that is directly related to the development of science fiction—and I stress that both of these hoaxes are science fiction—these hoaxes reveal the extent to which the newspapers as specific media are participating in the growing hegemony of the scientific episteme in the nineteenth century.

As John Pierce notes, in *Odd Genre: A Study in Imagination and Evolution*, "the roots of science fiction are lost in the confusion of the classical travel tale, the utopia, the satire, the gothic novel, the scientific hoax and other ur-genres." Despite this fact, it is a common critical tendency to posit Mary Shelley's *Frankenstein* as the first work of science fiction. Paul Alkon begins his study of science fiction as a genre, *Science Fiction Before 1900: Imagination Discovers Technology*, with this contention. Alkon bases his argument on the rejection of the supernatural in *Frankenstein*, noting that despite this rejection, terror "remains a desirable effect"—one that Alkon sees as providing an emotional dimension to science fiction that supplements the emphasis on the rational in science fiction in general.

Alkon goes on to argue that works of science fiction do not have to have plots that "necessarily command belief even as possibilities, much less as probabilities". Making specific reference to *Frankenstein*, and following Percy Shelley's Preface to the 1818 edition, Alkon argues that it "is not whether the scientific premise is believable—it was not—but whether a story based on such a premise can achieve a "valuable 'point of view to the imagination'". Thus, while Alkon thinks that "a scientific premise is important, belief in its possibility is not". Alkon's diminishment of possibility as a requisite may make sense at a certain level, but it fails to account for the continuing role of terror in the shift from the supernatural to the scientific in *Frankenstein*. If the supernatural is rejected, and the science that replaces it has no ground in possibility, what then is the source of the terror?

Is it sufficient to dismiss the scientific possibility of the work and to think that a reader will respond with fear? The answer to this problem derives from the difficulty of ascertaining, exactly, what is possible and how we entertain, accept, or otherwise come to believe it. In *Frankenstein,* the reader does not have unmediated access to the scientific creation.

Rather, the whole of the story is written by Walton in a series of letters, the majority of which recount Victor Frankenstein's telling of his life story. In this sense, the issue of possibility is inextricable from that of bias, memory, and veracity; and it is bound up by the internal perspectives of characters and narrators, especially as these characters and narrators exchange roles. (The monster must be included here, for he tells his own story to Frankenstein.) These perspectives inform and manipulate the relations between the suspension of disbelief and belief that a reader negotiates in the novel.

The shift from the supernatural to scientific possibility that occurs in *Frankenstein* is of particular interest because of what is at stake in the readers' investment of belief that occurs in the scientific hoax. In order to explicate the relevance of this shift to hoaxing, I will now consider Samuel Taylor Coleridge's discussion in *Biographia Literaria* of his use of the supernatural in *Lyrical Ballads* with special attention to "The Rime of the Ancient Mariner."

This focus is important for several reasons. First, Coleridge's poetry in general and *Biographia Literaria* in specific inform the immediate intellectual milieu of Shelley's *Frankenstein*. Second, Coleridge's interest in the supernatural is primarily directed at the suspension of disbelief on the part of a reader; and he extends his explication of the suspension of disbelief in terms of the way that belief and affect are figured by characters and by narrators within a literary work. Third, Coleridge is fundamentally interested in how the suspension of disbelief leads to the recognition of reading as a constitutive act. This type of recognition on the part of a reader helps explain both a general value for hoaxing and also Poe's tendency to point out the hoax, to deploy it as a sort of literary gesture.

In Chapter XIV of *Biographia Literaria,* Coleridge recollects the original plan for *Lyrical Ballads* in terms of experiments in a series of poems of two sorts. His efforts were to be directed toward the first sort and William Wordsworth's efforts toward the second:

In the one, the incidents and agents were to be, in part at least, supernatural; and the excellence aimed at was to consist in the interesting of the affections by the dramatic truth of such emotions, as would naturally accompany such situations, supposing them real. And real in *this* sense they have been to every human being who, from whatever source of delusion, has at any time believed himself under supernatural agency. For the second class, subjects were to be chosen from ordinary life.... (*BL* II 6, Coleridge's emphasis).

Coleridge's interest in the supernatural is directed at the psychological state of assenting to, or believing in supernatural incidents or agents, rather than in the supernatural itself. The "excellence" sought is specifically "in the interesting of the affections by the dramatic truth of such emotions..." if the incidents or agents were supposed to be supernatural. His choice of the word "delusion" is critical, because it emphasizes the lack of concern with the authenticity or truth of the event. He is interested in the attribution itself; and not in the representation of supernatural beings or agency.

For instance, in this sense, the status of the albatross in "The Rime of the Ancient Mariner" is far less interesting than the status attributed to it by the crew that hangs it around the mariner's neck ("Instead of the cross, the Albatross / About my neck was hung," lines 141,2). The crew assigns interpretations to the Albatross from the moment of its first appearance: "At length did cross an Albatross: / Through the fog it came; / As if it had been a Christian soul, / We hailed it in God's name" (*AM* 63-6). The marginal gloss interprets it as a "good omen" (*AM* 74) before the crew is explicitly noted as doing so. After the Mariner shoots the bird (*AM* 81,2) the crew connects the bird to the wind: "For all averred, I had killed the bird / That made the wind to blow" (*AM* 93,4). But when the sun burns the fog away they reverse their attribution: "Then all averred, I had killed the bird / That brought the fog and mist / Twas right, said they, such birds to slay, / That bring the fog and mist" (*AM* 99-102).

Whether the Albatross is a spirit, as the marginal gloss explains, or whether its death is the cause of the fate of the ship, are matters of conjecture. If we accept Coleridge's explanation in Chapter XIV, he is interested in the way that the differing attributions on the part of the crew would be accompanied by corresponding emotions. Regardless of the validity of the attributions, such emotions could not be disputed. The "dramatic truth" of such emotions, rather than the supernatural agency itself, interest the "affections" of a reader.

However, having said as much, it is difficult to know where to draw the line between the two. Does a reader merely respond to the emotional state of the characters without making some assessment regarding the validity of the supernatural agency that characters attribute to their experience? Coleridge blurs the distinction between character and audience when he continues his explanation in the next paragraph:

my endeavours should be directed to persons and characters supernatural, or at least romantic; yet so as to transfer from our inward nature a human interest and a semblance of truth sufficient to procure for these shadows of imagination that willing suspension of disbelief for the moment, which constitutes poetic faith. (*BL* II 8)

He seems interested in two levels of attribution: 1) the moment on the part of a character, wherein the belief is dramatically rendered as plausible; 2) the "suspension of disbelief" on the part of a reader, in which there is an assent to the attribution of the character. This second point is not necessarily a matter of participating in the belief itself. It is a matter of seeing it occur in the character, and of entertaining that belief as a possibility, or truth of the moment.

The line between these two levels of attribution is obscured by the prominence of the relation between character and reader within "The Rime of the Ancient Mariner." Coleridge situates the wedding-guest as an auditor to the Mariner's narration. The marginal gloss performs a reading of the poem. Just as various characters, spirits, and voices engage in different attributions to events and people within the narrative; the wedding-guest and the marginal gloss directly attribute belief to the Mariner's tale.

The wedding-guest suspends his disbelief to the point that the mariner has to calm him down: "Fear not, fear not, thou Wedding-Guest! / This body dropt not down". The marginal gloss expands on the supernatural details of several events. For instance, when the Mariner recounts that some of the crew "in dreams assured were / Of the spirit that plagued us so: / Nine fathoms deep he had followed us / From the land of mist and snow"; the gloss explains that the spirit is "one of the invisible inhabitants of this planet, neither departed souls nor angels; concerning whom the learned Jew, Josephus, and the Platonic Constantinopolitan, Michael Psellus, may be consulted".

Another obstacle to drawing this line between character and reader occurs because of a progressive attribution as the Mariner's tale proceeds. This progression can be illustrated by way of distinguishing between superstition and the supernatural. It almost suffices to say that superstition characterizes the outward journey, especially the movement from the southern ocean to the equator in the Pacific Ocean; while the supernatural characterizes the return to England. Especially early in his narration, there are attributions that belong entirely to the superstitious, without fully committing to the supernatural proper; or, the Mariner makes use of lively personifications that animate nature without extending such animation to the supernatural.

The crew's various interpretations of the Mariner's slaying of the albatross, noted above, are excellent examples of mere superstition. While the crew wants to attribute supernatural agency to the albatross, they do not know exactly *what* agency to attribute to it. Even when they hang the bird around the Mariner's neck, they are merely engaged in speculation. Such speculative attribution is considerably different from the events that occur when the Mariner falls in a "swound," while the ship is moving at an unbelievable speed, and he overhears two spirits attempting to understand what they are witnessing. In the same way, the personification that characterizes the outward journey of the ship differs considerably from its supernatural return.

As the ship crosses the equator, a "STORM-BLAST came, and he / Was tyrranous and strong: / He struck with his o'ertaking wings, / And chased us south along" (*AM* 41-4). Although the causality of this event is somewhat distorted—"southward aye we fled" (*AM* 50)—it is not presented as a problem or a mystery. The STORM-BLAST pursues "with yell and blow" but the attribution is left at the level of personified nature. Quite to the contrary, the return of the ship is entirely supernatural: "like a pawing horse let go, / She made a sudden bound...". The event is so mysterious that the two voices, overheard by the Mariner while he lies in a swound, cannot make sense out of it: "What makes that ship drive on so fast? / What is the OCEAN doing?" (*AM* 416,7). The Mariner does not attempt to explain the event. He simply recounts it, or the narration of it by the two voices. Nor do the voices, whom the gloss explains are "the Polar Spirit's fellow daemons", do anything more than describe it:

FIRST VOICE.
But why drives on that ship so fast,
Without wave or wind?
SECOND VOICE.
The air is cut away before,
And closes from behind.
(AM 426-29)

The only explanation is provided by the gloss, as if it is a matter of fact, as an answer to the FIRST VOICE's questions: "The Mariner hath been cast into a trance; for the angelic power causeth the vessel to drive northward, faster than human life could endure" (*AM* 426ff). Several points can be made here.

First, there is a distinct progression from casual attribution (e.g. personification) and superstition to the attribution of supernatural agency. Second, this progression is as dramatic at the level of the wedding-guest (an auditor of the tale) and the marginal gloss as it is on the part of the Mariner and the crew. For instance, the wedding-guest's last two outbursts both occur because he fears that the ancient Mariner is a ghost and that the ghosts of the dead crew have animated their dead bodies.

In "Word and 'Languageless' Meanings: Limits of Expression in The Rime of the Ancient Mariner," Raimonda Modiano focuses on the role of delusion in the Mariner's tale:

Until late in his life Coleridge maintained his view that the true subject of a supernatural poem is the mentality of its narrator and the circumstances that cause him to confuse reality with his distorted apprehension of it. In a notebook entry written in 1830, Coleridge points out that, to ensure the credibility and success of a supernatural tale, the poet "of his free will and judgement" must do "what the Believing Narrator of a Supernatural Incident, Apparition or Charm does from ignorance and weakness of mind,—i.e. mistake a Subjective produce (A saw the Ghost of Z) for an objective fact-the Ghost of Z was there to be seen."

The "mistake" consists in the forgetting, or the failure to recognize, that the mind has constituted something that it perceives as merely found. Coleridge's interest in the supernatural consists in the way that such incidents betray the mind's constitution of external reality. By extension, the apprehension of such error is critical because such apprehension reveals the active constituents of experience or knowledge. Thus, in Coleridge, we discover both a psychology of reading that exerts caution with regard to how a reader assesses possibility and an explanation for what is disclosed when a hoax is recognized or otherwise found out.

It is insufficient to argue, with Alkon, that the scientific premise behind the creation of the monster in *Frankenstein* was not believable. To do so would be to ignore the unstable and transitive nature of possibility with regard to representation and historical circumstance. Shelley's use of a nested narrative to render a scientific theme enacts a precise translation of Coleridge's use of the supernatural into a scientific register.

As a consummate reader of Colcridge, Poe is fascinated with Coleridge's interest in the psychology of reading from the outset. For example, both Poe's earliest successful tale, "MS Found in a Bottle," and the later "Descent into the Maelstrom" recast Coleridge's "The Rime of Ancient Mariner" in a way that accentuates the issues of belief at both the level of narration and in terms of the veracity of the piece as a whole. Interestingly, both tales are science fiction and both invoke the hoax as a literary gesture: like *Frankenstein*, "MS Found in a Bottle" involves a polar expedition; and "Descent into the Maelstrom" imagines the descent into and the escape from a whirlpool, with the escape being based upon supposed scientific principles.

"MS Found in a Bottle" alludes to John Clyve Symmes' 1818 theory that the earth is hollow and the later *Symzonia, A Voyage of Discovery* by Captain Adam Seaborn (usually considered to be Symmes). "Descent into the Maelstrom" uses a nested narrative to pose the believability of the narrator's tale as a central interpretative dilemma.

Poe not only consistently links his science fiction experiments with hoaxing; he also thematizes the hoax itself. For example, in "The Unparalleled Adventure of One Hans Pfaall," he explicitly interrogates the possibility that Pfaall's message is a hoax. This tale, which Poe claimed was inspired by Sir John Herschel's *Treatise on Astronomy*, was first published in the *Southern Literary Messenger* in June of 1835. It anticipates Locke's hoax by imagining a balloon flight to the moon.

The tale is striking as a work of science fiction insofar as Poe strives for extreme verisimilitude in his rendering of Pfaall's account of his ascent through the atmosphere: "In 'Hans Pfaall' the design is original, inasmuch as regards an attempt at verisimilitude, in the application of scientific principles [...] to the actual passage between the earth and the moon." The detailed empirical observations and scientific speculation that characterizes Pfaall's ascent is notable in this regard.

However, Poe undermines the veracity of the piece by drawing attention to its probable status as a hoax: "The letter, having been published, gave rise to a variety of gossip and opinion. Some of the over-wise even made themselves ridiculous by descrying the whole business as nothing better than a hoax". While he continues by speculating that "hoax, with these sorts of people, is, I believe, a general term for all matters above their comprehension", Poe has created a provocation to which readers are invited to respond. The hoax is deployed as sort of gesture that invites readers to evaluate their own interpretation of the tale. Furthermore, the endnote that Poe added when he republished the tale in 1840 discusses Locke's "Great Astronomical Discoveries" in considerable detail. This tendency to draw attention to the hoax, to turn it into a literary gesture, is symptomatic of Poe's Coleridgean interest in the psychology of reading. By revealing the hoax, even as it is being enacted, Poe points to the active constituents of knowledge that are at play in reading.

Like Coleridge, the interest is not the object—supernatural or scientific—but what the appearance of the object says about those who see it and the means by which they all see it together. In his Literati piece on Locke, Poe notes that as the supposed discoveries of Herschel "were gradually spread before the public, the astonishment of that public grew out of all bounds; but those who questioned the veracity of 'The Sun'—the authenticity of the communication to 'The Edinburgh Journal of Science'—were really very few indeed; and this I am forced to look upon as a far more wonderful thing than any 'man-bat' of them all".

Chapter 4

Coleridge and the Explosion of Voice

Coleridge is so often described in terms which are akin to the word, "explosive," and by all accounts he was at times an unusually dynamic, charismatic and unpredictable person. His writings themselves could also be termed "explosive" merely from their physical form; a fragmented mass, some pieces finished but most not, much of his writing subject to procrastination or eventual change of mind. Today I want to address a moment in his life which produced, as Richard Holmes has characterized it, an explosion of his poetic talent—Autumn 1799, when he first met Sara Hutchinson, and wrote, amongst other poems, the ballad, "Love."

In addressing this moment, I want to suggest that the voice of Coleridge at this time was explosive, vital and new, but only when set against the "ancient" balladic tradition with which he engaged. Whilst accepting the dynamism and the unpredictability of Coleridge, I want to show that his acceptance of a formal mode allowed him to find his own particular, romantic voice; for, as Stephen Parrish has pointed out, "for Coleridge, the passion was obscured unless the poet spoke in his own voice." The ballad revival of the eighteenth century supplied Romantic writers with an archive of voices from the past, a past which many seemed to idealize as a time of true feeling, when Nature not only had its place but was also imbued with a raw power.

Particularly in the late 1790s, Coleridge worked within such a tradition, and in so doing, found his own voice from the minstrelsy of the past. I want to begin by illustrating the literary environment in which Coleridge found himself at the end of the eighteenth century. Ancient ballad and song culture was being revived throughout Europe from the early eighteenth century onwards, possibly beginning with the "Ossian" fragments in Scotland.

Although most British commentators were skeptical of the authenticity of Ossian, as Hugh Trevor-Roper reports, they were feted in other parts of Europe; and Germany in particular. The title of this conference is "The National Graduate Romanticism Conference"; the proximity of "Romantic" and "National" in this tag is fortuitous, since it is important to realise the close relationship between the ballad revival and a sense of nationhood. In Johann Herder's famous essay on Ossian, the place of the song or ballad as a kind of national cultural archive is made plain. He refers to the ballads as "the gnomic song of the nation," and continues, in letter form, to his "friend":

What I wanted to do was remind you that Ossian's poems are songs, songs of the people, folk-songs, the songs of an unsophisticated people living close to the senses, songs which have been long handed down by oral tradition.

Herder locks into the fashionable Rousseauian notion of the "Noble Savage." He goes on:

Know then, that the more barbarous a people is - that is, the more alive, the more freely acting (for that is what the word means) - the more barbarous, that is, the more alive, the more free, the closer to the senses, the more lyrically dynamic its songs will be, if songs it has. The more remote a people is from an artificial, scientific manner of thinking, speaking and writing, the less its verses are written for the dead letter.

The attraction of this national voice is its proximity to nature; and thus, proximity to a kind of raw reality. Herder makes clear that this "ancient" verse is a superior form for it is from "Nature" and not from "Art." The present age, he observes, has made the mistake of foregrounding Art over Nature:

And if that is the way our time thinks, then of course we

will admire Art rather than Nature in these ancients' poems; we will find too much or too little Art in them, according to our predisposition, and we will rarely have ears to hear the voice that sings in them: the voice of Nature.

Indeed the general thrust of this essay is to cry out for a natural poetic voice, the kind of voice that he found so evident in the Ossian fragments. He complains at the recent German translation of Ossian, by Michael Denis, because he used the polished hexameters of the German neo-classical idiom; a hated, artful masking of the Natural Voice.

At the end of the essay, Herder calls to his countrymen for a collection of German folk-songs. They are badly needed, he feels, to remind the nation of their own collective voice, a voice that has been suppressed. Herder holds up England's Bishop Percy as the great example. He says that, "the sturdy Englishmen were not ashamed of [their ballads], nor did they need to be."

Whilst invoking the Elizabethan "Hearts of Oak" quality in the phrase "sturdy Englishmen," Herder reminds his public that they have theirs—and we should have ours. It is a national necessity. Eventually Herder fulfilled his own wish, and himself edited a two volume collection of folk-songs, entitled *Volkslieder*, which emerged in 1778-9. This collection was well-known among literary circles in Europe; when Coleridge visited Hamburg in 1798, he made a point of buying "a Luther's Bible, 3 marks & 4 pence — and Herder's Popular Songs, 7 Marks."

Herder was writing about Ossian around eight years after the first publication of Percy's *Reliques of Ancient English Poetry*, which came out in 1765. Although Percy was later to be hailed by many Romantics as a precursor to that movement, he underplays his contribution to any development in aesthetics, calling his collection "the barbarous productions of unpolished ages," and worrying that these poetic fragments are unworthy of patronage. However under this veneer of care and worry is a sly advancement of Herder's division between natural spontaneity and superfluous decoration. Percy immediately continues:

But this impropriety, it is presumed, will disappear, when it is declared that these poems are presented to your ladyship, not as labours of art, but as effusions of nature, showing the first efforts of ancient genius, and exhibiting the customs and opinions of remote ages.

Percy, in his famous phrase, "effusions of nature," anticipates the explosion of Romantic voices. But in a similar vein to Herder, he points to the collective importance of the ancient fragments. Voices are not singled out in these minstrels' lays; partly because they are anonymous, but partly also, I think, because Herder and Percy saw the fragments as in fact a kind of corpus, which in some way represented the collective ancient whole of a nation. Thus Percy refers to the works as the efforts of "genius," not "genii." For the generations who grew up with Percy's *Reliques*, this collection of songs would prove extremely influential.

By the end of the century, publication of songs had become even more popular and profitable. One of the most influential of these, as well as one of the most comprehensive, was Sir Walter Scott's *Minstrelsy of the Scottish Border*, of 1802. Here was the historical archive of ancient Scotland; the second chapter of Ossian, perhaps. Scott emphasized the link between poetry and national history, thus:

The historian of an individual nation is equally or more deeply interested in the researches into popular poetry, since he must not disdain to gather from the tradition conveyed in ancient ditties and ballads, the information necessary to confirm or correct intelligence collected from more certain sources.

Hugh Trevor-Roper states that, "Before he had ever written a novel, Scott had eclipsed the two founding fathers of the romantic revival. He was at once the new Percy of his country, the new Ossian of his time." Trevor-Roper's thesis in this 1969 Coffin Lecture is that Scott changed the writing of history, by peopling it. Enlightenment historians—Hume, Gibbon and Robertson, for example—"saw history as a process, and a process, moreover, of improvement, of "progress." "But", as he goes on to say, if they thus penetrated to the inner meaning of history, they did so, too often, by overlooking the human content. The men of the past entered their story only indirectly, as the agents or victims of 'progress': they seldom appeared directly, in their own right, in their own social context, as the legitimate owners of their own autonomous centuries. The romantic writers changed all that.

Appearing "directly," in one's "own right," becomes of crucial importance when considering the emergence of an individual voice in Coleridge's early ballads.

Thus Britain at the end of the eighteenth century, according to Dianne Dugaw, "was being swept, bottom to top, by a spirit of antiquarianism, a sentimental and revivalist love for old ballads and histories." Wordsworth and Coleridge were caught up in this surge of sentimental interest and, whilst walking on the Quantock Hills in the late nineties, would conceive the idea of the *Lyrical Ballads*. In the later *Supplementary to the Preface* (1815), Wordsworth makes clear his, or their, debt to Percy:

I have already stated how much Germany is indebted to this ... work; and for our own country, its poetry has been absolutely redeemed by it. I do not think that there is an able writer in verse of the present day who would not be proud to acknowledge his obligations to the Reliques; I know that it is so with my friends; and, for myself, I am happy in this occasion to make a public avowal of my own.

Wordsworth and Coleridge were undoubtedly influenced by Percy. But, as Mary Jacobus points out, the English romantics were equally stimulated by a descendent of Herder, the German balladeer, Gottfried Bürger. In the nineties, ballad imitations—rather than the ancient originals so praised by Herder and Scott—were becoming increasingly sensational and poorly written. Bürger was a welcome relief. Jacobus comments: "As no-one in England had done, Bürger transformed the traditional ballad into something both novel and contemporaneous." Bürger's ballad, "Leonore," had been in circulation in England from the early nineties, and it thrilled the English writers. Charles Lamb wrote to Coleridge in 1796,

"Have you read the Ballad called 'Leonora', in the second Number of the 'Monthly Magazine'? If you have!

Coleridge found himself at a time of intense interest and debate over the ballad form. His closest friends were writing to him about the Bürger ballads; he talked about the ballad form with Wordsworth, in particular; and he was deeply interested in German aesthetics. He had taught himself German in the mid-nineties, because, as Richard Holmes puts it, "he considered [it] to be far more advanced, both scientifically and philosophically, than French and English." During the *Lyrical Ballads* months, he composed many experimental ballad poems: between September 1797 and April 1798 he began *The Rime of the Ancient Mariner, Christabel,* "The Three Graves," and "The Ballad of the Dark Ladie." Soon after, he traveled to Germany with the Wordsworths; he spent virtually a year there, reading German philosophy and aesthetics voraciously, particularly Kant, Schelling, and the Schlegels. It was during this visit that he bought Herder's *Volkslieder*.

He returned to England in July, 1799. And in the autumn of that year, amid his failing marriage, he traveled to Durham and met Sara Hutchinson whilst with the Wordsworths. He fell in love with her. Holmes comments: "This love affair underlay, and to some degree undermined, almost everything he did and wrote in the next ten years. It broke his marriage, it helped to break his health, and it very nearly broke his will to go on with his work." But at this time, Coleridge was ignited, regenerated in a passion for life and for writing.

"His notebooks, previously used largely for memoranda of his reading, lists, addresses and accounts, suddenly explode into life with descriptions of the rivers and mountains, and the subtle effects of light and weather." From this regeneration, came immediately the poem "Love"—another experimental Gothic ballad. It was the only other ballad apart from the *Mariner* which he actually completed.

Coleridge's personal explosion here, although important, is somehow not unexpected. His life seemed to be a series of violent outbursts and then of silences, of tremendous energy, and then of procrastination. Dorothy Wordsworth, impressed by Coleridge in at least the early years of their friendship, describes the energy of his arrival at Racedown in June 1797: "he did not keep to the high road, but leapt over a gate and bounded down the pathless field by which he cut off an angle." One of the more famous, early, descriptions of Coleridge is from William Hazlitt. Hazlitt describes the scene, when Coleridge arrived at his local town to preach in 1798:

He did not come till late on the Saturday afternoon before he was to preach; and Mr Rowe, who himself went down to the coach in a state of anxiety and expectation, to look for the arrival of his successor, could find no one at all answering to the description but a round-faced man in a short black coat (like a shooting jacket) which hardly seemed to have been made for him, but who seemed to be talking at a great rate to his fellow-passengers.

Mr Rowe had scarce returned to give an account of his disappointment, when the round-faced man in black entered, and dissipated all doubts on the subject, by beginning to talk. He did not cease while he staid; nor has he since, that I know of. He held the good town of Shrewsbury in delightful suspense for three weeks that he remained there.

Coleridge himself, in describing his habit of procrastination, says, castigating, "it is a deep & wide disease in my moral Nature ... Love of Liberty, Pleasure of Spontaneity, &c&c, these all express, not explain, the fact."

Such "Pleasure of Spontaneity" is, as Thomas McFarland notes, most fully felt in Coleridge's notebooks and marginalia. These fragmentary effusions of the poet's mind work well with McFarland's thesis, which to simplify, sees expressions of ruin and fragmentation as a core or bedrock of Romanticism. He says, "It is my judgment, and I believe of many and perhaps most scholars actively engaged in Coleridge studies, that Coleridge's most pregnant, vital and idiosyncratic work is to be found in his pure fragments: in the haphazard entries of his notebooks, and in the immediacies of marginal notations in books he was reading." Many of Coleridge's poems are fragmented, too; *Christabel* was written in a series of pieces, over a period of time; and *Kubla Khan*'s form, actually described by the poet as "A Fragment," is a result of interruption and forgetfulness. Friedrich Schlegel, in one of his own "Fragments," responds to this modern habit, and relates it to the ancient tradition: "the works of the ancients have become fragments; the works of the moderns are fragments at their inception."

But the poem "Love" is a completed ballad. If there is fragmentation here, it seems to be of a more subtle kind. I suggest that the "ruin," to use McFarland's word, is that of the ancient national tradition. In this balladic experiment, Coleridge works within the by now predictable voices of the tradition, and from their ruins builds a personal emergent voice. The poem "Love" reminds us that you cannot have ruins without having a castle in the first place; Coleridge's own voice is new, but it is the product of a knowledge and love of the historical voice which Herder and Scott refer to in their own ways. Stephen Parrish, in his article, "The Wordsworth - Coleridge Controversy," simplifies nicely the difference in approach for Wordsworth and Coleridge in writing songs and ballads:

the crucial difference lay in Wordsworth's adoption of the dramatic method in his ballads. and Coleridge's rejection of it. To put it in the simplest way, the passion that Wordsworth expressed in poetry was likely to be that of his characters, the passion that Coleridge looked for was mainly that of the poet. For Wordsworth, the passion could appear only if the poet maintained strict dramatic propriety; for Coleridge, the passion was obscured unless the poet spoke in his own voice.

Coleridge approaches the balladic tradition and takes what he needs in order to experiment with his own voice. The voice speaks out of generations of voices.

At the time when he met Sara, Coleridge's notebooks teem with jagged shards of life, to use a McFarland turn of phrase. Not only are the entries for November 1799 about as long as all the entries for the preceding six months, but the mental leaps of imagination, excitement and wonder as revealed in the entries is disorienting:

576 — O God! when I now think how perishable Things, how imperishable ideas — what a proof of My Immortality — What is Forgetfulness? —

577 May not Time in Association be made *serviceable* & evidence Likeness/.

578 The Long Entrancement of a True-Love's Kiss.

579 In the North every Brook, every Crag, almost every Field has a name — a proof of greater Independence & a Society more approaching in their Laws & Habits to Nature–

Less than a month after these entries, "Love" was published in the *Morning Post*, on 21 December 1799, as "Introduction to the Tale of the Dark Ladie." It was considerably edited and newly titled "Love" for the 1800 edition of the *Lyrical Ballads*. It appears on the page as a controlled, completed, twenty-five stanza poem; evidence of romantic fragmentation here will certainly not come from the format of the verse. The ballad structure is rigid; every stanza is four lines long, the first three of eight syllables, and the last of six syllables.

Coleridge dots the poem with the obligatory archaisms of the "ancient tradition": for instance, "ladie," "lay," and "minstrel." The story within the poem is recognizably of the antiquarian tradition, too: the wooing of a Lady by a Knight, "that wore / Upon his shield a burning brand." This story is told by a minstrel, who himself is wooing a woman. When it first appeared, the poem was prefaced by a letter which Coleridge wrote to the editor of the newspaper, and the letter makes a case for his modern balladeering. Coleridge's list of excuses makes interesting reading in the light of our discussion today:

As it is professedly a tale of ancient times, I trust that 'the affectionate lovers of venerable antiquity' (as Camden says) will grant me their pardon, and perhaps may be induced to admit a force and propriety in it. A heavier objection may be adduced against the Author, that in these times of fear and expectation, when novelties *explode* [Coleridge's emphasis] around us in all directions, he should presume to offer to the public a silly tale of old fashioned love; and, five years ago, I own, I should have allowed and felt the force of this objection. But, alas! explosion has succeeded explosion so rapidly, that novelty itself ceases to appear new; and it is possible that now, even a simple story, wholly unspired [sic] with politics and personality, may find some attention amid the hubbub of Revolutions, as to those who have resided a long time by the falls of Niagara, the lowest whispering becomes distinctly audible.

Coleridge is coy in this letter. We should not believe that he, of anyone, has not been affected by the explosion of "novelties" in "these times of fear and expectations." "Personality," or the individual person, is actually deeply involved in this poem; we do not need, in this case, the benefit of Holmes' and other modern biographical scholarship, for E.H. Coleridge glosses the history of this poem in the *Poetical Works*, and he points out a clear connection between this pseudo-medieval fable and Coleridge's personal life.

He details the visit to Sockburn, and goes on to show direct links between the poem and this visit; for instance, he says that lines 13-16 describe scenes from Sockburn church and the "field near the farm-house."

More than plain biographical and topographical links, an individual personality or voice emerges from the story of the minstrel singing to his princess, the story which frames the Knight's tale.

Because the minstrel/poet is the real subject of the poem, the ballad form is taken from historical fragment to personal, romantic song. The poem becomes less of an ancient imitation, less of a "simple song," than an expression of love, and at the same time, a statement of personal poetic ambition.

The poet's love for Genevieve seems more concrete, more real, than the Knight's story, which is transparent by comparison. The Knight's story is constantly interrupted by the poet observing Genevieve react to him; her blushing, and finally, their embrace. "Love" does not end with the Knight, but with the minstrel: "And so I won my Genevieve, / My bright and beauteous bride." The poem foregrounds the minstrel's vocation as a poet, a singer and a teller, by repeating verbs which emphasize such a role: "I told her of the Knight"... "I told her how he pined"... "I sang an old and moving story." From this, the reader is encouraged, I think, to realise the triple relationship occurring; at the same time, three sets of voices compete for love's sake; Knight and Ladie, Minstrel and Genevieve; Coleridge and Sara. The ninth stanza in particular seems to indicate the importance of finding your way through a poem's voices:

I told her how he pined: and ah!
The deep, the low, the pleading tone
With which I sang another's love,
Interpreted my own.

At the same time as the minstrel is interpreting his love from the Knight's, so too do we interpret Coleridge's love for Sara from the minstrel; Sara seems very close to the text here. But there are other issues of interpretation going on, too. In this poem, Coleridge has moved the balladic voice from an impersonal story-teller to a doubly personal voice: the minstrel/narrator *and* Coleridge behind the scenes. Layers of interpretation unfold in this poem: from historical legend to ancient minstrel to romantic poet. Coleridge, in the letter to the editor, complains at "novelty," but in fact what he is doing here seems new and characteristically Romantic.

He delves into the historical, cultural archive of songs and ballads - the univocal, raw, voice of a nation as described by Herder - and works within such a frame to produce his own voice. It is a voice both of love and of individual poetic vocation.

Parrish reminds us that, for Coleridge, "passion was obscured unless the poet spoke in his own voice." In his ballads, as shown in this example, Coleridge's is not the only voice; but in competing with other, older voices his emerges as dominant and individual. Coleridge, the explosive romantic, becomes one of the writers, according to Hugh Trevor-Roper, who would influence the way people thought and wrote about history. He did this by creating his own voice from the old voice of the nation; by writing "directly," and in his "own right."

DREAMING: ROMANTICISM, DREAMS AND THE MEDICAL IMAGINATION

A full-length study of Coleridge's concern with dreams has long been a desideratum. Select writings, especially the notebook entries recording dreams and commenting on them, have been studied for such varied purposes as elucidating Coleridge's poems, assessing the effects of his opium use, revealing his ambivalence about women, evaluating his psychological insight, and determining his place in the history of oneirology. But before the appearance of *Coleridge on Dreaming*, no book was wholly occupied with surveying and interpreting Coleridge's oneirological writings, and it looked as if Coleridge's inability to 'devote an entire work to the subject of Dreams' (a hope he expressed in *The Friend*) had extended to his critics.

Hitherto the most comprehensive examination of Coleridge and dreams took the form of a special double-issue of the psychological journal *Dreaming*, edited by David Miall and Don Kuiken. But precisely because this was a collection of essays by divers hands, it was not expected to demonstrate a uniformity of approach or even of subject. A book by a single author, in contrast, may reasonably be expected to demonstrate one kind of uniformity or the other.

Let me define these terms for the present context. Uniformity of approach would consist either in interpreting Coleridge's recorded dreams themselves (whatever one conceives dreams to be) or in interpreting his comments about his dreams, but not in doing both. Uniformity of subject would consist in confining one's attention either to dreams, as products of the nocturnal mind, or to 'dreams', as products of the waking mind (i.e. poetic constructs), but not in treating both as if they were the same. A psychoanalytic study, because it is uniform in approach and assumes that both dreams and poem can reveal the contents of the unconscious, may neglect the formal differences between the texts it studies.

But an 'historical exploration', which seeks to investigate 'Coleridge's responses to his dreams and to contemporary debates on the nature of dreaming' (I quote from the dustjacket blurb of *Coleridge on Dreaming*), needs to adhere to both uniformities, so to speak. It has no business interpreting Coleridge's dreams for him or interpreting his poems as if they were dreams, for neither kind of interpretation contributes to an understanding of his relation to contemporary oneirology.

By these criteria of assessment, *Coleridge on Dreaming* is a disappointment. The problems begin on the title page with the concepts of *dreams* and *medical imagination*, neither of which is sufficiently defined in the book. The failure to distinguish between the literal and metaphorical use of the word *dream*, for example in the discussions of drama and *Christabel*, permits in turn a more serious confusion between different senses of the word *imagination*.

Thus on the one hand imagination is identified with association, as when we are informed that in 'Dugald Stewart's *Elements of the Philosophy of the Human Soul* (1791), dreams are seen as the product of the imagination, which is the tendency in the 'human mind to associate or connect its thoughts together'', while on the other it is identified with the formative power that Coleridge theorized in explicit rejection of associationism.

Admittedly, Coleridge himself confused the issue by occasionally using the word *imagination* indiscriminately, and by falsely opposing imagination (conceived in German idealist terms) to fancy (conceived in British empiricist terms). But these facts make it especially imperative for the critic to sort out, rather than to reproduce, the confusion.

If there is one respect which Coleridge is perfectly consistent, it is in his insistence on the suspension of volition, or will, in sleep and nocturnal dreaming. Ford acknowledges this and correctly notes Coleridge's agreement on the matter with earlier oneirological writers, including Andrew Baxter and Erasmus Darwin, but she underestimates the importance of the fact, which is the key to understanding Coleridge's fundamental differentiation of poetic creations from oneiric aggregations.

His definition of poetry as a 'rationalized dream' is quoted several times, but without due consideration of the adjective:

because reason, for Coleridge, presupposes the presence of will, a rationalized dream is no dream at all, at least according to his usual description of dreams as phenomena produced during sleep by an unrestrained process of association. And just as the presence of will distinguishes poetry from dreams, so the absence of it prevents dreams from containing symbolic meaning.

It is one thing to assert that Coleridge's recorded dreams *are* symbolic, as Ford does, but quite another to assert that he *considered* them to be so. (To make both assertions, and to interpret the dream-texts accordingly, is to violate the principle of uniformity of approach.) Coleridge was certainly capable of entertaining the possibility that dreams have a language distinct from but analogous to spoken languages, but it is an exaggeration to say that he was 'firmly convinced' of it. In fact the notebook entries in which he recorded his dreams are remarkable not only for their detailed accounts of the content of the dreams, but also for their refusal to interpret those contents.

The extent to which Coleridge was unable or unwilling to relinquish the associationist view of dreams as meaningless is revealed in his dismissive comments on precisely that book which, if he had attributed symbolic significance to dreams, he should have embraced: G. H. Schubert's *Symbolik des Traumes*, which he read in the second edition of 1821. Coleridge could hardly have failed to notice the similarity between Schubert's concept of the symbol and his own (as formulated in *The Statesman's Manual*), so why did he reject Schubert's argument that dreams can reveal to modern man the cosmic harmony which nature had revealed to ancient man—and on the grounds that Schubert's symbolic dreams 'ought not to have been confounded with those of proper sleep' (qtd. on p. 62)?

The answer is not, as Ford argues, that Coleridge believed there were 'many different dream languages', but rather that he was unwilling to attribute symbolic significance—which would imply the operation of the rational mind—to phenomena whose rationality he steadfastly denied. The thought that dreams might be meaningful could only increase their terror to someone who, even while explaining them in mechanist and associationist terms, often kept himself awake at night to avoid them.

There is much of value in *Coleridge and Dreaming*, not least in its diligent assembly of Coleridge's scattered writings on dreams and its extensive attention to the Enlightenment contexts of those writings, particularly associationist psychology; but the book's methodological faults militate against its conclusions and prevent it from being considered a 'definitive' treatment of its various subjects.

Chapter 5

Coleridge's Muses and Feminist Criticism

According to Thomas De Quincey, the poetics of Romanticism were organised around a gender opposition: 'the Sublime... in contraposition to the Beautiful, grew up on the basis of *sexual* distinctions - the Sublime corresponding to the male, and the Beautiful, its anti-pole, corresponding to the female'.

The principal proponent of these gendered poetics was Edmund Burke, for whom the sublime was characterised by the masculine traits of power, terror, strength, greatness, and the beautiful by the feminine qualities of softness, sympathy, and feeling. Burke's view of the feminine was criticised by the contemporary feminist Mary Wollstonecraft, who argued that it amounted, when used to define women's social role, to a prescription for libertinism. Burke's views, she asserted, rendered women helpless, ill-educated beings.

Valued (if at all) only for their bodily appearance and compliance, they were rejected when their looks faded because men found them mentally dull. No longer entranced by their beauty, men became contemptuous of the very weakness they had encouraged women to adopt. They cast them off, to replace them with other mistresses whose weakness was still attractively accompanied by beauty. In the process, both men and women were degraded. Inequality was perpetuated; men became tyrants, women became victims.

Coleridge was briefly a friend of Wollstonecraft. He was, in the 1790s, a political enemy of Burke. But he was not a feminist. Despite his political differences from the *Reflections on the Revolution in France,* he often viewed the feminine in a way similar to its author. And, according to a number of recent critics, he adopted a Burkean view of the feminine in his poetry.

His poetry and poetics, it is suggested, borrowed a gendered sublime and beautiful, in order to empower the masculine and disempower the feminine. The male poet, it is argued, was the principal beneficiary. He became sublime, whereas he made of the female a beautiful but subordinate muse. Marlon B. Ross, for instance, sees Coleridge as participating in male Romanticism's struggle for a transcendent 'power of self-possession, a power that is repeatedly willed in the poetry by both overt and subliminal appeals to the virility and masculinity of his creative project'.

Ross's view of male Romanticism has as its test case Wordsworth's poetic treatment of women. For Mary Jacobus too, Wordsworth's poetic power was gained at the expense of the feminine, and at women's cost. She shows that in Wordsworth's poetry Dorothy is enlisted as a muse, only for her insights and words to be absorbed into Wordsworth's contemplation of his own superior genius. For Anne K. Mellor, Wordsworth's silencing of Dorothy was replicated by Coleridge in 'Kubla Khan'.

The treatment in that poem of the Abyssinian maid is paradigmatic of the procedure of male Romantics: they effect a 'total absorption' of the feminine which leaves it - and the women who feature in their work - 'conquered' and 'enslaved'. Margaret Homans declares that Wordsworthian Romantic poetry 'states most compellingly the traditional myth ... of woman's place in language as the silent or vanished object of male representation and quest'. The male Romantics, in other words, far from being opponents of the gender inequality which Burke, and the social order he defended, perpetuated, were complicit with his defence - and with the social order itself (at least in so far as it concerned women). They were not, in this area, radicals, and if they were not libertines they were, in their poetry, conquerors.

In what follows I want to take issue with the idea that Coleridge participates in a conquest and enslavement of the feminine. By investigating the poetics of 'Kubla Khan' and the implications of his verse correspondence with Mary Robinson, poet and spurned mistress of the Prince of Wales, I shall offer a more historically nuanced account of Coleridge's versions of femininity. I shall contend that he undermined (sometimes even as he set out) what Ross calls male Romanticism's strategy of presenting poetry as 'a form of masculine empowerment' and 'a paradigmatic form of manly action'. Rather than blame Coleridge for a poetic 'conquest' of the feminine, we need to see him as an unstable writer, who, at his best, opens gender roles and gendered poetics to question.

Unsure of his own masculinity, in poetry as in life, Coleridge often leaves masculine and feminine, men and women, in undetermined relationships, their gender and sexual identities uncertain and fluid (Geraldine in 'Christabel' being an example of this). As Laura Claridge notes, the economies energising the majority of [male Romantics'] poems aimed at recuperating the special potency that accrues to marginalised forces, in this case, woman as that which is not always already written. Saying this is not the same as accusing the poets of appropriating such female voices.

I. 'Kubla Khan'

'Kubla Khan' is Coleridge's most concentrated dramatisation of the conflicts, sexual and implicitly political, produced through the adoption of the gendered sublime and the beautiful. It features a male figure of power, the Khan, who is a sublime genius - a conqueror, a statesman, a master-builder. It also features a poetic genius, sublime in his capacity to command awe, who also builds - builds domes in the air, or the imagination. Each of these figures is associated with a female: the Khan with the 'woman wailing for her demon lover', the poet with the Abyssinian maid, who sings rather than wails.

Critics of the poem divide on the crucial question of whether the sublime conqueror Kubla Khan is analogous to, or contrasts with, the sublime poet, and whether the Abyssinian maid resembles, or differs from, the wailing woman. If one accepts that conqueror and poet, woman and maid are analogous, then the poem seems to suggest that the poet's vision seeks desperately to preserve, in transcendent form, the masculine creativity that has built the pleasure dome. For the Khan is like God in Genesis: he decrees and the dome is erected. His word has immediate and direct power in the world: it seems neither to require mediation nor the assistance of another. The Khan is a creator who needs neither a muse; nor a wife. But his creation is flawed: being a production of masculinity, and of a violent masculinity to boot, it is haunted by a dominance that issues in violent and libertine sexuality:

A savage place! as holy and enchanted
As e'er beneath a waning moon was haunted
By woman wailing for her demon-lover!
And from this chasm, with ceaseless turmoil seething,
As if this earth in fast thick pants were breathing,
A mighty fountain momently was forced:
Amid whose swift half-intermittent burst
Huge fragments vaulted like rebounding hail.
(PW, I, 297; ll. 14-21)

Shaped by a masculine sexuality to which women become victims, the Khan's dome is a place in which women's suffering and desire are heard as one in the sound of a 'savage' wail. But if the dome is characterised by conquest and violence, it is threatened by it too, for it is vulnerable to destruction, to 'ancestral voices prophesying war' (l. 30). The dome that the sublime poet proposes to build is not similarly vulnerable, for it exists only in the imagination. But it is not clear whether the poet can ever build it, for he doubts his own creative power.

He ends not with a successful construction, but with a vision of the awe he would inspire, the sublimity he would acquire, could he envision the dome in words. In a recent article Jane Moore has construed this outcome as a failure by the poet to attain the potency he desires. Reading the poet at the poem's end as being analogous to the Khan, she sees him as trying, but failing, to become a Khan himself, to become a sublime creator whose masculinity is produced through the conquest of the feminine. She declares

it is exactly at the moment when the poet fails to master woman that he fails also to be master of himself, of his own actions: the dome is never built and the poem, at least the poem the preface promises, is never finished.

For Moore, the poet cannot 'revive within me / [the]symphony and song' of the Abyssinian maid (ll. 42-43) and therefore can neither master the feminine nor complete the poem. Moore's argument is an intriguing one, for it highlights the extent to which sublimity, creativity, and masculinity are bound together in the poem, over and against visions of femininity. But in assuming that Khan and poet are simply analogous Moore overlooks some of the poem's distinctions in its portraits of women and of master-builders. The damsel with a dulcimer is to be distinguished from the 'woman wailing for her demon-lover!'.

She is from the start an apparition in a 'vision', and she is not subordinated to a masterful and evil lover. She does not wail, but sings and plays - signs of culture. She offers 'deep delight' with her lyric; she gives a gift of poetry. In other words, she is a muse, one who communicates the arts of an ancient culture to which a poet might aspire - especially as she unites words and music, like the minstrels and bards whom Coleridge idealised. She does not resemble, but differs from, the unidentified woman who wails for her demon lover, defined as that woman is by her bodily cry of desire/suffering. Coleridge, that is to say, sets up an opposition, not an analogy, making the poet and maid represent a cultured relationship, a communication of spirit through song, to contrast with the tyrannical and violent sexual relationship of the Khan's building.

The building which the Abyssinian maid's symphony and song sponsors is significantly different from the Khan's. Whereas Kubla tries to conquer nature by his decree, to shape it to his will, aping God and producing a dome vitiated by 'ancestral voices prophesying war' (l. 30), the poet's dome exists only as a possibility registered in the consciousness of writer and reader. The poet's dome of air, no more substantial than the breath of speech, is a more beneficent creation than the Khan's, is an alternative to Kubla's mastery and to the subjugation it demands, precisely because it exists *only* in the other-world of fiction - a world in which the conditional has, through imagery, the visual intensity of the apparently real.

By the end of the poem the dome can only be held together in suspension - not in a scene imagined which might exist beyond the poem but as a possibility of renewal held for as long as it takes to read the lines - a tentative half state in which to say 'I would build that dome in air' is to build it - a castle in the air of poetry.

The poet's dome, then, is dependent not on a Satanic conqueror of women, but on the revival of their envisioned song in the self-conscious creativity of the male poet. The damsel with a dulcimer is a muse, a feminine song-within, without the acceptance of which the male poet's creation is vitiated by exclusivity and mastery as was the Khan's. The poet's remodelling of creative power, for Coleridge, is dependent upon his (for it is a he) willingness to be sponsored by the feminine, to incorporate (his ideas of) a woman's voice into his own: as he put it in a late notebook, 'in every true and manly Man there is a translucent Under-tint of the Woman'. It is, of course, the male poet who sets this agenda, forms this vision of the feminine, but it is one of revival, of sponsorship (in *Coleridge's* terms, reciprocity) not mastery in the sense that Moore suggests.

Nor is it one of conquest or enslavement: it is the male poet's failure to revive within himself the maid's song that makes his building of the dome doubtful. It is the willingness to hear another's voice within, *but still to recognise it as another's voice,* that he seeks. The male poet does not absorb, or wish to absorb, the feminine; rather, he seeks to retain it as the other within the self.

To do this is not to conquer or enslave, but neither is it to allow the female her own independent position: her voice remains hers, but it is valued for its ability to complete the male's creative masculinity. Coleridge does not reverse the process - value his masculinity in so far as it may complete the femininity of the maid (or any female poet).

In 'Kubla Khan' Coleridge constructs a feminine voice in order to licence the masculine to create a poetry which both envisions and itself enacts a fragile and timeless harmony. In this sublime state male poet, poetry and audience are united in rapture. They participate in a paradisial sublime to contrast with the demonic and tyrannical sublime which the Khan's masculinity creates. Coleridge, in other words, had made a version of masculinity in opposition to the version, so powerful in eighteenth-century politics and poetics, that defined a man as a sublime conqueror of women.

He had made the sublime man dependent on a feminine Muse, thus replacing mastery with sympathy, dominance with poetic chorus. In doing so, he offered himself - and his readers - a more inclusive masculinity, one attentive to and completed by a feminine voice. If, however, this voice is not absorbed, silenced, or conquered, it is registered in order that it may sponsor the semi-divine vision which the male poet builds. It is he who gains, via a more inclusive masculinity, a vision that seems to encompass both masculine and feminine, centre and circumference, reason and sensibility. It is because it can sponsor him, and lift him beyond the vitiating gender stereotype provided by the Khan, that the maid's voice is valued. Reviving her song allows the male poet a transcendent wholeness that she herself does not attain:

His flashing eyes, his floating hair!
Weave a circle round him thrice,
And close your eyes with holy dread,
For he on honey-dew hath fed,
And drunk the milk of Paradise.
(ll. 50-54)

What the Abyssinian maid would think of this is not recorded.

If Coleridge's new man's sublime is not built on or vulnerable to violence, it is accessible only in renewed readings of the poem - or hearings of the maid's song. In the Preface he added later to the poem, Coleridge further qualified its already tentative conclusion. He argued that the poem was a 'psychological curiosity,' a fragment from 'reverie' whose vision he could not consciously revive once the person from Porlock had interrupted him. Thus he placed limits on his poem's visionariness and on its revision of gender roles, denying it the status of poetry and removing from himself the power to consciously modify his own masculinity through poetic vision.

The Preface, that is to say, blurs the poet's responsibility for what he has achieved. It implies that he provides no detailed model for the revision of masculinity and sublimity in society or self save by the example of the poem as a language of social and sexual harmony accessible only in dreams and drug-induced reveries. It is, apparently, only whilst half-asleep that Coleridge can discover a new sublime and a new manliness in which the feminine completes the masculine.

II. Coleridge and Mary Robinson: Feminising the Sublime

After 1798 inspiration by a feminine muse seemed, for a while, no dream. Coleridge found a poet prepared to act as his Abyssinian maid, willing to sponsor his bardic song with her own music. He found Mary Robinson, the former actress whose appearance as Perdita in *The Winter's Tale* had, in 1778, brought her to Prince George's attention. He had wooed her under the name Florizel, and turned the Shakespearian 'shepherdess' into his mistress. But he had later abandoned her, leaving her to the life of the kept mistress of a series of well-known public men, including Charles James Fox and Banastre Tarleton. Robinson had turned to poetry to support herself after being deserted by Tarleton.

Robinson's desertion by the Prince had led to a public scandal in 1781; in 1796 George's desertion of his wife for another mistress reminded the public of what had formerly happened to Robinson. George's tyrannical treatment of women attracted widespread criticism, for it seemed to epitomise the aristocratic immorality which was thought to be undermining the constitution. Coleridge had himself published a poem critical of George's treatment of his wife,

'On A Late Connubial Rupture in High Life,' in which he hoped that George would mend his ways and act, as he was supposed to do, as protective husband and father: 'And ah! that Truth some holy spell might lend / To lure thy Wanderer from the Syren's power' (*PW*, I, 152).

Robinson's sexual life became a political issue. To conservative supporters of the social order she was an emblem of female immodesty, an example of the dangers posed to Britain by radical change. Richard Polwhele attacked her along with Wollstonecraft as 'female Quixotes of the new philosophy'. His phrase saw them as self-deluding knights, seduced by the romance of radical French ideas, when they should have been innocent damsels. Similarly, the *Annual Review* reminded women readers of her sexual past in order to deny her the power to speak for them; Robinson, it proclaimed, wielded a 'pen of vice':

Before a tender-hearted young lady has committed to memory the invocation to 'Apathy', or learned to recite with tragic emphasis the 'Ode to Ingratitude', let her at least be aware from *what reflections* the author wished to take shelter in insensibility, and for *what favours* her lovers had proved ungrateful.

Opposition Whigs and radicals saw Robinson differently: to them she became a symbol of the injustice perpetuated by the aristocratic establishment which they were seeking to change. Her status as a victim of royal libertinism was cemented by the fact that she was, in fact, suffering from a paralysing disease. Coleridge pitied her for this, but also admired her writing. He did not seek to silence her authorial voice but promoted it in publications over which he had influence. He and she published poetic compliments to each other in the anti-ministerial newspaper *The Morning Post*, the paper which printed his political criticism of the government.

In the newspaper Coleridge presented their poetic relationship as one of mutual sympathy, in noticeable contrast to the sexual despotism Robinson had suffered as George's mistress. This gave gender relations a political context because sympathy for Robinson was implicitly a criticism of the Prince who had abandoned her, undermining his chivalric duty to protect. If George was Robinson's demon lover, abandoning her to wail, Coleridge was, as he represented it, her fellow poet, she his maid - as much French as Abyssinian. Coleridge placed his 'The Visions of the Maid of Orleans' immediately before Robinson's 'The Snow Drop' in the *Morning Post* of 26 December 1797. Taking advantage of the seasonal emphasis on peace and forgiveness, Robinson's poem used the flower as an image of herself as an abandoned, tender, crippled female:

All weak and wan, with head inclined,
Its parent breast, the drifted snow;
It trembles while the ruthless wind
Bends its slim form; the tempest lours,
Its em'rald eye drops crystal show'rs
On its cold bed below.

Coleridge's 'Visions' (an extract from 'The Destiny of Nations') use similar maternal and sentimental imagery to link Robinson with a French maid. He portrays Joan of Arc as a paragon of female virtue: Joan encounters a family frozen to death as they tried to escape the sacking of their village:

She meantime,
Saw crowded close beneath the couverture
A mother and her children - lifeless all,
Yet lovely! not a lineament was marred -
Death had put on so slumber-like a form!
It was a piteous sight! and one, a babe,
Lay on the woman's arm, its little hand
Smooth on her bosom. Wildly pale the maid
Gaz'd at the living wretch ...

Coleridge's poem had a political purpose: by arousing sympathy for innocent French womanhood besieged by war it opposed the government's current war with revolutionary France. And preceding Robinson's poem, it contextualised her work in an implicitly political way as that of another innocent female who, like Joan, was sacrificed to the cruelty of the British aristocracy.

Robinson herself did not simply play upon her status as

a suffering victim of libertinism. She also offered herself as a muse and respondent. In her 'To the Poet Coleridge' Robinson positioned herself as the sympathetic admirer of a poet already known for his radical opinions. She also positioned herself as a fellow lyricist, as a woman whose song responded to, but also inspired, Coleridge's words. Specifically, she associated herself with the Abyssinian maid of 'Kubla Khan':

I'll mark thy 'sunny dome', and view
Thy 'caves of ice', thy fields of dew!
Thy ever-blooming mead, whose flower
Waves to the cold breath of the moonlight hour!

Here Robinson offers herself as the delighted viewer of and believer in Coleridge's poetic landscape; her own verse appears as the offspring of his fertility, his 'ever-blooming mead'. Mutual sympathy replaces the sexual servitude Robinson had suffered (or was agreed to have suffered) at the hands of the libertine Prince. Coleridge's literary masculinity, Robinson suggests, is productive through sympathy, rather than dominant through sexuality. She shares the Abyssinian maid's song with Coleridge, and then gives him a song of her own inspired by it:

And now, with lofty tones inviting,
Thy Nymph, her dulcimer swift-smiting,
Shall wake me in ecstatic measures,
Far, far removed from mortal pleasures!
In cadence rich, in cadence strong,
Proving the wondrous witcheries of song!
I hear her voice! thy 'sunny dome,'
Thy 'caves of ice,' aloud repeat,
Vibrations, maddening sweet!
Calling the visionary wanderer home.
She sings of thee, O! favoured child
Of minstrelsy sublimely wild!
Of thee, whose soul can feel the tone
Which gives to airy dreams a magic all thy own!
(ll. 59-72)

Reading Kubla Khan, she is inspired to write, rather than reduced to being the wailing victim of a demon lover.

If Robinson found her poetic field enriched by Coleridge's, Coleridge found in her - at least briefly - a lyric voice capable of modifying his own. He admired her for exactly that for which he praised the Abyssinian maid - her music. Recommending her 'Jasper' for inclusion in the *Annual Anthology,* he 'thought the metre stimulating'.

He also praised 'the fascinating metre' of 'The Haunted Beach'. This latter poem was derivative of 'The Ancient Mariner' in subject matter but succeeded in intertwining lines of different metrical balance with an intricate and unusual rhyme-scheme:

The Spectre-band, his messmates brave
Sunk in the yawning ocean,
While to the mast he lash'd him fast
And brav'd the storm's commotion.
The winter moon, upon the sand
A silv'ry carpet made,
And mark'd the Sailor reach the land,
And mark'd his murd'rer wash his hand
Where the green billows play'd.

The last three lines of what Coleridge publicly called 'that absolutely original Stanza' suspend the expected resolution, protracting the verse by introducing a couplet which, conclusive though its rhyme might normally be, is itself superseded. Suspending the reader's expectations of narrative sequence was, of course, vital to Coleridge's own supernatural poetry, and in appreciating Robinson's music Coleridge was paying tribute to an ability which he understood to be more than merely technical.

It was, he thought, through control of metre and rhyme that poetry could make readers suspend their disbelief in the supernatural. Prosody, Coleridge knew, could lull audiences into 'poetic faith', make them temporarily believe in events they had thought to be beyond nature. What was, and was not, natural might then become a matter of doubt. And this process, of course, was potentially radical, since what had been assumed to be natural might include the established social and political order.

Robinson's control of music intrigued Coleridge with the possibility of modifying the understanding of gender on which the established order was dependent. It was through a lyrical revision of the sublime, made in reply to Robinson, that Coleridge again attempted, as he had in 'Kubla Khan', to undo the Burkean assumption that authority takes the form of a dominant masculinity.

He did so in a poem called 'A Stranger Minstrel' (1800). This poem replied to Robinson's tributes to him. It alluded to her poem to his son Derwent, in which she imagines, via allusions to Coleridge's own verse, his son wandering through 'Romantic Mountains' with 'brows sublime'.

It echoed Robinson's description of herself as a 'Stranger' and an 'untaught minstrel' in comparison with 'his loftier Muse'. In that poem Robinson had concluded with the hope that her poetic sublime would outlive the sublime mountains of his birthplace: 'Still may thy name survive, sweet Boy! till Time / Shall bend to Keswick's vale - thy Skiddaw's brow sublime!'.

Coleridge's 'A Stranger Minstrel' takes up the questions Robinson had posed to the natural sublime. It too is set on Skiddaw. It too considers the role of the poet, even as it alludes to her poems:

In that sweet mood of sad and humorous thought
A form within me rose, within me wrought
With such strong magic, that I cried aloud,
'Thou ancient Skiddaw by thy helm of cloud,
And by thy many-colour'd chasms deep,
And by their shadows that for ever sleep,
By yon small flaky mists that love to creep
Along the edges of those spots of light,
Those sunny islands on thy smooth green height,
And by yon shepherds with their sheep,
And dogs and boys, a gladsome crowd,
That rush e'en now with clamour loud
Sudden from forth thy topmost cloud,
And by this laugh, and by this tear,
I would, old Skiddaw, she were here!

A lady of sweet song is she,
Her soft blue eye was made for thee!
O ancient Skiddaw, by this tear,
I would, I would that she were here!'
Then ancient Skiddaw, stern and proud,
In sullen majesty replying,
Thus spake from out his helm of cloud
(His voice was like an echo dying!):-
'She dwells belike in scenes more fair,
And scorns a mount so bleak and bare'.
(PW, I, 351, ll. 9-33)

So far, so conventional: Skiddaw speaks through the Burkean sublime. But as he reads and quotes Robinson in the poem, Coleridge seems to challenge his own need to have his nature poetry confirmed as a protective and powerful masculine authority. The masculine Skiddaw ('His voice was like a monarch wooing') redefines his own sublimity in the words of Robinson's poetry:

Now to the 'haunted beach' can fly,
Beside the threshold scourged with waves,
Now where the maniac wildly raves,
'Pale moon, thou spectre of the sky!'
No wind that hurries o'er my height
Can travel with so swift a flight.
I too, methinks, might merit
The presence of her spirit!
To me too might belong
The honour of her song and witching melody,
Which most resembles me,
Soft, various, and sublime,
Exempt from wrongs of Time!
(ll. 55-67)

A strange shift has occurred, for although Skiddaw says that Robinson's song 'resembles me' it seems rather that he now resembles it in being 'soft, various and sublime' rather than 'stern and proud' and sublime (l. 28). The masculine majestical sublime has been modified from within by Robinson's words as, for the sake of the nation's moral health,

Coleridge wished the Prince of Wales to have been. Here Coleridge was publicly providing an alternative version of masculine authority in which monarchical mountains and the male poet are presented as softened into feminine sensibility and yearning:

Thus spake the mighty Mount, and I
Made answer, with a deep-drawn sigh:-
'Thou ancient Skiddaw, by this tear,
I would, I would that she were here!'
(ll. 68-71)

This conclusion is as near as Coleridge comes to a poetry in which the sublime is feminised. Here the conventionally masculine is not just redefined as a power capable of encompassing the feminine in an all embracing vision. Instead, the mountain is both sublime and feminine, its masculinity in abeyance. Borrowing the words of Robinson, words offered in poetic correspondence as those of a muse writing of/from Coleridge's own poetic landscape (the Lake District), Coleridge lets woman's verse and a feminine discourse reset his own.

He was able to accept and adapt those words because they were offered in poetic friendship, indeed in tribute, in terms with which he identified himself. In a sense, then, Robinson, the self-appointed Abyssinian muse, had colonised Coleridge's landscape from within, by moving to Skiddaw and making it a feminised ground. Coleridge, in response, neither acts as fatherly protector, nor as a male poet bolstering his threatened mastery with the admiring verse of a subordinate poetess. He envisages not just a suspension of sublime power but a feminine occupation of the traditionally masculine.

As was the case in 'Kubla Khan', Coleridge did not succeed in developing a way in which the visions conjured up in his poem could be translated into actions in the world beyond. That he did not succeed was due in part to his own fear of the radical unorthodoxy of the poetics he had sketched out. Susan Luther has written astutely of both his unorthodoxy and his fear. He was, she argues, groping towards a redefinition of the sublime in which authority would be based not on subordination but interchange, one that 'attempts to bring the lady's terms to his own'. Ultimately unsuccessful, it was flawed by Coleridge's desire simply to incorporate Robinson as woman and as poet in his own self-reflection. In Luther's words it displays 'the difference between the WOMAN and the MUSE as well as their unsettling similarity, the hazards encountered when the sublime of "SENSIBILITY!" and Fancy meets the sublime of ... Imagination'. Coleridge's feminised sublime proved too hot for him to handle.

After having written 'A Stranger Minstrel', Coleridge tended to retreat from its implicitly radical version of femininity. He reinscribed Robinson within a more conventional relationship, in which sublime authority was again gendered as masculine. In a letter of 1801, for example, he wished for Robinson the protection of a good husband and of his own poetry. And he quoted a letter of hers which suggests that she was ready to appeal to such chivalric values. The quotation suggests that Coleridge took refuge in the belief that Robinson simply confirmed him in the role of powerful man and sublime nature poet:

Poor dear Mrs Robinson! you have heard of her Death. She wrote me a most affecting, heart-rending Letter a few weeks before she died, to express what she called her death bed affection & esteem for me - the very last Lines of her Letter are indeed sublime -

'My little Cottage is retired and comfortable. There I mean to remain (if indeed I live so long) till Christmas. But it is not surrounded with the romantic Scenery of your chosen retreat: it is not, my dear Sir! the nursery of sublime Thoughts - the abode of Peace - the solitude of Nature's Wonders. O! Skiddaw! - I think, if I could but once contemplate thy Summit, I should never quit the Prospect it would present till my eyes were closed for ever!'

O Poole! that that Woman had but been married to a noble Being, what a noble Being she herself would have been. Latterly, she felt this with a poignant anguish. - Well! -

O'er her pil'd grave the gale of evening sighs;
And flowers will grow upon it's grassy Slope.
I wipe the dimming Water from mine eyes -

Ev'n in the cold Grave dwells the Cherub Hope!
(CL, II, 669)

Here Coleridge's lines of verse respond to Robinson's own idealisation of the mountain as an abode of peace and a 'nursery of sublime Thoughts'. They depict her death as a release of the kind she sought when her 'eyes were closed for ever'. Her grave becomes a nursery of the cherub hope; in the poetry of the man who himself dwelt under Skiddaw pity for her is able to release her from her thraldom to the sensible world of nature. Not Skiddaw, but the male poet who writes under its authority, becomes the locus of a sublime of translation from the sensible to the spiritual, from bondage to nature to hope of heaven.

Coleridge, as the Lake District man and poet to whom Robinson appeals in her dying weakness, becomes, in his own eyes, the poetic husband who restores her lost nobility and respectability. It is his capacity for pity and grief ('the dimming Water') that allows her a possible future existence. Burkean subjection before natural power is transformed, through a feminine appeal to masculine pity and protectiveness, into a discourse which allows the woman a limited (but subordinate) position of freedom. Here though it is after death, and through the man's nature poetry, that the freedom is possible. Coleridge here falls short of his achievement in 'A Stranger Minstrel': he flatters rather than questions himself as he imagines himself in the conventional role of the strong male protector of the helpless female.

Coleridge continued to fight shy of the implications of his poem. In 1802 he rebuked Robinson's daughter for planning to publish in a collection of her mother's works a poem of his own alongside ones by Moore and 'Monk' Lewis, 'men, who have sold provocatives to vulgar Debauchees'. Idealising Robinson as a pure and dear Mother, 'of all names the most awful, the most venerable, next to that of God', Coleridge wished to save Robinson's posthumous reputation from the notoriety of the writers she had been associated with, to reinscribe her within the discourse of literary as well as personal propriety. But he also wished to save himself: faced with the prospect of publicly appearing as one of a company of libertine men who were associated with her, Coleridge was afraid. No longer able to see himself as her private literary protector, he panicked. He wished to avoid having his verse seem to be indebted to a poetic muse known for her loose morals and the bad company she kept.

Coleridge was neither disinterested nor feminist: he was trying to shape an authority-in-writing that he could himself adopt. He needed to be lord of his own utterance, to gain a position at the top, but through words that rejected the prevailing kinds of manliness. Robinson had inspired in Coleridge what his Abyssinian maid inspired in the idealised poet of 'Kubla Khan', a poetry which can escape the kind of masculinity set out by Burke and practised by the Prince, the kind predicated on its capacity to inspire awe and fear.

As in 'Kubla Khan', however, Coleridge found difficulties in making this kind of poetic masculinity that on which he took his public stand. He remained unable and unwilling to risk staking his poetic character on a language of suspension and enchantment which flourished from positions that were culturally unconventional - from drug induced reverie, from the inspiration of a feminine sublime, from dialogue with a woman whom many regarded as notorious.

Luther sums up Coleridge's problems in doing justice to what Robinson had shown him as she had become a more challenging and creative muse than at first appeared:

> If the problem for [the female lyricist] is how to recreate for herself the space of the beautiful within the sublime, or the sublime within the beautiful, how to claim her erotic and lyrical power without having to deny their contiguity so as to escape being once more (negatively) defined as her flesh, the problem for [the male lyricist] seems to be how to assimilate, accommodate, encompass and compose those moods, rhetorical modes and human impulses that his own and his culture's values deny him, unless he is willing to relinquish his position at the top.

Coleridge may have been unable wholly to relinquish his desire for a position at the top, yet his Romanticism should not as a consequence be seen as a consistent 'conquest' and 'enslavement' of the female. If it often idealises a role for women that is at best supportive of and at worst subordinate to male creativity, if it often presents the feminine as merely a supplement to masculine power, it nevertheless also often calls women's subordination to those languages into question.

Coleridge did sketch - but only sketch - an alternative model of poetic power through a feminising dialogue with a woman poet and muse. In doing so he revealed some of the limitations of the traditional (and interlinked) discourses of/about political and poetic power.

Chapter 6

Romanticism & Ecology

Were a seventeenth-century English painter to travel in time to a gallery in the latter half of the eighteenth century he or she might well exclaim, wide-eyed, "Where did all the animals come from?" For the animals depicted in those portraits and landscapes had somehow migrated from the backgrounds they had previously inhabited to become foregrounded pictorial subjects in themselves: cattle in fields, dogs and horses standing alone or beside proud owners, horses arranged like Grecian statuary, wild birds, exotic lions, and inquisitive monkeys painstakingly depicted in quasi-natural habitats. Where indeed had all these animals come from, and why were they here?

The phenomenon of George Stubbs (1724-1806), the renowned English "horse painter," would itself have shocked our traveller. Consider, for example, Stubbs's portrait of "Captain Samuel Sharpe Pocklington with His Wife, Pleasance, and possibly His Sister, Frances" (1769). Although anthropocentrically enough titled and most likely commissioned as a marriage portrait, this painting is really a study of Captain Pocklington's horse. Whether or not the Captain or his wife was cognizant of the fact, Stubbs, whose popular *Anatomy of the Horse* had been published three years before in 1766, was clearly using the much-prized, status-confirming animal not just as the group portrait's focus but also as its main point of interest. It is the horse around whom the three human figures are posed, and it is the horse, not the good Captain, who receives Mrs. Pocklington's affectionate attentions. In his life-time Stubbs painted many such animal-oriented works, including horse portraits like the well-known "Whistlejacket" (1762) and the series of equine formal studies, "Mares and Foals" (1762-68, 1776), as well as numerous paintings of dogs and more exotic creatures—lions, zebras, and the occasional rhinoceros. Stubbs had made a career of it.

Similarly, John Constable's landscape paintings are populated by as many animals as people, with animals frequently serving as a work's focus or focusing agent, as in "The Haywain" (1821) and "Salisbury Cathedral from the Meadows" (1829). In each tableau a lone, attentive dog—the sole depicted observer—mediates the viewer's gaze, directing it to a dramatic animal scene of wain-pulling horses. These and other creative works of the Romantic period interconnect human perception and animal perception or being, human economy and animals' various places within it or outside it, and by so doing foreground both human-animal similarities and differences, among other things. In the late eighteenth and early nineteenth centuries such representations of animals indeed are by no means merely familiar (or exotic) subject matter or handy rhetorical tools readily substitutable by other signs. On the contrary, in these years animal depictions are fundamentally tied to Englishmen's shifting social existence, as indices of cultural change, of difference, and of identity.

Not coincidentally, and for more than a few thinkers of the time not a little fortuitously, the human monarchy of nature had itself recently been toppled and reconceptualized under a new system of animal classification. A Copernican revolution all its own, the Linnaean taxonomy, as utilized by English natural scientists like Erasmus Darwin, resituated *homo sapiens* as one animal among many similar, interconnected species. Hence, in the preface to his epidemiological taxonomy, *Zoonomia* (1794), Darwin could argue that, although the "Creator of all things has infinitely diversified the works of his hands," he has also "stamped a certain similitude on the features of nature, that demonstrate to us, that the whole is *one family*of one parent" (B; original emphasis).

Darwin's metaphor of the family aptly sums up the then-emerging view of the biological commonality of all creatures, a view that posited creatures' mutual bonds and shared affections—and also significantly implies the social connections within and between species. In the widely popular natural histories by Buffon and Bewick one similarly finds animals' social nature to be a foregrounded concern, these histories' illustrations depicting animals in "clearly defined social setting[s]," with careful attention also given to their relationship to human economy (Potts 18).

In a manner equally typical of the Romantic era, Darwin moreover holds the source of human virtue itself to rest in "our intellectual sympathies with ... the miseries, or with the joys, of our fellow creatures". Our connection *to* animals is for him, as for others of his time, dependent upon our sympathetic identification *with* these "our fellow creatures." In this way, eighteenth-century natural history presented to British men and women not just a further blow to traditional notions of the place of human beings—"a dissolution and reconstitution of conceptual patterns by which natural phenomena had been understood" (Kroeber 18)—but also an important means of re-envisioning humankind's proper place in the social and natural fabric: as a part of a unifying (albeit for some thinkers also a dislocating) whole of interconnected species—even of a dynamic "family" of people, horses, dogs, and other, undomesticated creatures.

In *Romantic Ecology* Jonathan Bate argues that what poets like William Wordsworth added to this new matrix of an interrelated ecosystem or "economy of nature" (the English title of one of Linnaeus's essays) was their "emphasis on a symbiosis between the economy of nature and the activities of humankind": the Wordsworthian "'one life' within us and abroad".

And, as James Turner observes, this is where animals "came in," answering the psychological call on the part of late-eighteenth-century men and women for a "bulwark" against "the wrenching changes wrought by factory and city". The enormous popularity of animals in the period, both in paintings and in zoos, can of course be attributed to other factors as well, ranging from an urban population's nostalgia for rural times and places past to a growing empire's appetite for exoticism.

But turn-of-the-century animal representations particularly responded to the anxieties and desires prompted by social and political change—by revolution, war, domestic disrule, and reform—and by the era's wrenching economic transformations. At a time when age-old "securities of class and status and theological assumptions" were themselves being shattered (McFarland 20), when distrust of government and the old orthodoxies was at an all-time high, and when deep fissures could be glimpsed within England's social, political, and economic landscape, artists responded to these historical pressures by attempting in their works to discover and represent new forms of social organization and subjectivity. And it is in this cultural project that animals came into the picture.

Indeed, for Romantic artists animals particularly satisfied a desire to find alternative, local, and noneconomic means of human connection, a social appeal that is especially prominent in the late-eighteenth-century poetry of Wordsworth and Samuel Taylor Coleridge. During the increasingly turbulent years from 1794 to 1800, including the nadir of the Terror, these two poets depict new forms of social cohesion and identity based upon lasting bonds able to "bind all men together" (Eisold 122). The poets' sociological project leads them to represent communities articulated by mysterious human-animal linkages, as in Wordsworth's "Lines Written in Early Spring," from his and Coleridge's *Lyrical Ballads* of 1798.

Here Wordsworth describes his experience of nature as a product of his abiding belief (most likely owed in part to Erasmus Darwin) that the "human soul" is intricately linked to nature's "fair works" (ll. 5-6). For Karl Kroeber this provocative hypothesis in fact implies the speaker's understanding that "all human cultures are constructed by natural creatures". And the poet's belief indeed suggests not just his pantheism but also his understanding of a profound social connection between human beings and animals, one with the potential to form a "true community ... / Of many into one incorporate," as Wordsworth describes matters in *Home at Grasmere* (MS. B.819-20). To a diseased social-political world "where no brotherhood exists" (*The Prelude* 2.404), human and animal relationships offered to these poets and to other artists important potential bonds for human connection: "mysteries of passion which have made, / And shall continue evermore to make ... / One brotherhood of all the human race" (10.84-88).

Although Coleridge himself winced at Wordsworth's lingering "One Life" pantheism (despite the fact that Wordsworth had gleaned much of it from him) and, in Kroeber's words, would in later years "devote major energies ... to defending a transcendental vision of divinity hostile to Romantic proto-ecological nature poetry", in the waning years of the eighteenth century he generally shared his friend's "proto-ecological" orientation and belief in the divine, and deeply social, power of nature's animals. Notably, in Coleridge's "Fears in Solitude" (1798), the poet, fearing the rumored French invasion of England, finds consolation that in a "spirit-healing nook" a man still may

...lie on fern or withered heath,
While from the singing lark (that sings unseen
The minstrelsy that solitude loves best),
And from the sun, and from the breezy air,
Sweet influences trembled o'er his frame.... (12-21; *emphasis added*)

Communion with nature's "best" minstrel produces in the quiet listener "[r]eligious meanings" and "dreams of better worlds" set in stark contrast to a violent world of "[i]nvasion," "fear and rage, / And undetermined conflict" (36-38), a world made all the more despicable by these contrasting, nature-bestowed dreams of more tranquil "society". Nature's harmony here has the power to guide the self from such alienating political preoccupations to "[l]ove, and the thoughts that yearn for human kind"—thoughts of one's natural connection to his or her "brethren". Like the well-known dictum of Wordsworth's *Prelude,* that love of nature leads to love of humankind, these lines by Coleridge describe nature's active involvement in fostering community. And, although the lark's music is missing from the poem's concluding description of a now "silent dell" (and even may have been owed to the poet's recollection of a past visit), at the outset that songbird, singing "unseen / The Minstrelsy that solitude loves best," like some "angel in the clouds," singularly contributes to those vital "sweet influences" that tremble over the speaker (19-21, 28) and elicit both his "melancholy" thoughts about his warring "human brethren" and his more hopeful visions of "better worlds" populated by animals and (animal-) loving human beings.

Coleridge's earlier poem "To A Young Ass" (1794), popular enough to have been lampooned by Lord Byron, similarly represents animals as makers or markers of community and communitarian feeling. It also presents the animal as an emblem of oppression, the "[p]oor little Foal of an oppressed Race". The speaker exclaims, "I hail thee *Brother*—spite of the fool's scorn! / And fane would take thee with me, in the Dell / Of Peace and mild Equality to dwell". The latter reference is to Coleridge's and Robert Southey's ambitious utopian scheme, "Pantisocracy," but we should not let their failure ever to realise that idealized dell overshadow the poem's more immediate aims, akin to the French Revolution's own, by then vanishing, goals of *liberté, égalité, fraternité*.

The "*Brother*" foal, italicized in Coleridge's text arguably to emphasize precisely this revolutionary significance, is to be set free—so the speaker would wish, anyway—to dwell in "mild Equality" with the poet and his fellow pantisocrats, in a life of work and playful "bray[s] of joy". The poem's animal addressee thus serves not just as an exemplum of rural poverty's brutalizing effects but also as a sign and source of resistance to such economic brutalization. For the speaker, true brotherhood, not to mention true equality and liberty, must include the foal.

In this Coleridgean manifesto of sorts the principal source of social cohesion rests in the socializing sympathies the foal itself occasions and which its brays repeatedly confirm, in stark contrast to the caged bird in the imprisoning city, whose "warbled melodies" merely "soothe to rest / The aching of pale Fashion's vacant breast!".

Wordsworth's "Poor Susan," from *Lyrical Ballads* of 1800, also describes a caged bird's song, heard by Susan from a London street corner. The lone thrush's singing prompts her to daydream of remembered "Green pastures ... in the midst of the dale, / Down which she [had] so often ... tripp'd with her pail". In lines later excised at Charles Lamb's urging, the poem's speaker goes on to chastise Susan as a "Poor Outcast" (perhaps a prostitute, then no uncommon condition) who should return to her father's rustic home and, having replaced her fancy loomed dress for a "plain russet" home-spun gown, once again hear a "thrush sing from a tree of its own". Here, too, the countryside is depicted as an ideal dell of free animals and concomitantly liberated human beings. By contrast, the city is a place of imprisoned humans and animals alike. At the same time, of course, such liberating communitarian contact with animals is in some manner occasioned by, or is at least responsive to, their past and present suffering.

To return for a moment to Wordsworth's "Lines Written In Early Spring," we find its poet similarly seeking social connection and belonging, his desires' fulfillment resting in his firm "faith that every flower / Enjoys the air it breathes" (11-12). Yet the flowers' enjoyment of their life processes is, like the thoughts of the birds hopping about nearby him, something he "cannot measure". This conclusion of his is more than a poetical jab at Enlightenment rationalism's tendency to quantify and calculate all things. For these creatures, although sentient and pleasure-loving like the speaker himself, serve as a "measure" of his *difference* from them as well as from those men unable or unwilling to accept a faith established in opposition to "[w]hat man has made of man".

Such faith implicitly seeks a missing or lost form of social cohesion, a form the poem's speaker lacks and fervently desires. Still, despite his depressing awareness of his alienation from his destructive fellow human beings, the poet points to what in Wordsworth's and Coleridge's poetry proves to be an implicit basis for human connection and for humanity's amelioration: that, in spite of, or because of, animals' difference from human beings, nature's creatures nevertheless have this power to "link" together the "human soul" that runs as one life through living things. As other works by Wordsworth and Coleridge reveal, it is in fact this irreducible difference between animals and human beings that ultimately makes such linkages between modern people possible, and even necessary. "What man has made" of animals, and what animals in turn can make of man, becomes a basis, in places even the sole basis, for community.

Coleridge's "The Nightingale: A Conversation Poem," also from *Lyrical Ballads* (1800), while of paramount importance in this social articulation of human beings and animals, may well at first seem an odd choice, for it is clearly skeptical about at least some of the connections poets discern between humankind and nature's animals (those animals' thoughts being immeasurable even in Wordsworth's more optimistic "Lines"). Indeed, Coleridge's poem starkly decries our narcissistic tendency to transform nature into but a distorted mirror of ourselves. In a notable turn against classical and Miltonic tradition, and against the "pity-pleading strains" of his own prior poem "To A Nightingale," Coleridge's speaker insists instead that the singing nightingale, rather than being "melancholy" (in accordance with the Greek myth of Philomela), is "full of love / And joyance".

The *Oxford English Dictionary* notes that the Spenserian word *joyance* was, according to Samuel Johnson's own lexicographical judgment, obsolete by the eighteenth century. The antiquated term was then reintroduced by Coleridge (and Southey), to become a favourite archaism of later poets like Percy Shelley, as in his avian poem "To A Skylark." Coleridge had recoined the word "joyance" in "Lines on an Autumnal Evening" (1796), and then chose to redeploy the term in "The Nightingale," with the reasonable expectation of the word's antique strangeness to his readers.

The term "joyance" interestingly denotes as much an activity as a state of feeling or being, referring, unlike the common word "joy," both to feeling joy and to the action of showing it (*OED*). The archaism thus serves to underline animal nature's active role in altering human feeling: its power to help compose in the listener an active, participatory joy similar to animals' own. Yet while the word "joyance" suggests an active role for nature's creatures and their "sweet influences," at the same time the term's use in these lines also reveals its human authors' limits. Coming as the word does on the heels of the poet's impassioned condemnation of past writers' attributions of "melancholy" to the famed songbird, his own corrective perceptions of "love" and "joyance" in the bird's song must raise suspicions.

Is not his revisionist view but the narcissistic antithesis of the rejected Miltonic, and prior Coleridgean, perspective, too simply exchanging avian sadness for avian happiness? While one should think it true that in nature there indeed is "nothing melancholy," given such anti-anthropomorphic, anti-anthropocentric logic as the speaker has proposed, can sentient nature be said to be full of active "joyance" either? In this particular context, the word *joyance* itself becomes increasingly suspect: as a term that signifies not just being but *showing*: display, semblance, and, by implication, perception.

The reader might also raise a skeptical eyebrow when the poet proceeds to describe the singing nightingale as "disburthen[ing]" his "full soul" in an expressive activity analogous to the actions of Coleridge's own proper poet, who similarly "surrender[s] his whole spirit". Such identifications again smack of anthropomorphic narcissism, not to mention of the pathetic fallacy, especially in light of the poet's prior indictment of the solipsistic *penseroso* whose "melancholy" personifications—bad figures of speech—merely tell back "the tale" of his "own sorrows". Given Coleridge's staunch rejection of just such artificial "conceit[s]", his treatment of the bird's "joyance" generates troublesome contradictions indeed, contradictions that in turn point to significant problems of perceiving and representing animals (miring the "One Life" doctrine in something of an epistemological quandary). The singing bird, appropriately and traditionally unseen, in this way remains intriguingly beyond the culturally constraining powers of human categorization and understanding. And, in this way, as a text "The Nightingale" provides within itself a curious resistance to its own anthropomorphic reductions, a resistance significant, as it turns out, to the poem's representation of human/animal community.

This social lesson is revealed principally in the closing lines' repeated adieus to the bird and to its human audience of friends: "Once more, farewell, / Sweet Nightingale! once more, my friends! farewell". The salutation forms a chiasmus of addresses and addressees:

farewelllxxxxxxnightingale
X
friendsxxxxxxfarewell

This rhetorical figure serves, along with the associative repetition of the lines' adverbial phrases ("Once more," "once more"), to conflate the avian singer with its human audience. In fact, the chiasmus figuratively connects the bird and its crowd of listeners as one community, engaged in a type of nocturnal conversation.

The human friendships of course to some extent precede this meeting in the company of the nightingale (and of its fellow singers in nearby fields), yet the meeting of friends is occasioned by the bird's audible presence. Indeed, the propinquity of these "loitering" listeners is made possible only by the animal "joyance" produced by the nightingale's "love-chant[s]"—chants that will in turn lead to the next night's consolidating farewells: "till tomorrow eve,... a short farewell". For, as the poet proclaims, such bird-song is the stuff of answer and provocation, of "skirmish and capricious passagings, / And murmurs musical and swift jug jug".

The phrase "jug jug" itself merits attention. The word *jug* was one commonly used to signify the notes of nightingales and other songbirds, and so has more sense than nonsense about it (although even such onomatopoeic words as *jug* are conventional and arbitrary rather than strictly motivated and, for lack of a better word, natural). Coleridge's poet strikes a position between cultural revision and traditionalism, arguing for nonmelancholy, perhaps even nonjoyful, "skirmish," and for so customary a description as "jug jug." At the same time, such *jugging* does "bid us [to] listen", while at the same moment importantly frustrating our attempts to interpret, let alone to reproduce, the intricate song. Rather like the poet's child, who though "Nature's playmate" yet "[m]ars" all its sounds "with his imitative lisp", the speaker and his friends mar the bird's inimitable singing, and in fact seem to be drawn together night after night by what the nocturnal scene precisely does *not* provide them: by what their language of poetic archaisms, onomatopoeias, and other suspect figures of speech cannot reproduce "once more."

For the adult friends, as for the child, the nightingale's "love-chant" remains a "fast thick warble" of notes "delicious" for their difference, resistance, complexity, and mystery. Such resistance to knowing bids the bird's human listeners return to become more "[f]amiliar" with enchanted song that remains strange. And in seeking this familiarity with animals the listeners are thereby themselves nightly associated in a ritual-like gathering of initiates poised on the epistemological verge of delimiting perceptions. "The Nightingale" is in this way very much a "conversation poem," as Coleridge subtitled it, but one of limits and transgressions, in which human and animal discourse produces a kind of social conversion based upon linguistic and other forms of discord, violence, and desire.

And, as shall now be shown, this marring and atonement are themselves really key parts of a deeper, darker Coleridgean and Wordsworthian schema of human and animal "society" as a collective of "sweet influences" prompted by animal "mysteries of passion," including animal suffering and sacrifice.

Although it might at first appear to be a quite different human/animal scheme that we encounter in Coleridge's well-known lyrical ballad, *The Rime of the Ancyent Marinere* (1797-98), in fact this poem makes even clearer the violence—a markedly physical violence—and atoning acts of sympathy and story-telling that frequently underlie animal-based community. James McKusick sees the story's Mariner, a seafarer cursed for his thoughtless shooting of an albatross, as at the outset "a Cartesian dualist, a detached observer cut off from any feeling of empathy or participation in the vast world of life that surrounds him," but who is eventually transformed into a Linnaean or Darwinian self "released from his state of alienation from nature".

For, according to McKusick, the Mariner learns "what the Albatross came to teach him: that he must cross the boundaries that divide him from the natural world, through unmotivated acts of compassion between 'man and bird and beast'". This moral, which Coleridge later criticized as being too explicit, is well known even to those unfamiliar with the poem, being a message also proffered by *Goody Two-Shoes* and other children's books of the eighteenth century:

He prayeth best who loveth best,
All things both great and small:
For the dear God, who loveth us,
He made and loveth all. (647-50)

Oddly, and in contradistinction to Anna Barbauld's, Erasmus Darwin's, and others' belief that the humane treatment of animals was a key means to human moral improvement—for Barbauld, specifically for improving the lower and middle classes—it is because of the Mariner's murderous *dis*regard for one of God's beloved creatures that he comes to be morally improved. His release from the curse placed upon him is earned, as he himself sees it, by his unconscious blessing of other, decidedly less desirable creatures: "water-snakes" swimming alongside his ship. "O happy living things!" he cries in a heart-felt "spring of love" (274, 276). By blessing them "unaware", without ulterior motivation, the Mariner earns the pity of two local nature spirits, one of whom he overhears proclaim to the other that, "the man hath penance done, / And penance more will do" for having offended a fellow-spirit who "lov'd the bird that lov'd the man / Who shot him with his bow".

However just or unjust the Mariner's divinely bestowed punishment may be, his show of love for animals spares him the gruesome, zombie-like life-in-death inflicted upon his shipmates (who had first condemned but then praised his murder of the albatross, making them, in the words of the poem's later-added commentary, "accomplices in the crime"). It also leads him, by these mysterious rites of suffering, to regard all life, both human and animal, as sacred and interconnected. But "penance more" is nonetheless owed the natural world, and it is in this indebtedness that the social aspects of Coleridge's sea-tale are revealed.

At his tale's end the Mariner relates how, his ghost ship having sunk off the shore of his native land, he at once found himself stricken

With a woeful agony,
Which forc'd me to begin my tale
And then it left me free.
Since then at an uncertain hour
Now oftimes and now fewer,
That anguish comes and makes me tell
My ghastly aventure. (612-18)

The Mariner thereupon must tell that chosen listener the tale and its compassionate moral. The narrative in this way provides an explanatory coda of its origins: that "penance" owed for animal murder, what the shipmates misinterpreted as beneficent sacrifice, drives the narrative to be rehearsed (reproduced and exchanged), in order, one must suspect, to disseminate this hard-won wisdom about humankind's treatment of, and moral dependence upon, animals.

Hence, the Mariner's story is one we overhear as it is told by him to a diverted, spell-bound "wedding-guest," at that most traditional and social of rituals, a marriage—a setting that underlines the tale's social significance. "[S]tunn'd" and "of sense forlorn" from the tale's telling, the guest arises the next day a "sadder and a wiser man", his altered condition a result of that narrative. Such learning about animals and human beings completes what might well be called an eco-communitarian circuit, manifesting as it does a system of intertwined human and animal relationships transgressed against in the Mariner's ignorant slaughter of the albatross and then repaired, in part, by his benediction to the water-snakes and his subsequent transmissions of wisdom to a series of distraught but enthralled "guests."

Accompanying this animal-oriented wisdom is the underlying guilt upon which such narratives and their implicit cultures are based: a sacrificial originary before whose knot of sin cannot be undone but whose irredeemable violence makes atonement and its totemic human-animal wisdom possible. Narrative in *The Rime of the Ancyent Marinere* is in this way eucharistic and guilt-ridden; hence, perhaps, the poem's oddly irreconcilable Christian imagery, including the Mariner's "cross bow", a weapon that for McKusick embodies both the "destructive tendency" of technology and "the traditional Christian imagery of sacrifice and atonement".

(The dead albatross itself substitutes for a cross when the sailors hang it around the Mariner's neck). Coleridge's poem presents a genealogy of human violence and atonement regarding animals, and reveals itself to be predicated, as a narrative, upon such transgressions and their authors' attempts to amend them. Yet, as the text makes clear, such acts of atonement are never enough. The mariner's guilt is, rather like his tale, and like Adam's own sin, irrevocable and perpetual, and yet also, in its case, consolidating of relationships ("love") between human beings and animals and between those who grieve and atone; in this instance, between a saddened guest and his haunted mariner-host.

Like other such transformational tales, the Mariner's story of sacrifice and atonement is ambivalently predicated upon animal difference and relatedness ("He made and loveth all"). It acknowledges the commonality and otherness upon which human-animal relationships, here as in "The Nightingale" and in Wordsworth's "Lines," are inherently founded and structured. Coleridge's *Ancyent Marinere* is in this sense an allegory not just of human benevolence toward animals—an RSPCA forerunner of sorts—but of the binding invisible connections between human and animal realms. It tells how such connections can form communities of human beings bonded by their shared observance of past transgression and present or future atonement. The perpetuity of the narrative and its serial community of tellers and listeners indeed argues for the long journey such wisdom requires. In fact, as we find in Wordsworth's "Hart-Leap Well" (1799) and in *Home at Grasmere* (1800, 1806), such community is never won easily nor ever entirely; it is attained through violence and the post hoc lamenting of what "man" has done to animal.

In *Home at Grasmere* Wordsworth describes his and his sister Dorothy's journey into Grasmere's inclement vale. He lingers, as they lingered then, entranced in the locale of Hart-leap Well, which auspiciously intimated to them a "milder day" and "fairer world" to come. This locodescriptive passage is also an intertextual one, alluding to Wordsworth's previously mentioned, appositely titled lyrical ballad "Hart-Leap Well." The latter poem recalls the medieval knight Sir Walter's renowned chasing down of a hart, which then killed itself in its last of three desperate leaps, leaving the spot "curs'd" (124, 141-42).

As Raimonda Modiano points out, "by voluntarily leaping to its death" the deer transformed a hunt into a sacrifice; hence Sir Walter's ritualistic raising of three stone pillars to commemorate the dead stag. And yet Walter's act of memorialization seems ultimately inconsequential or even impious, due to its lack of the atonement required for such acts of sacrifice and commemoration. "Without mourning," Modiano observes, Walter's action becomes "profane", a "murder," in the words of the poem. David Perkins sees this hunter's killing of the hart as an act of "solipsistic egoism," similar in its way to the Mariner's own "egoistic self-assertion" and rightly memorialized not just by the pillars but by the adjacent pleasure house Walter builds as an expression of his selfish, libidinal desire ("Wordsworth").

In lieu of its proper mourning, the hart's death is lamented, we learn, not just by the poem's narrator and tale-telling shepherd but also by nature itself. "This beast not unobserv'd by Nature fell," the poet states, "[h]is death was mourn'd by sympathy divine". The animal's "murder" has for the narrator two important "lesson[s]" to teach: first, that we ought never to "blend our pleasure or our pride / With sorrow of the meanest thing that feels", and second, as in the *Ancyent Marinere,* that nature's "Being" "[m]aintains a deep and reverential care" for those "quiet creatures whom he loves" (167-68, 177-80). Yet, although "Hart-Leap Well" does in some sense represent an ecological interpenetration of cultural and natural observances—"how the conventionally antagonistic 'cultural' and 'natural' may in fact felicitously interanimate" (Kroeber 55)—the poem ultimately presents a picture less of human-animal felicity than of struggle, at least of past struggle.

In *Home at Grasmere* it is at this ambivalent topographical and intertextual spot of Hart-leap Well that Wordsworth and Dorothy, still transfixed in "awful trance," receive the quasi-religious "intimation of the milder day / Which is to come, the fairer world than this". This prognosis or prophecy, owed to their more proper observance of animal suffering, becomes its own form of sacred election, raising them up:

...dejected as we were
Among the records of that doleful place
By sorrow for the hunted beast who there
Had yielded up his breath.... (240-43)

In their "trance" the poet and his sister experience a religious "Vision of humanity and of God / The Mourner, God the Sufferer", of God the Paschal Lamb, that re-emphasizes this passage's intertextual connection to animal sacrifice and to the ritualized eucharistic fellowship that such death or suffering can make possible. In their ambivalent intermingling of "sadness" and "joy" at this past prospect of a creature "suffer[ing] wrongfully" the thoughtful couple finds, significantly, a "promise": that through their observance of past sacrifice—their Christian-like sacralizing of a prior, profane "murder"—their "love" and "knowledge" might "secure" them a "portion" of nature's benevolence. On the one hand, Wordsworth of course simply hopes that in a world where the death of a hart is signified by nature the lives of humans will receive a similarly blessed accounting. But, on the other hand, as this strange "episode in mourning" shows, it is humans rather than nature spirits who must first undertake such rectifying work (Modiano 499). Their requisite mourning in turn implies that animal death, nature's "tribute of inevitable pain" (l. 841), is what provides the lasting basis for Wordsworthian dwelling and community in Grasmere's vale: first profaning violation (botched animal sacrifice, "murder"), then sacralizing compensation of human sorrow, and finally the hoped-for blessings of fellowship and dwelling such observance may bequeath—blessings that, the poet and his sister hope, may extend beyond a solitary "pair seceding from the common world" to encompass "all the Vales of the earth and all mankind".

And yet, in the intertextual domain of these closely linked poems, at least one question remains. Might this couple's aforementioned "joy" at a retrospect of animal suffering, given such joy's proscription in the first of the two lessons of "Hart-Leap Well," profane their commemoration of the hart, thus marring their communitarian fortunes? If such mingling of "joy" and "sadness" at the hart's death makes mourning incomplete or improper, would matters then require, as in Coleridge's sea-tale, that further narratives or revisitations be proffered? Profanation may be unavoidable here, as animal death in Wordsworth and Coleridge ever wavers between murder and sacrifice. At the same time, such ambivalently registered failure and incompleteness may also serve to afford people, in *Home at Grasmere* as in both "The Nightingale" and *The Rime of the Ancyent Marinere,* further possibilities for mourning and for its continuing promise of social cohesion.

However one in fact sorts out this dilemma, the couple's sense of belonging to a place, and their concomitant sense of belonging to one another—of "twain" made "pair"—is grounded in their, and in their hoped-for community's, uneasy relationship to (past) animals. Their prospect of dwelling in the death-shadowed valley will be secured by their love for the sacred murdered hart and their (insufficient) sadness at its loss, in a community that is, in contrast to what the poem's speaker espouses, necessarily *not* "without dependence or defect, / Made for itself and happy in itself, / Perfect Contentment, Unity entire". For such community in Grasmere is neither independent nor even necessarily "happy in itself"; it is uneasily dependent upon prior animal death for its blessings.

This communal dependency upon animal loss is the subject also of another episode, where the poet ponders the likely fate of a missing "lonely pair / Of milk-white Swans" that had frequented the lake:

These above all, ah, why are they not here
To share in this day's pleasure? From afar
They came, like Emma and myself, to live
Together here in peace and solitude,
Choosing this Valley, they who had the choice
Of the whole world.... We knew them well—I guess
That the whole Valley knew them—but to us
They were more dear than may be well believed ...

With regard to the actual fate of the swans, Wordsworth speculates that some local shepherd may "have seized the deadly tube / And parted them, incited by a prize / Which ... / He should have spared; or haply both are gone, / One death, and that were mercy given to both". In reasoning thus he knows he seems to "wrong" the very community he and Dorothy are seeking to join. But the birds' loss nonetheless requires explanation, and seems to threaten the isolated human pair's own place in the vale. Yet, in thus mourning and questioning the swans' likely fate something different results: "No, we are not alone," the poet assures his sister, "we do not stand, / My Emma, here misplaced and desolate, / Loving what no one cares for but ourselves". As with their mourning of the hart, this grief over putative past animal suffering or death also promises to earn them inclusion in Grasmere. "Look where we will," the poet holds, "some human heart has been / Before us with its offering.... Joy spreads and sorrow spreads"—at Hart-leap Well and now here by the lakeside, as a further covenant formed of profane sacrifice and of memorializing, (re)sacralizing grief.

If their community in Grasmere is a "unity," then, it is for Wordsworth a profoundly totemic and eucharistic one, comprised of mournful humans and mourned, missing or dead animals and founded both in violence and in ensuing, responsive practices of commemoration. As in Coleridge's *Ancyent Marinere,* such society is uneasily based upon past human/animal difference and transgression, as it is upon present and future acts of responsive, supplemental human atonement.

It is in the end a troubling "knowledge" imparted to (or by) him and Dorothy, but at the same time it is social knowledge that transforms the vale of Grasmere into a prospect of a "community ... / Of many into one incorporate": of a social formation of "[c]ompanions, brethren, [and] consecrated friends" sanctified by the communion and "brotherhood" that human and animal relationships—forms of animal sacrifice and human atonement—"once more" provide.

For Wordsworth and Coleridge, and for other Romantic-period artists, human beings' relationships with animals are vitally social and efficaciously vexed. "Love" for animals seems, often as not in the above poems, and in others such as Wordsworth's "There was a Boy" (a.k.a. the "Boy of Winander"), to arise out of the gulf of difference between humans and animals. In poems like Coleridge's "Nightingale" and Wordsworth's "Lines" we find speakers mindful of the marring effects of human cognition and action upon animal otherness. We also discover that community is repeatedly represented as a product of such difference and of its violent clashes. As Wordsworth's *Home at Grasmere* and Coleridge's *Ancyent Marinere* even more clearly reveal, animal otherness, more than human/animal sameness (as Erasmus Darwin proclaimed), is the principal foundation for community, a community ever observing, belatedly, its difference from and violence toward the myriad animals with which it identifies.

In these Romantic-era representations, animals help to realise alternative, perhaps truer or more legitimate, forms of community founded not upon the vagaries of political revolution, reform, or even nationality but upon ritual observance: a working-through of what remains deeply problematical in human beings' relationships with animals.

In the later eighteenth century and early nineteenth century, animals' "preeminent utility to mankind" (William Kirby, ca. 1835; cited Thomas 28) indeed was, for writers and painters, a social utility: a capacity to produce communities founded upon observance and the playing over "once more" of that which remains unsung or unmemorialized, even violent, in human beings' troubled relationships with nature's creatures.

And while Wordsworth's and Coleridge's desire for such animal-derived community would appear to wane in subsequent years, owed in part no doubt to the poets' restored confidence in the institutions and religious orthodoxies they had previously questioned or condemned, at the turn of the century their longing for new, alternative means of social cohesion was acute. Animals uniquely answered their call, as they did the calls of other artists, both for a broader notion of "brotherhood" and for "a transformative process" (Fulford 124) capable of constituting or renewing communitarian connections.

One thus finds in Stubbs's portrait of the Pocklington family that the foundational relationship of husband and wife is triangulated and emblematized by the horse, to whom Mrs. Pocklington gives her hand and affections, and beside which the captain stands, legs mimetically poised like the animal's own. Such formal human-animal, quasi-familial similitude of course also serves to emphasize actual human-animal *difference*. As Onno Dag Oerlemans observes, "[w]hat makes Stubbs' paintings distinctive ... is that they also very often attempt to render the animal strange, distant, and 'other' than its would-be owner".

For Oerlemans, Stubbs represents such domesticated animals "as having an energy and presence *not* possessed or even understood by the humans around them," a vitality subtly encoded by just such likenesses of "expression" as we find between owner and horse. And yet the structure of the Pocklington community is established in the human figures' attention to this most valued of Britain's animals, without whose presence and differential tension, it seems, given

Stubbs's arrangement, there could be no proper marriage, or minimal community, at all.

In this foregrounding of animals and of animal-oriented economies of various kinds, the late eighteenth and early nineteenth centuries ultimately represent something of a historical bubble in the cultural articulation of the human and the animal. At no time before or since have domestic and wild animals been so conspicuous within and so central to Western conceptions of human social interconnection and subjectivity. But it was a time that passed. Stubbs and even his more emotive artistic successors fell out of public favour (Vaughan 171). As Britain's social and political structures changed it would appear that animals were less needed as the subjects of these artists' social reimaginings. Animals thereupon receded into the pastoral backgrounds and rural memories from which they had come.

As Lyle Rexer contends, the French Romantic painter Eugène Delacroix (1798-1863) "was, perhaps, the last great Western painter for whom animals really mattered." Since that time animals have been "increasingly absorbed into a corner of the public's consciousness" as trivial symbols "of times past and places elsewhere". Polly Chiapetta similarly perceives animals' decline in the paintings of the English Victorian artist Edwin Landseer (1802-73), whose works anthropomorphically represent animals in such a manner as to bring "the sublime and the ridiculous ... perilously close". For his part, John Berger mourns the loss even of such distorting anthropomorphisms, for their loss marked animals' definitive cultural disappearance. Today, he laments, "we live without them". Despite the advent of Charles Darwin's evolutionary theory, in our era we are perhaps farther than ever from his grandfather Erasmus Darwin's social conception of humans and animals as "one family," and from Wordsworth's, Coleridge's, and other artists' depictions of human/animal intra- or inter-familial difference as a basis for cohesion.

And yet, as Rexer argues, even in our time, on some level, animal-oriented artists continue to seek "to 'make a connection,' to reforge a broken bond". It may be that these artists' and their Romantic predecessors' representations of animals still retain a certain cultural "utility," providing alternative visions of identity, difference, and community—even for a post-Romantic age.

Conscious of perceptive critical studies that have traced the interstices between "Yeats, Shelley, Blake, Keats and Wordsworth", Matthew Gibson's Yeats, Coleridge and the Romantic Sage is, sympathetically, attuned to the shortcomings of previous efforts to map this important artistic relationship — notably, Robert Snukal's High Talk: The Philosophical Poetry of W.B. Yeats and Anca Vlasopolos's The Symbolic Method of Coleridge, Baudelaire and Yeats — and purposefully re-describes an important line of influence between the poetry and prose of Samuel Taylor Coleridge and W.B. Yeats. Gibson deliberately avoids conceiving of this artistic and philosophic influence in terms of Harold Bloom's creative oedipal struggle, preferring instead to interpret those distorted figural representations of Coleridge's character and repeated Coleridgean patterns of imagery and thought in Yeats's esoteric works as manifestations of "John Hollander's theory of metalepsis and echo".

Although Coleridge was familiar to Yeats in his younger days, Gibson argues, that only in Yeats's writing, after 1925, did Coleridge as man, poet, and theosophist became a significant lens through which Yeats refracted his understanding of "Anglo-Irish ancestors, Classical and Modern philosophers, as well as [...] his own identity". In this later period, Yeats's endeavour "to reconcile the passion of the artist with the abstraction of the philosopher" centred on a (re-)figuring of Coleridge's received reputation from the Victorian era. By the end of the nineteenth century two divergent views of Coleridge held sway, for some he was regarded, in Arnoldian vein, as "a fabulous failure in all but a few seminal poems and all but a few prose pieces" and, by others, after Arthur Symons, as an ethereal dreamer and "forerunner of symbolism and the new, fin-de-siècle trends in France".

Typical of Yeats's moulding of "literary history", his scarce references to Coleridge in those early writings avoid shaping the romantic poet into a "literary hero" and instead illustrate Yeats's "own ideas". Reviewing the poetry of R.D. Joyce (Irish Fireside, November 1886) and Douglas Hyde's Beside the Fire (National Observer, February 1891), Yeats appreciates Coleridge as an "aesthetic poet" of self-reflexive consciousness — dramatised, for example, in "Frost at Midnight" and "The Eolian Harp" — and as a mystic symbolist steeped in Swedenborg. These youthful depictions of Coleridge's poetic sensibility and personality extend beyond an impressionistic sense of the "reflective nature of conversation poems", acquired in Yeats's school days, to a studied engagement with Coleridge's Table Talk.

Such serious study is further evidenced, for Gibson, by the fact that "Yeats may even have read Coleridge's marginalia to his Swedenborg editions in the British Library". In this formative phase of Yeats's imaginative development, he found creative interests akin to his quest for "the dissolution of self in symbol" more readily available in works by "Romantic forebears such as Blake and Shelley". In initial reviews and an essay on "William Blake and his Illustrations to the Divine Comedy" (1896), Yeats's portraiture of Coleridge is ambivalent, at one moment, Coleridge exemplifies an "aesthetic, visionary and ultimately Symbolist bent" and, at another, emerges as a traitor of his own "mystic powers" (Gibson 17-18).

With the advent of the twentieth century, Gibson delineates, Yeats's decisive swerve away from a pure aesthetic of mystic Symbolism to a revised understanding of aestheticism "which was [...] grounded in the common experience of the people" and apparently re-enacted his own previous condemnation of Coleridge's betrayal of mysticism. Drawing on Romantic precedents, especially those established by Coleridge and Wordsworth, Yeats as organiser of the Irish National Theatre and playwright had ascertained a sense that "imaginative literature could be founded upon the language of real people rather than upon the artifice of cliques" (Gibson 18). Yeats did not relinquish his commitment to the word as transcendental signified, but "modified the symbolist aesthetic to [the] new environment" of social, cultural, and political change.

In "Literature and the Living Voice" (1906), Yeats praises Coleridge's creative collaboration with Wordsworth to produce the Lyrical Ballads (1798), for "the discovery of a popular language — a living voice — which appeals to an entire people" through an unpretentious simplicity (Gibson 19). Eulogising the literary life and work of J.M Synge ("J.M. Synge and the Ireland of his Time", 1910) Yeats, vitally, connects such linguistic primitivism to "the passive man who shapes and selects themes from common experience" as opposed to those artists, Goethe and Shelley among them, who are regarded as "active re-creator[s]" (Gibson 20).

These essays by Yeats of 1906 and 1910, coloured by Wordsworthian poetic theory and practice, Gibson suggests, redefine Coleridge's artistic attributes to accommodate Yeats's altering relationship with Aestheticism and Symbolism, presenting a newly drawn figure of Coleridge, distinct from other past manifestations of Wordsworth's literary associate in Yeats's prose, as "a poet of experience, passivity and simplicity" (Gibson 21).

Yeats's projection of Coleridge, Gibson believes, into "the role of visionary and Aesthete" is galvanised by the favourable comparisons Yeats draws, in "The Tragic Generation" (1922), between Coleridge and Ernst Dowson, Lionel Johnson, and Monroe Beardsley. Following Arthur Symons's editorial commentary on Coleridge's poetry as the product of a sleeping state and prescient of Stéphane Mallarmé, Yeats felt compelled to "reconstruct Coleridge's personality on the lines of Baudelaire, Johnson, and Dowson". According to Gibson, Yeats comprehends Coleridge as a "tragic poet" and "precursor of the Tragic Generation of Aestheticist and Symbolist poets" whose "intellectual schizophrenia" translated into "a division between Christian morality and aesthetic purity". This tragic conceptualisation of Coleridge marks the beginning of a separation, in Yeats's mind, of the co-authors of Lyrical Ballads.

Yeats's segregation of these prominent first-generation

romantic poets coincided with his growing fascination for Coleridge's sense of religious guilt and "renewed interest in [his] 'supernatural' poems, and consequent dissociation of [Coleridge] from Wordsworth". With this division of Coleridge from Wordsworth, Yeats moves away from his youthful conceptions of a unifying cultural and linguistic primitivism that he had extolled in 1910. Despite "some patterns of consistency" between Yeats's sketches of Coleridge as "tragic Aesthete" and mystic, no coherent pattern or opinion on this subject is evident in Yeats's writing "up until 1922". Instead the shadow-play of Coleridge's personality and poetic reputation is endlessly performed and "variously understood in Yeats's phantasmagoria as Aesthete and Symbolist poet, as a source for mysticism and as adherent to primitive and popular forms of art".

In his diary entries from 1930 onwards, Yeats was increasingly preoccupied with adequately defining the philosophic and poetic sage who, eventually, in more Nietzschean mood, come to encapsulate artistic sentiment with intellectual logic, capable of a tragic, joyous, affirmation of existence and, as such, no longer an enemy to the creative artist by virtue of being "antithetical, 'demonic' and passionate in character" — distinct in kind from "the Sage of A Vision".

Having established "the Daimonic nature of the sage", Gibson explores how, Yeats sought to ascribe this "Romantic figure" a social function and found in Coleridge a model for one "who can make his work accessible to the masses without compromise". Yeats's derived his template for these socially purposeful sages not from Coleridge the poet, but from Coleridge as man, philosopher, and seer. Yeats regarded, Gibson writes, "Coleridge the philosopher as conforming to the new ideal of sage who struggles tragically with his Daimon to a joyful despair, but also to expand the powers of the archetype still further to include a greater social appeal and clarity".

The influence of Symon's edition of Coleridge's poetry extended to this later Yeatsian "construction of Coleridge's personality", as Yeats found many of the editor's opinions corroborated and expanded in John Charpentier's study of Coleridge the Sublime Somnambulist (translated and published in 1929). Yeats agreed with Charpentier's analysis of Coleridge as "a different sort of teacher" (Gibson 49), an accomplished communicator and educator of mankind, he dissented from Charpentier's acquiescence with Thomas Carlyle's "less laudatory recollections of the great man" (Gibson 48) and his portrayal of Coleridge as the reclusive seer of Highgate, who had become utterly estranged from ¯and a mere observer of the battlefield of ordinary life.

In rejecting "the view that the end of [Coleridge's] life was merely a symbol", Yeats forged the "the man of passion to the man of society" in his re-conceptualisation of the sage as a combatant in the incessant struggle to discover "the Unity of Being [...] with social relevance" (all Gibson 49). Diffused through Symon's editorial apparatus, Charpentier's critical interpretation, and Yeats's own "recent reading of 'Fears in Solitude' and 'Hexameters'", Coleridge's personality and artistry became the standards of the archetypal philosopher-poet to which Yeats "aspired in rewriting A Vision".

Throughout the 1930's the image of Coleridge as the epitome of what it is to be a philosophical poet profoundly effected Yeats's creative and theoretical endeavours "to end abstractions in three major spheres: the transcendental, the political and the life after death". When Yeats wrote an explication of his Principles, in The Completed Symbol (1937), he discovered in Coleridge's The Friend (1818) a Platonic restatement of Kantian epistemology that asserted "a Platonic ontology for Kant's pure Theoretic" between Reason, Understanding, and Sense (Gibson 58). Grosvenor E. Powell's assertion "that Coleridge's distinction between Reason and Understanding allowed Yeats to see Spirit as transcendental" (Gibson 65) is persuasively contested by Gibson's argument "that Coleridge allowed Yeats to see the 'Divine ideas' as appertaining to the soul of individual man" so enabling him "to link microcosom with macrocosom". Coleridge's Platonic re-interpretation of Kant permitted Yeats to work through his own difficulties with the transcendental abstractions of

Plotinus's Enneads and revealed to the Irish poet the possibility of discovering "the primal oneness of God within one's own self" (Gibson 66).

During this time Yeats's reading of Coleridge became an important catalyst for his political reflections on governmental institutions, the nature and dispensation of just rule, the relationship of art and architecture to the socio-political dynamics of a given era, and the wider patterns and implications of historical change. "The Friend acted," Gibson claims, "as an arbiter between [Yeats's] own system, the cyclical theories of anthropology which he was reading and the autocratic Tory politics of [Jonathan] Swift and [Edmund]Burke, allowing him to see their systems as cyclical and predestined, when in fact they were not". Outside of the 1930 diary, however, Yeats makes no mention of Coleridge in "a political context" as his political traits are elsewhere in Yeats's writing (for instance, in his "Introduction to The Words upon the Window-pane") subsumed into the figure of Swift who, for Yeats, "becomes political prophet or sage".

When meditating on the nature and purpose of mortal existence, Yeats's sense of the universe as comprised of "embattled contraries" (for example, between Husk and Passionate Body and Spirit and Celestial Body) and his desire to render the spiritual realm physically incarnate also found a vocabulary in "the relation of light to dark in Coleridge's poems" and their often supernatural aspect. Yeats's introduction to The Oxford Book of Modern Verse (1936) unequivocally associates Coleridge's poetry with "a sense of enchantment" (Gibson 87). Much of Yeats's later work unfurls, in Gibson's reading, as an intense dialogue with the poetic creations of other romantic sages, including the perceived magical wonderment of Coleridge's "Christabel" and "Kubla Khan", "the nature philosophy of Wordsworth's 'Pedlar'" in The Excursion, and the sensory tactility of Shelley's Ahasuerus in The Revolt of Islam.

Consciously and unconsciously, Yeats's poetics from The Winding Stair and Other Poems (1933) onwards echo "[t]he phantasmagoric qualities of Coleridge's poetry", embarking on an artistic and philosophic quest to ensure that "the spiritual become[s] materially immanent rather than transcendent". In particular "Kubla Khan" and "The Rime of the Ancient Mariner" presented a "concretising of abstractions which Yeats had sought in Coleridge's prose" and signposted art as the appropriate medium for the manifestation of "this passionate philosophy of the sage" which became the aspiration of Yeats's poetry "of the early thirties".

The final and third part of Gibson's Yeats, Coleridge and the Romantic Sage shifts in focus from Yeats's recreation of Coleridge's personality as a means of negotiating the complex relationship between the transcendental and the immanent – the subject of the previous two sections – to a consideration of Yeats's adaptation of Coleridge's metaphors for describing mental and spiritual processes. Reading Coleridge's refutation of the mental passivity involved in the process of perception, advocated by David Hartley's Doctrine of Vibrations, Yeats lighted upon Coleridge's image, in Biographia Literaria (1817), of the mind being "the mere quick-silver plating behind a looking glass" (Coleridge 119), as one that subsequently informed those "metaphors of mind which represent a drive towards organicism and synthesis in Yeats's [...] apprehension of spiritual reality" attendant to a variety of different "kind[s] of unity" and their peculiar incarnations.

Yeats understood the Coleridgean metaphor to indict Hartley's system for its reduction of "the mind to the state described by the image" and adopted "the looking glass" as a motif to represent "the movement way from Unity of Being in its individual manifestations" that encompassed "[John] Locke's 'mechanical philosophy', [G.E.] Moore's realism, Modernism in literature and the mind of the war poets" – all of which were perceived by Yeats as "Daimonic influences" that had caused the denigration of "our own time" (all Gibson 148). Yeats's "creative misconception" of the meaning of Coleridge's "looking glass" metaphor, as Gibson remarks, is both shrewdly perceptive and erroneously inventive, chiming perfectly with how Yeats misconstrued (often wilfully) at other points along the trajectory of his literary career Coleridge's personality and theosophy. Yeats's persistent return in his writing life to the image of the Eolian harp (first encountered through his father's admiration of Shelley's A Defence of Poetry and then in Coleridge's 1795 poem of that title) to express the ineffable, internal, invisible, machinations of "the mind as a pure act" underscores the centrality of a self-invented hagiography built around Coleridge to Yeats's conception of the gyres and definition of sage as tragic philosophical-poet and antitype to the Victim. Spiritually and intellectually, Yeats discovered in Coleridge an ontological basis to render the rarefied concretely palatable and art's potentiality to make the fine abstractions of "passionate philosophy" (Gibson 113) felt on the pulses.

In Yeats, Coleridge and the Romantic Sage, Gibson's scope extends beyond an illumination of the creative and philosophic exchange of imagery and ideas with Coleridge in Yeats's artistic and mystical thought to a recent, broader, and timely area of critical interest — most notably explored by Richard Cronin's Romantic Victorians (2003) — in the Victorian era as an important moment of confluence between what is now regarded as Romanticism and Victorianism. This historical locus affords an invaluable opportunity to reassess Romanticism's cultural legacy in the late nineteenth century and early twentieth century. Disseminated through the writings of W.B. Yeats and others, Romanticism persisted as the perpetually self-spawned spectre of the Victorian and Modern age.

THE CHALLENGE OF COLERIDGE

Peter Larkin, at the 2002 Coleridge conference in Somerset, spoke warmly of David Haney's The Challenge of Coleridge as an exemplary contribution to recent debate within the hermeneutical community, and it is not hard to see why. It is a comprehensive and erudite reading of the ethical dimension of Coleridge's thought, and one which is written with a certain kind of clarity. And it contributes to one of the central problems of post-structural discourse over the last fifteen years or so: the problem of how (if indeed it is possible) to bring an ethical dimension into a discourse which in its earlier phases was marked by an all-corrosive scepticism. But I am less sure exactly what it contributes to that discussion, a reservation which will emerge in the course of this review.

The first chapter deals, appropriately enough, with the very question of whether ethics and hermeneutics can meet. As Haney points out, borrowing Harpham's analysis:

ethics has been seen as complicit with everything that literary theory has attempted to subvert, from logocentricism to autonomous selfhood [...]. However, ethics is in this scenario a repressed that inevitably returns in the wake of the 1987 exposure of Paul de Man's pro-Nazi wartime journalism, at which point polite discussions of language gave way to charges of personal immorality, collaboration [...], opportunism and deception.

The question, then, was how to bring ethics back into hermeneutics, a question which is closely related to Hume's problem of how to get an ought from an is. As the Oxford Companion to Philosophy suggests, the usual response is to try to argue that ought and is interpenetrate—a strategy Barbara Hernstein Smith adopts in her argument that all interpretation (or attention to the world) is value laden. But the problem here is, of course, that the values spoken of are not necessarily ethical. The male gaze, for instance, is certainly evaluative, but much less certainly ethical.

Haney thus prefers to argue that "there does seem to be an unavoidable ethical element in the hermeneutic act: a demand for a certain generosity toward the other," an idea he takes further by referring to Aristotle's view that speech often involves "a kind of communality[,] in virtue of which reciprocal taking of counsel [...] is at all meaningful in the first place". This sounds like a version of what Anglo-American philosophy calls "epistemic charity": a willingness, for instance, to interpret a passage so as to render it coherent with the text's presumed broader purposes.

But if this is the note on which Haney ends his introductory discussion of the problem, it is not easy to see how we have got beyond his earlier warning that it is "a mistake to see interpretative activity as fundamentally ethical". For when Derrida accused Gadamer of depending on a Kantian concept of "good will" in his hermeneutics, Gadamer replied that hermeneutic understanding is ethically neutral. It has "nothing to do with ethics," Gadamer said, because "even immoral beings try to understand one another". This is not a conclusion Haney can rest content with, and Haney suggests that "even evil doers must listen to each other generously if they are to work together". That claim is open to some question.

And so I take the argument to have shown that hermeneutics often will be characterised by an ethical impulse, even if of no greater significance than a common epistemic charity. But in the absence of metaphysics or foundations, I am still left wondering what the status of this ethical impulse might be and whether it is really consonant with the hermeneutical approach.

In the remainder of his first chapter, Haney does not answer these question but moves instead to a criticism of New Historicism for what he sees as its too easy assumption that "history can simply be reconstructed in its original form"—the Schleiermacherian or Romantic position. The critique is interesting in its own right but also a necessary means by which Haney creates space for his own kind of hermeneutic approach. He suggests "a kind of Levinasian humility before the otherness of the past [...] an approach that refuses to assimilate the other into the categories of my ego [...] but that by the same token refuses agreement [with it]". It is this move (one again characterised by a certain ethical openness) which licences his Gadamerian "transhistorical conversation" (xii), his hope:

> to produce a kind of criticism which will see Coleridge's writing, not as embodying a set of concepts [...] to be affirmed or critiqued by modern theory, but as [...] a set of perspectives that can be put into a mutually illuminating ... relationship with more recent perspectives.

We are in a critical universe where there are no foundations or essences, and so what we are offered instead is a conversation—a conversation between Coleridge and Gadamer, Ricoeur , Levinas, and others. Let us turn, then, to some of the details of that conversation.

Chapter 2 is entitled "Ethics and Art" and was for me perhaps the least rewarding in the book. It begins with Aristotle's distinction between techne (the artistic skill involved in the creation of aesthetic objects) and phronesis ("a state grasping the truth [...], concerned with action about what is good or bad for a human being"). This distinction is inflected through the works of various recent thinkers, and a set of increasingly fine, not to say ethereal, distinctions is used to interrogate Coleridge. And yet we are presented with no evidence that Coleridge was aware of Aristotle's distinction, nor with much help on what Aristotle might have understood by the distinction, nor with much sense of its importance or lack thereof in the poststructural sphere.

And by the time a page-long discussion of Heidegger reveals that the mariner has treated the albatross as a merely utilitarian object, we may reasonably wonder whether all of this erudition is serving any useful purpose. Haney does rightly assimilate techne to Fancy, and phronesis to Imagination, but I was left with little sense of why this assimilation might be enlightening. And when we are told that "Coleridge [...] was perhaps less confident than Heidegger in the possibility of the Greek reunification of techne and poeisis", I wonder whether the Greeks had indeed reunified the concepts and whether Coleridge had any views on the matter at all.

In chapter 3 things improve considerably with a discussion of Coleridge's reaction to Kant's essential, but at the same time arid and rationalistic, categorical imperative. As Haney observes, Coleridge avoids talk of special and extra-rational moral faculties, such as moral sense or conscience, preferring to argue that reason itself is grounded in conscience. This derives from Coleridge's well-known argument that consciousness derives from conscience, that God the Father is able to instantiate himself as a person (along with consciousness and reason) only by recognising the alterity, or otherness, of the Son. Reason is thus grounded in ethics rather than vice versa, and moral obligation is intensely and unavoidably personal.

The second part of chapter 3 moves to a sustained and interesting discussion of Coleridge's higher critical views (83-93). Haney makes good use, here and elsewhere, of Coleridge's marginalia, pointing to a note in which Coleridge wonders of his own post-Kantian theology, "Do I believe that the Writers of the old Testament were conscious of any such Ideas? What if they were not?—The Bible is that which is capable of reflecting—It is the Mirror of Faith" (qtd. in Haney 86; Marginalia 2:423). Haney's understanding of this is anti-intentionalist and anti-psychologistic. And he very usefully quotes Gadamer, who argues that when subjective intentions are put "at risk" in conversation, the result is "something [...] that is not only mine or the author's, but common".

This points to something important and true about meaning in texts and about Coleridge's grasp of the historicity of biblical texts. But it is important to remember that even if for Coleridge the Old Testament writers were not aware of the implications Coleridge draws from them, there is a broader authorial presence in the form of the Divine Spirit. For as Haney himself shows, Coleridge claimed that "The Prophets do not describe their inspiration as Poets; but relate sudden changes produced without any conscious act of their own will [...]. This state was used instrumentally by the Divine Spirit as the [...] base [...] of his spiritual Agency" (qtd. in Haney 88; Marginalia 2:402). And so, while Coleridge did not believe in divine dictation, he did see a role for the Spirit in the writing of the Bible. Chapter 3 offers a useful and discriminating account of Coleridge's position in relation to Eichorn, Schleiermacher, Herder, and "the German School" (Coleridge, Notebooks 4:5322).

Chapter 4 builds on Ricoeur's analysis of narrative as an attempt to mediate between first person, phenomenological experience and the desire to give meaning to that experience by treating the self as a third person within a life story. Haney's analysis of the Mariner's response to the question, "What manner of man art thou?" is thus suggestive, though by its nature it is not the kind of argument which can be extended far. Chapter 5 is more substantial, covering a number of large topics like freedom and necessity, and the psychology behind the famous "willing suspension of disbelief." But much of the chapter is taken up by a complex discussion of the idea of sacrifice, which Haney claims is central to Coleridge's view of tragic effect.

Unfortunately, the evidence Haney adduces is far from persuasive, consisting of a passing remark in "Satyrane's Letters" (merely the claim that Christian morality demands more than just sympathy towards the suffering of others), a passage in which Coleridge analyses the sublime effect of certain Miltonic images, while making no mention of sacrifice at all, and a passage from Aids to Reflection in which Coleridge basically argues against any notion of sacrifice. In chapter 6 we discover that Coleridge allows us to avoid the isolated, autonomous self of the Enlightenment, and the chapter contains interesting discussions of Christian "otherness" and sin. The chapter also contains a well-informed and detailed discussion of the Trinity and the relation between the Ground and the three existential persons of God.

Haney suggests that this relation is marked by an unsayable transcendence of the kind which Levinas finds at the heart of the (ethical) recognition of the other. I might mention that Haney disagrees with my views here, though in ways which do not affect his underlying point. Since God is unlikely to pronounce on the issue in the near future, I am not sure how we could resolve the issue, but I do point out that Coleridge himself repeatedly claimed that his formulation was not Plotinian and thus did not involve any "process of development" within the Godhead.

Readers of this review will have noticed a certain ambivalence within it, for I am aware that I am not the book's ideal reader—and that the book will have to find its ideal reviewer elsewhere. For me, the book is like a rich Christmas pudding: one is never quite sure whether one likes the cake, but the plums are juicy. For I am torn between a genuine admiration for Haney's evident learning and the breadth and fluency of his range of reference on the one hand and a nagging suspicion that this is a book which will have only a very limited readership on the other.

Its later chapters contain interesting discussions of key Coleridgean concepts, and I would certainly direct my students to those passages. But taken as a whole, this is not a book for those who are not already experts in hermeneutical discourse.

I realise that to ask for something more foundational is antithetical to the genre, but nonetheless I read with a growing wish for a rather different book: a book which made some more concessions to the uninitiated reader and which might have explained to the Coleridgean community why a hermeneutic approach is rewarding. Perhaps that will be Haney's next book.

Chapter 7

Poetic Failure in Coleridge

'Kubla Khan' is now one of Coleridge's best known and most widely read poems, yet it still presents twentieth-century scholars and readers with many of the same critical problems that confounded its contemporary reviewers. It's textual history remains unclear, Coleridge's prefatory explanation of the poem's production is often considered dubious, and scholars just can't agree on what it 'means' or if it means anything at all. Most readers interpret 'Kubla Khan' as an allegory for the creative process, relying heavily upon a perpetuated Romantic formulation of the redemptive imagination as described separately by M. H. Abrams and Geoffrey Hartman. Such critics as Humphry House, Harold Bloom, and Kathleen Wheeler ignore the melancholia of the preface and the last stanza, and decide that the poem celebrates the creative imagination.

Other readers like R. H. Fogle and Peter Huhn argue that Coleridge achieves thematic and structural unity by reconciling the celebratory and melancholic opposites evident in the poem. Finally, readers such as Kenneth Burke, Paul Magnuson, and Anne Mellor suggest that Coleridge sustains a contradictory duality in which he bemoans the poet's creative limitations while simultaneously hailing the power of the imagination and celebrating the process of life, thus expressing what Mellor calls Romantic irony.

While seemingly different in their final readings of the poem, these various critical stances locate the redemptive power of the creative imagination within the poet. Further, these readings do not explore in any great detail the rhetorical relationship between the preface and the poem proper and the ways in which this relationship informs Coleridge's complex representation of the creative imagination and the poet figure.

If we analyse the subtitle and preface as metalinguistic keys to the poem's interpretive and performative context, we will discover that the poem is not about imaginative redemption or Romantic irony. Rather, 'Kubla Khan' offers its readers a series of false poetic figures, ultimately demonstrating that the ideal (pro)creative and redemptive imagination lies beyond the grasp of the mortal poet, remaining an external and unobtainable other.

The subtitle and preface to 'Kubla Khan' are indeed curious aesthetic and thematic elements that elicit numerous interpretive responses, editorial practices, and critical perspectives. One of the most common readings views the subtitle and the preface as rhetorical apologies added by Coleridge in an attempt to assuage his guilt and/or to avoid harsh criticism. Such a reading ascribes a biographical legitimacy to the introductory note, assuming that the speaker is indeed Coleridge.

As a result, the preface is elevated to the literal and (mis)construed as an expository addition to the imaginative poem, a supplement that should be distinguished from the aesthetic experience of the poem itself. But what if we denature this (artificial) separation between the prose preface and the imaginative poem and thus include it in the reading experience or, more accurately, in the performance context of the poem? Indeed, critics such as David Perkins, Fred Milne, Marjorie Levinson, and Paul Magnuson have considered this question, analyzing the rhetorical dimensions of the preface and noting the ways in which it informs the reader's interpretive horizon. I am much indebted to these critical perspectives, for they indeed begin to answer my question concerning the relationship between the prose preface and the imaginative poem. However, they limit their discussions to textual considerations.

On the one hand, the preface and the poem are obviously (printed) texts, and it makes sense to address the interpretive relationship between these texts in terms of rhetorical theory. On the other, however, the reading experience—that dialectic between the text and the reader which produces the aesthetic work—is also characterized by a performance context. In other words, the dialectic constituting the reading experience is itself a (cognitive) performance space, and as such presupposes a performance context. Understanding the poem more fully, then, involves a textual analysis that is coupled with a study of the poems performance contexts. I argue that the preface serves as a rhetorical monocle that allows us to glimpse the poem's performance context and thus better to understand Coleridge's ambiguous poetic metaphysics. 'Kubla Khan' exhibits metacommunicative devices that remind its audience they are reading a fabricated narrative (the preface) and verse (the poem proper) tale and that reveal a specific understanding of this tale.

The very existence or, more properly, the coming into being of the preface suggests that it is itself a rhetorical device that foregrounds the poem's performance context. Critics and literary historians have extensively debated the date of the poem's composition, suggesting dates that range from as early as 1797 to as late as 1800. The most convincing date of composition is Autumn (October or November) of 1797, for this is the date given in the Crew Manuscript endnote in which Coleridge writes, 'This fragment with a good deal more, not recoverable, composed in a sort of Reverie brought on by two grains of Opium, taken to check a dysentery, at a Farm House between Porlock and Linton, a quarter of a mile from Culbone Church, in the fall of the year, 1797.'

Furthermore, in a letter to John Thelwall dated 14 October 1797 Coleridge mentions a brief absence that probably corresponds to his stay at Porlock where the poem was composed, and Coleridge goes on to say, 'My mind feels as if it ached to behold & know something *great* —something *one* & *indivisible*—and it is only in the faith of this that rocks or waterfalls, mountains or caverns give me the sense of sublimity or majesty!'. Here, Coleridge seems preoccupied with the sublime and very specific natural imagery that appear in

'Kubla Khan', helping to confirm further that the poem or some version of it was most likely composed in the fall of 1797. We cannot know if the poem initially had textual supplements; but the 1810 autographed Crew Manuscript contains a short explanatory endnote, and the published 1816 manuscript begins with an elaborate preface. Why did Coleridge feel it necessary to supplement his later manuscripts with such addenda? One explanation concerns Coleridge's role as orator and his ability to affect audiences deeply through verbal performance.

Coleridge was indeed a powerful speaker, drawing crowds for his sermons and lectures. William Hazlitt remembered being awe-struck by Coleridge's preaching in January of 1798:

As he gave out this text, his voice 'rose like a steam of rich distilled perfumes', and when he came to the two last words, which he pronounced loud, deep, and distinct, it seemed to me, who was then young, as if the sounds had echoed from the bottom of the human heart, and as if that prayer might have floated in solemn silence through the universe. Coleridge also captivated his audiences with his poetic recitations, and 'Kubla Khan' left a significant impression on many of its listeners. For example, Sir Thomas Noon Talfourd noted a particular occasion sometime between 1815 and 1817:

But more peculiar in its beauty than this [Coleridge's recitation of 'Christabel'], was his recitation of Kubla Khan [sic]. As he repeated the passage—

A damsel with a dulcimer
In a vision once I saw:
It was an Abyssinian maid,
And on her dulcimer she played,
Singing of Mount Abora!

his voice seemed to mount, and melt into air, as the images grew more visionary, and the suggested associations more remote. (Armour, 351)

And Leigh Hunt recalled the time Coleridge recited this poem to Byron, an event instigating the poems eventual publication: 'He recited his *Kubla Khan* one morning to Lord Byron, in his lordship's house in Piccadilly, when I happened to be in another room. I remember the other's coming away from him, highly struck with his poem, and saying how wonderfully he talked. This was the impression of everybody who heard him' (Armour, 269).

These accounts suggest that Coleridge had a commanding presence and elicited intense reactions in his audiences. He was a master orator who performed his poetry effectively, and a portion of this poetic performance involved some kind of performative contextualization. For example, in 1811 John Payne Collier remembered engaging in a literary discussion of dreams with Coleridge and Charles Lamb, a discussion 'having been introduced by a recitation by Coleridge of some lines he had written many years ago upon the building of a Dream-palace by Kubla-Khan: he had founded it on a passage he had met with in an old book of travels' (Armour 177). Even though Collier did not specifically mention a preface or endnote, he did note that Coleridge contextualized the poem for this audience by locating (as far as Collier remembers) its impetus in 'an old book of travels', a performative strategy anticipating the 1816 preface.

The endnote of the Crew Manuscript, the information concerning the possible source of the poem that Coleridge shared with Collier, and the later more developed preface to the 1816 published text suggest that Coleridge felt it necessary to contextualize this poem. However, Coleridge is not apologizing for this poem; rather, his contextualization provides an intellectual and epistemological performance context through which Coleridge attempts to assert his poetic authority (yet, as we will later see, he ironically fails in this effort) and with which Coleridge's audience (auditors of his recitations or readers of his printed text) can better understand the poem.

The first sentence of the preface is significantly set off from the rest as its own paragraph, implying that it holds a singular importance for our understanding of the preface and for the way we position ourselves in relation to the poem. On the surface, this first statement is simply an authorial disclaimer, whereby the speaker discounts his own poem as a 'fragment', a 'psychological curiosity' that caught the interest of some other poet (Lord Byron). One could read this disclaimer quite literally, as do many critics, and thus conclude that indeed Coleridge is dismissing his own work as a mere triviality or curiosity in an attempt to avoid charges of blasphemy (Mellor, 157-58) or poetic and artistic ineptitude (McFarland, 225) contrasting his attempt to argue for creative individuality in the preface to 'Christabel'. However, if we read the preface to 'Kubla Khan' as a key to performance, then an other reading presents itself, resulting in a more rich and complex understanding of the poem and Coleridge's poetic project.

Kathleen Wheeler provides one possible alternative reading, suggesting that the opening sentence of the preface is an advertisement for the poem that encourages the reader to approach the poem specifically as a 'psychological curiosity' and as a fragment. However, this reading focuses on the interaction between printed text and reader without sufficiently exploring the poem's performative dimensions. Many storytelling performances are initiated by the teller disclaiming his or her tale, attributing the source to some other storyteller or discrediting his or her storytelling ability. Such a strategy conditions listeners to the storytelling act and implies that what they are about to hear will indeed be an interesting and well-told story.

The disclaimer is a sign of a good storyteller. Therefore, by subtitling his poem 'A Vision in a Dream. A Fragment' and classifying it as a 'psychological curiosity', Coleridge actually encourages his audience to consider the poem as more than a meaningless dream. Also, by deferring his own poetic authority to that of the celebrated Byron, Coleridge provides more authority to his poem than if he were to assert himself—as if boasting—that he has produced a poetic masterpiece.

Interestingly, this performative disclaimer differs from the traditional storytelling disclaimer in that Coleridge creates a speaker who presents himself as an editor of the printed text (or the orator of a poem he did not necessarily write) who is clearly separate from the Author figure. That is, this speaker is not reciting his own poem but that of some other poetic agent, and this rhetorical move identifies a poetic context in which the performance itself pertains specifically to poets and poetry.

Furthermore, by imposing an artificial tension between psychological curiosity and aesthetic poetry, Coleridge effects the opposite: he conflates psychology with aesthetics, ultimately demonstrating that the workings of the (poetic) mind is indeed proper material to constitute a poetics. In effect, readers are not to dismiss the poem as a 'psychological curiosity' but to look for ways in which Coleridge creates a poetics concerning the faculty of poetic imagination. Coleridge's disclaiming the poem as a mere vision or reverie makes the psychology of poetic creation the subject of his poem.

The rest of the preface narrative outlines and foreshadows the ways in which the poet's mind becomes the subject of the poem, thus rhetorically schematizing the reader's horizon of interpretive expectation. By developing a narrative of failed poetic activity, the second section of the preface establishes the poem proper as an allegory of imaginative failure. In the preface narrative, readers encounter a clearly mortal and ill poet figure who possesses limited creative abilities. This figure is not the image of a divine creative entity; on the contrary, he is a frustrated poet who is contrasted later to the supremely powerful Kubla Khan and the demonic poet/seer in the last section of the poem proper. This contrast is foreshadowed and, simultaneously, concretized at the moment in his dream when the poet figure encounters his own subconscious double.

He sees the imaginative other who he himself is not (and can never be). The Khan figure of the poet's dream whom the poet tries to render (and, thus, poetically and imaginatively resurrect) in his poem is the mirror image of the poet's creative desire (a mirroring that is thematically reinforced by the reflection image in the quotation from 'The Picture') a desire that can never be satisfied but, instead, can only remain as an eternal process of becoming. As the poet tries to obtain his desire in the form of the poem, as he tries to contain this personal *objet petite a* , it becomes a Lacanian gift of *merde*—a fragmented, lost vision. And it is this very narration of desire—coming to terms with poetic failure and coping with the longing to become a supremely powerful decreer of divine grandeur and splendor—that becomes the thematic context of the poem proper.

In other words, the preface provides a context through which to interpret the poem proper as an imaginative representation of failed poetic figures. It can be argued that the headnote (a fragment itself) abstracted from 'The Picture' posits a hopefulness that the vision may return. However, because this moment of re-vision, as the preface notes, 'is yet to come' this hopefulness is indeed ironic, thus suggesting that 'Kubla Khan' is not about poetic rediscovery but, instead, poetic failure. Xanadu—the fantastic realm where the Khan decrees his stately pleasure dome, where the sacred river Alph meanders down to depthless caverns, and where a constructive/destructive fountain breaks through the rocky surface—represents the creative cognition and the phenomenal mind. In this creative realm there are three key agents: the Khan, the sacred river Alph, and the fountain. In terms of the Coleridgean ideal imagination, these three agents correspond to the three faculties constituting Coleridge's phenomenological model—the fancy, the primary imagination, and the secondary imagination respectively.

Coleridge had not yet outlined his phenomenological model when he first composed 'Kubla Khan' in 1797, and readers like Paul Magnuson (viii) find it too reductive to suggest that the poems exemplify Coleridge's later metaphysics. Wheeler answers this charge by deciding that in the very least, this phenomenal model is implicit in the poem (*Creative Mind* , 33). But we can safely say that Coleridge's metaphysics is more than just implicit in his poetry; for while his poetry may not have been written to exemplify his prose metaphysics, his studies in philosophy and metaphysics indeed informs his poetic musing. We know that Coleridge was versed in German and familiar with German philosophy as early as 1796-97 (before and during the creative process generating 'Kubla Khan') because in May of 1796 Coleridge wrote Thomas Poole that he was already studying German and planning to study German metaphysics (*CL* , I: 209). By December 1796 he had already begun to read Kant, referring to the German metaphysician as 'the most unintelligible Emanuel Kant' in a letter to John Thelwall dated December 17, 1796 (*CL* , I: 283-84).

Furthermore, by 1796 Coleridge had become disillusioned by 'Mechanic Philosophy' and converted to 'Constructive Philosophy' which conceives the mind as a more active (as opposed to passive) player in the creation of knowledge and the structuring of perception. Even though Coleridge's specific position on the creative imagination is not formally published until 1817 in *Biographia Literaria* , he had been struggling with these various formulations of the imagination, and his continual work with theories of the mind, passive versus active imagination, and conceptions of the will (dating back as early as 1796) informs the thematics and aesthetics of his early poetry.

In relation to the poem proper, these philosophic theories and models of the creative imagination take the form of multiple poetic figures or creative agents. The first creative figure or agent in this phenomenal realm of Xanadu that we encounter is the Khan, a figure identified immediately with the creative process: 'In Xanadu did Kubla Khan/ A stately pleasure dome decree'. The Khan appears to be the ultimate poet/creator, for his utterances shape his material reality. His active will shapes not merely a poetic text but an aesthetic masterpiece of staggering proportions. The Khan produces an enchanting paradise:

So twice five miles of fertile ground
With walls and towers were girdled round:
And there were gardens bright with sinuous rills,
Where blossomed many an incense-bearing tree;
And here were forests ancient as the hills,
Enfolding sunny spots of greenery. (ll. 6-11)

This pleasure dome is clearly an Edenic realm infused

with (masculine) virility ('walls and towers') and seething with sensuality (blossoming incense-bearing trees and soft hills enfolding spots of greenery) and sexual potency ('fertile ground' through which run 'sinuous rills'). It is therefore understandable that so many readers associate the Khan with the creative imagination. However, if we examine this Khan figure more closely, we will see that he is not an agent of the pure imagination but, instead, of what Coleridge called the fancy.

While the Khan, as the object of the Author's desire, appears to be the reflection of what the poet cannot be, he ultimately embodies the same poetic failure represented by the Author figure in the preface. That is, in terms of creative ability these figures are opposites, but in terms of Coleridge's model of the imagination they are the same—failed poets of the fancy who do not achieve the Coleridgean ideal. In Chapter XIII of *Biographia Literaria* , Coleridge describes the fancy as a non-creative faculty that is more empirical than the imagination. It is a lower cognitive faculty related to and influenced by the will, but not dependent upon the will for its operation: 'Fancy ... has no other counters to play with, but fixities and definites.

The fancy is indeed no other than a mode of memory emancipated from the order of time and space; and blended with, and modified by that empirical phenomenon of the will ... '. It may appear as though the fertile gardens of the Khan's creation conforms to Coleridge's organic aestheticism; however, the Khan's kingdom—with its symmetric dome and rigid towers and confining walls—is more akin to a material, ordered realm of 'fixities and definites' that is controlled and mastered by the Khan. It is not an imaginative, ideal realm in which the individual can unite with the infinite. The Khan, rather than being associated with the powers of the pure imagination, is portrayed as a poet of the fancy.

As a poet of the fancy, the Khan is thus a failed poet who is unable to achieve the Coleridgean ideal. Khan's kingdom, with its caves of ice and sunny domes, is an oxymoronic realm inhabited only by the Khan himself. There is no mention of any other human being (the woman wailing for her demon lover is not a literal inhabitant of the pleasure dome, but a metaphor reinforcing the heterosexist perspective of the [pro-]creative process). Instead of establishing self-unity through community, the Khan's creative act effectively isolates him from outside human contact, like the Ancient Mariner who becomes lost on the cold, wide sea and like Christabel who is separated from her dead mother and becomes estranged not only from her lover Geraldine but also her father.

This communal estrangement is paralleled in the final section of the preface, where the Author, just on the brink of poetic genius, is interrupted by a member of his surrounding community and ironically loses the imaginative image. This loss is ironic because imaginative creation, in German and Romantic Idealism, represents an attempt to restore a fractured, disunified self. Because the community is an icon for social unity, it is ironic that an agent from the poet's community—an agent who attempts to conduct business and, thus, to include the poet in the (commercial) workings of that community—effects disunity of the poet's consciousness, resulting in further isolation from the community.

In addition to isolating him from human contact, the Khan's creative acts do not elevate him to prophetic heights as is expected by the Coleridgean ideal. Instead of actually prophesying the coming of war (a war that signifies further the destruction of the Khan's realm and a denial of imaginative creation) the Khan only hears it amid the tumult of the surging and plunging river Alph. Much like the Author figure of the preface (and the crazed poet in the last stanza) the Khan receives the prophecy, via inspiration, instead of originating it as would the true prophetic poet of the pure imagination. It is also important to note that the Khan never becomes united with these eternal ancestral voices: he remains finitely separate from the infinite.

The Khan's eternal separation from the infinite is reinforced by his oppositional relationship to nature. His stately pleasure dome is interrupted and shaken—much like the vision that fades from the Author figure's mind in the preface after being interrupted by the business man from Porlock—by the upheaval that the seething fountain and the tumultuous river Alph initiate. As Regina Hewitt notes, 'the Khan's [creative] method results in an illusory order, a shaky structure on the brink of overthrow by the elements it could momentarily ignore but not permanently exclude'. The Khan, as a false poet, creates a phantasmagoric realm that ultimately drifts away from him and fades into the prophetic ancestral voices, thus signifying and sealing his eternal isolation and separation from Coleridge's ideal 'infinite I Am'.

If the first stanza represents the Khan as the failed poet of the fancy, then the second stanza—clearly marked as a contrast to the preceding stanza (of the fancy) by the textual break and the dramatic 'But oh!' (l. 12)—allegorizes the pure imagination. For Coleridge, the pure imagination exists as a procreative duality consisting of the primary and secondary imagination. These two faculties are not individually distinct; rather, they are dialectically distinguishable. In other words, they are separate only insofar as they serve vaguely different functions. Yet at the same time these faculties are interrelated and dependent upon each other for their individual functioning and for the operation of the imagination. Again in Chapter XIII of *Biographia Literaria* , Coleridge describes the primary imagination as that creative power which links the individual with the eternal creative force of the 'infinite I Am' or the transcendental whole (*Biographia* 1: 304).

In 'Kubla Khan', this faculty is best represented by the sacred river Alph(a)—the beginning, the signifier of original and eternal creativity, 'the unifying first principle of all mental activity' (Milne, 21)—that produces and releases the prophetic ancestral voices. The river Alph is the source of the poet's prophetic powers that are achievable only by the primary imagination which unites the finite poet with the 'infinite I Am'. If the river Alph is the primary imagination, then the fountain, as the 'echo' of the river, represents the secondary imagination. According to Coleridge, the secondary imagination is a reflection of the primary creative force, a preliminary sensory processor that attempts to unify apparent perceptual disunities into understandable perceptions before presenting them to the primary imagination (*Biographia* 1: 304). Arden Reed explains that 'the secondary imagination is obliged to 'dissolve, diffuse, dissipate' original perceptions before 'recreating' them, in a way that 'idealizes and unifies'. The fountain, with its heaving rocks and seething pants clearly represents this preliminary faculty that dissolves, diffuses, and dissipates phenomenal impressions, unifying them with the primary imagination or, in the context of the poem, the river Alph:

And from this chasm, with ceaseless turmoil seething,
As if this earth in fast thick pants were breathing,
A mighty fountain momently was forced:
Amid whose swift half-intermitted burst
Huge fragments vaulted like rebounding hail,
Or chaffy grain beneath the thresher's flail:
And 'mid these dancing rocks at once and ever
It flung up momently the sacred river. (ll. 17-24)

The fountain and the river are dynamically related, for out of the sexually destructive/constructive fountain bursts the prophetic, eternal river Alph, thus allegorizing the way in which the primary and secondary imaginations are dialectically interrelated.

Finally, Coleridge describes the primary and secondary imaginations as dynamic and vital, contrasting them to the fixed and dead nature of objects as objects. In other words, objects in themselves are fixed, dead, indeterminate material, but the powers of the imagination are life-giving in the sense that they transform the indeterminacy of objects in themselves into discernible meaning. We know objects only as phenomena, and it is the dialectic of the imagination that intuits (in the Kantian sense) or gives meaning to or represents (*darstellen*) the object in our minds and assigns an idea or image to that object. Of the elements in 'Kubla Khan', the river Alph and the fountain clearly represent vital agents, always in sensual motion and disruptive (yet constructive) turmoil.

The Khan's pleasure dome is but a fixed structure enclosing the pulsing fountain and the meandering river, two agents that destroy in order to construct and to unify. This unifying process is of a sublime order that provides access to the 'infinite I Am' as signified by the ancestral voices. It is clear that the Khan is a failed poet of the fancy who attempts to contain the primary and secondary imaginative faculties, as his walls attempt to enclose the river, only to be left eternally isolated from his ancestral spirits and human community and from the imagination that makes such connections possible.

This middle stanza representing the integrated workings of the primary and secondary imaginations is interrupted by a final stanza that completes the frame of the preface: the Author figure is abruptly reintroduced, effectively jolting the reader back into the consciousness of the failed poet. The primary and secondary imaginations, in the context of this poem, are purely fanciful (that is, products of the Author's fancy) and remain eternally illusive.

As the Author breaks from his vision and bemoans its loss, he fixates not on the river Alph or the fountain but on the aesthetically tangible caves of ice and pleasure dome: 'It was a miracle of rare device,/ A sunny pleasure dome with caves of ice!' (ll. 35-36). Instead of recalling the sublime river Alph or the fountain (images that would be more attractive to the poet of the imagination) the speaker attempts to revive the image of the Khan, to become a poetic agent akin not to the imaginative river Alph but to the fanciful Khan. He wishes to be inspired by the Abyssinian maid and to build his own dome and caves of ice, oxymoronic structures that would separate him from imaginative redemption; for to build this dome and caves of ice would necessitate a poetic possession, a succumbing to an external inspirational force.

This prostrate position relative to an external force is rhetorically paralleled by the Author in the preface who is overtaken by an opium trip and thus receives (instead of creating) the image of the Khan. A poetic process based upon inspiration, as Ken Frieden explains, is an unconscious process and, as such, a passive cognitive mechanism. As early as 1796 Coleridge had rejected 'Mechanic Philosophy' that casts the mind in a passive role, and by the time he publishes *Biographia*

Literaria, the mind to Coleridge is a dynamic and willful agent, divided into the more active primary and secondary imaginations and the more passive fancy. The Author figure clearly rejects the faculties of the active primary and secondary imaginations in favour of an unconscious, passive process that is antithetical to Coleridge's ideal poetic process. Furthermore, this inspiration invokes fear in his community:

And all who heard should see them there,
And all should cry, Beware! Beware!
His flashing eyes, his floating hair!
Weave a circle round him thrice,
And close your eyes with holy dread,
For he on honeydew had fed,
And drunk the milk of Paradise. (ll. 48-54)

The poet given in to inspiration becomes an ostracized individual, akin to the Khan figure who is isolated in his pleasure dome and caves of ice and possessing a hypnotic gaze not unlike that of the Ancient Mariner or Geraldine in 'Christabel'. This crazed poet is a demonic figure who becomes inscribed and (textually) enclosed within a mystical circle marking him as an oddity. This poet/seer whom the Author holds as an exemplary creative figure is actually a contained failed poet like the Khan who is girdled with walls and towers. In the end, this Author is doubly failed: first, he does not situate himself with the proper imaginative faculty represented in the poem, choosing instead to identify with the Khan figure and thus missing the real vision in his dream—the nature of the pure imagination; and second, his desire to be a (false) poet secures his eternal isolation from human community.

At first glance the Khan and poet/seer figures that the Author longs to emulate appear to represent the poetic ideal—an ideal the speaker fears he may never be able to achieve. Actually, they reflect the Author's own poetic failure. That is, as he attempts to internalize the various poet figures into a unified vision of himself as poet, he ultimately denies himself true identification with the (Coleridgean) poetic ideal, for what he desires is nothing but a projection of his own imaginative inadequacies.

'Kubla Khan' is indeed a 'psychological curiosity' in the sense that it establishes and foregrounds an aesthetics of the imagination. More specifically, the poem aesthetically represents Coleridge's formulation of the imaginative process that he began formulating as early as 1796 and that becomes most clearly articulated in his *Biographia Literaria* . However, in this poetic representation, the imagination is elevated to a naturalistic realm forever out of reach of the human poet, thus disillusioning all Romantic hope of imaginative redemption through artistic creativity. This Romantic disillusionment is contextualized by Coleridge's preface, for without the preface to the poem, it would be impossible not to identify Khan and the poet/seer at the end of the poem as ideal agents of the imagination.

However, when read from the context of disillusionment, we see that Coleridge actually represents these poetic figures as failed poets. Instead of simply apologizing for his poem via the preface and the subtitle, Coleridge was trying to establish a performance context (as he did when he recited this poem in person) in an attempt to foreground his aesthetic and philosophic insecurities and skepticism. As Hewitt concludes, 'the tensions in 'Kubla Khan' may be seen as a tension between the extant theories of poetic creation—represented by the false poets—which Coleridge rejects and the new theory of imaginative creation that Coleridge embraces but cannot quite completely work out'. And H. R. Rookmaaker suggests that, in the context of Coleridge's writings, 'Kubla Khan' allegorizes the metaphysical and aesthetic struggles through which Coleridge was attempting to work. While I agree for the most part with these conclusions concerning imaginative failure, I am suggesting that the poem foregrounds not a tension so much as a melancholic recognition and subsequent re-vision or relocation of vision.

That is, poetic vision is located not within the individual poet but, rather, in an external other. The poem depicts not what poetic creativity is but, instead, what it is not and cannot be. In this sense, the poem is negatively purposive, for it does not effect a celebration of the poet's divine ability to create sublime aesthetic moments that link the poet to the universal whole (the 'Infinite I Am') thus achieving imaginative redemption. On the contrary, 'Kubla Khan' underscores a disillusionment resulting from the recognition of the poet's imaginative lack, namely the inability to achieve redemption and unity of self through divine acts of poetic creation.

This lack or failure on the part of the various poet figures directs the audience to the moment in the vision that the Author misses, namely that the river Alph and the fountain signify the ideal imaginative faculty or, at least, the nature of the creative process and the rewards it brings in terms of a reunification with the community of the past and the future. 'Kubla Khan', then, is a poem about poetic failure, where agents of the pure imagination are represented not by human personae who are to be emulated but, rather, elements of a sublime natural realm that remain external to the individual and, thus, an always already unobtainable other.

Any attempt to colonize this other, to girdle it with walls and towers—to fulfill the desire to become an ideal poet of the imagination—is effectively to destroy this other, to nullify the desire. Becoming the poet of the imagination for Coleridge is a desire always in process that cannot be obtained. For to obtain (and, thus, contain) this other is to render it as the self and, thus, to disable or destroy it. The imagination as aesthetically represented in 'Kubla Khan' is a natural other that cannot be obtained, contained, or harnessed by the poet.

Furthermore, 'Kubla Khan' underscores more specifically Coleridge's personal poetic disillusionment resulting from the recognition of his own imaginative lack, namely his inability to achieve redemption and unity of self through divine acts of poetic creation. As David Riede points out, Coleridge lost faith in his own poetic faculties, viewing himself as 'diseased in will almost to the point of madness'. Ironically, even though Coleridge bemoans his imaginative lack in this and other of his poems ('The Eolian Harp', 'Dejection: An Ode', and, to some extent, *The Rime of the Ancient Mariner*) his performance abilities suggest that he was a poet of great imagination and authorial command.

Yet the literary reviews of 'Kubla Khan' demonstrate that he failed in the eyes of most of his contemporaries, many of whom ignored this poem, cast it in the critical shadow of 'Christabel', or simply dismissed it as a confused and disappointing effort, a fragment generated from his opium-induced sleep that should never have been printed. In the end, the poem not only depicts and explores poetic failure, but its nineteenth-century reception mirrors and reinforces this failure in Coleridge's self-imaging. The goal of becoming the sublime imaginative poet for Coleridge was a desire he could not fulfill; for even as many of the reviews of his earlier poetic works praised his genius and poetic promise, his later poems often confounded and frustrated most reviewers who felt his Germanic aesthetics to be childish, ineffective, and/or overdone. Thus he focused his attentions on proclaiming the imaginative authority of such poets as Milton, Shakespeare, and Wordsworth and establishing his own intellectual authority as literary critic, metaphysician, and theologian.

Romantic Anti-Jacobins or Anti-Jacobin Romantics?

Kenneth R. Johnston

I propose to set two scenes of writing in a fundamentally parodic relationship to each other. One was famous in its day but is almost forgotten now, the other unknown then but forever famous now. The first was in a house next to No. 169 Piccadilly, opposite Old Bond Street, connected by a hidden passage to the bookshop of James Wright, the 'morning resort' of savvy young politicians like George Canning, who gathered there to throw together the weekly issues of the *The Anti-Jacobin; or Weekly Examiner*, from November 1797 to July 1798. The other was somewhere "a few miles above Tintern Abbey," where Wordsworth started composing his famous poem of that title, finishing it as he walked down Clifton Hill into Bristol on July 13, 1798, and delivering it next day to the printshop of Joseph Cottle in Wine Street for last-minute inclusion in the volume titled *Lyrical Ballads*.

We know a great deal about these latter, Somerset scenes. Indeed, since the publication of Jerry McGann's *The Romantic Ideology* in 1983, and especially since Marjorie Levinson's provocative 1986 essay, "Insight or Oversight?," we have learned more new things about "Tintern Abbey"-a poem on which the community of Romantic scholarship thought it had a very good grasp-than anyone might have believed possible, in 1983.

About *The Anti-Jacobin,* however, we have known, until very recently, only about as much as we have ever known, and that has seemed enough. But I want to suggest that it is not, and that these two scenes of writing have more to do with each other than we have thought. Considered as "text" and "context," they provide a good working model of an older form of literary-historical scholarship: *viz., The Anti-Jacobin* and its last polemical satire and cartoon, "New Morality," have remained deep in the background of Wordsworth and Coleridge's careers, thanks to its one-line reference to "C—-dge and S-th-y, L—d & L-b & Co."

Usually this reference has been treated as something of a joke, if not downright slander, on the order of the "Spy Nozy" incident in Somerset the year before, or the Pantisocracy fiasco-almost always referred to as a "fiasco"-the year before that. At most, it is understood as a reference to the *formerly* radical writings of Coleridge and Southey, and a sign that the powers-that-were had not yet got the word that the two young poets had, in Coleridge's calculated phrase, "snapped their squeaking baby-trumpets of Sedition" and were no longer radicals but something else, something that we now call "Romantics."

Instead, I want to suggest, following a newer model of historical interpretation, sometimes called "*The* New Historicism" (though its practice is not so unified), that these two scenes cannot be neatly divided into foreground "text" and background "context." At the very least, in 1798, their roles were reversed: *The Anti-Jacobin* was very much in the London foreground, *Lyrical Ballads* very far in its anonymous Bristol background. But, since the apparent reversal in value of these two scenes, over the intervening two hundred years, might still look like "poetic" or "historical" justice to some, I want to complicate that mere reversal, and suggest that the two scenes (i.e., texts, places, and authors) were mutually implicated in each other-and further (here I advance beyond suggestion to speculation) that the two sets of writers knew this, and were "in some sense"-those invaluable weasel words-communicating with each other. My instrument for creating this complicating mutual implication is the theory of parody developed by Linda Hutcheon, which derives in turn from the inter-textual theories of Mikhail Bakhtin, especially 'dialogism' and the phenomena of texts-speaking-through-texts, with or without conscious authorial intention. The historical hypothesis I am developing is that "New Morality" is to some extent a coded call to Wordsworth, and perhaps also to Coleridge and Southey, to return to the establishment fold-from whence they came by birth and class origin-and join in the work of cultural regeneration which the bright young men of *The Anti-Jacobin* saw themselves engaged in.

I have put forward some of this interpretation in my recently published *The Hidden Wordsworth*. But I want to extend it further, suggesting that not only do certain lines in "Tintern Abbey" appear to *reject* this coded invitation ('evil tongues, / Rash judgements [and] the sneers of selfish men'), but that certain lines of argument in the Preface to the second edition of *Lyrical Ballads* (1800) constitute a revisionary *acceptance* of that invitation. This becomes especially clear when the two sets of texts/contexts are placed together with the almost wholly unknown plans that Wordsworth and Coleridge were hatching, especially between 1798 and 1800, that Wordsworth should become the new Milton of England, the prophetic author of *The Recluse,* "On Man, on Nature, and on Human Life."

Finally, at my furthest point out on this shaky limb, I want to suggest that Wordsworth's qualified acceptance of that invitation is signaled-perhaps "sealed" is the better word-by his acceptance of yet another invitation that might be implied in the larger context of these two scenes of writing: namely, that he should, on his way through London en route to Germany, meet with some of *The Anti-Jacobin's* authors, in their daytime jobs as under-secretaries in the Home Office and the

Foreign Office, to set up an arrangement whereby some or all of his expenses in Germany would be paid by putting him on the payroll of William Cavendish, third duke of Portland, head of the Home Office and chief architect of the new "secret department," which was the nucleus of the modern British Secret Service.

All that is quite a mouthful. Now let me try to shore up the limb I am standing on. Assuming that we have the various "scenes" of Tintern Abbey quite firmly in our collective cultural memory, I will concentrate on *The Anti-Jacobin* and the ways in which it would have been known to our semi-anonymous young authors in and around Bristol. Some of these are demonstrably biographical.

Others are more abstract, involving a critical sense of the various ways in which *The Anti-Jacobin* and what we may call the 'textual milieu' of *Lyrical Ballads* (its poems, prefaces, advertisements, and revisions from 1798 to 1800) can be seen as engaged in a critical re-writing of each other, a polemical engagement or duel in which parody is the weapon chosen by the antagonists. This is obvious in the case of *The Anti-Jacobin;* less obvious but still relevant in the case of Wordsworth and Coleridge, if we expand our sense of parody to include not just humorous writing and debunking intentions, but also serious intentions that might (or might not) be expressed in humorous terms.

The Anti-Jacobin was a very powerful and largely successful weapon in what we can now recognize as a "culture war" being fought for the hearts and minds of the British people during the Parliamentary session of 1797-98, the precise term of its existence. (Thus I distinguish sharply between it and its much tamer successor, *The Anti-Jacobin Review and Magazine*, which ran until 1821.) It was established by its primary authors, George Canning (the future prime minister), John Hookham Frere (college acquaintance of Wordsworth and Coleridge and later close friend of Byron), George Ellis, and William Gifford, its actual editor (not to be confused with the John Gifford who later became the editor of the *Edinburgh Review*).

Canning and Frere were under-secretaries in the Foreign and Home Offices, respectively, and they proposed *The Anti-Jacobin* as a semi-official attack mechanism to discredit opponents of Pitt's unpopular "Minister's War" with France. It would be something like a *Private Eye* written by M.P.s or, in American terms, an *American Spectator* or *National Review* receiving over-the-transom submissions from the White House or Congress. (Forms of authorship and contribution certainly not unknown today, if we think of Joe Klein's originally anonymous novel, *Primary Colors*.) These young men realized that though the British people still supported Pitt, they did so with their heads, not their hearts, and more from fear of a French invasion than out of any affection for Pitt-who, whatever his many qualities, was not a man to inspire affection.

Furthermore, the *Anti-Jacobin* writers wanted to distance themselves and their leader from the merely reactionary anti-Jacobins, those "King and Crown" mobs who sprang up in many towns and terrorized the populace by their attacks on their liberal opponents, who were frequently some of those towns' most distinguished citizens. (The burning and sacking of Joseph Priestley's house and laboratory in Birmingham is the clearest case in point here.) Instead, *The Anti-Jacobin* writers wanted to immobilize their opponents by making them appear ridiculous: laughter, not lynching, would be its weapon. With the Gagging Acts of 1795 and subsequent repressive legislation and successful trial convictions firmly in place, the young men of *The Anti-Jacobin* turned to ridicule and co-optation to complete the government's mopping-up operation against its opponents.

As such, it was a type of media watchdog, like Steven Brill's recently launched *Brill's Content* in the U.S., which set journalists of every stripe howling with its first issue, analyzing the media's sloppy coverage of allegations about Monica Lewinsky. But, unlike *Brill's Content*, *The Anti-Jacobin* was a government attack-dog against the media-Pitt's pit bull, so to speak. Each of its substantial weekly issues (30 pages or more) divided the previous week's news coverage into 'Lies,

Misrepresentations, and Mistakes.' Given the relative anonymity of its authors, this was a brilliant fail-safe device, especially the "Lies of the Week" section, which was something like the 'Top Ten' feature on David Letterman's *Late Night* television show, providing each week a new set of reasons demonstrating that Pitt's opponents in the liberal press were stupid, foolish charlatans.

It was as hard to answer as a long-running "when did you stop beating your wife?" joke. On the few occasions when the *Morning Courier* or *Post* or *Chronicle* tried to answer it (as the *Chronicle* did in early 1798, submitting an 'Epistle to the Editors of *The Anti-Jacobin*,' which was printed along with a deflatory answer by Hon. John Courtnay), they found themselves, like the hapless opponents of Swift and Pope earlier in the century, helplessly ensnared in the net of their own distorted language-like the astrologer Partridge in Swift's *Bickerstaff Papers*, hopelessly protesting to a laughing world that he was *not* dead. Answering the *Anti-Jacobin* was a no-win proposition, and since "The New Morality" satire appeared in its very last issue, it was even less answerable-unless its attack were picked up and carried on-unannounced and disguised, but clear to those in the know-in another publication, such as *Lyrical Ballads*, whose address to the issues at hand was as oblique, but as pointed, as *The Anti-Jacobin* was in its.

Though most of every issue was devoted to "exposing" Lies, Misrepresentations, and Mistakes, and often included long pieces on government finance (for the taxes were the most unpopular part of the war), every issue nevertheless had a substantial poetry or 'Arts' section. From the outset and frequently throughout the year (especially at the beginning of 1798), these sections discussed the kind of poetry-and the kind of poet-that was most needed at this time of national crisis. In its introductory number (November 20, 1797), *The Anti-Jacobin* announced its search for the ideal poet for the troubled times: "we have not been able to find one good and true Poet, of sound principles and sobre practice, upon whom we could rely for furnishing us with a handsome quantity of sufficient and approved verse." And in its last number (July 9/16, 1798), in

"The New Morality," it appeals to a "bashful genius" to emerge from rural retirement and "pour th'indignant strain" of "lofty satire" against the "stage, verse, pamphlets, politics, and news" that are England's "just alarms."

That the Somerset poets were well aware of *The Anti-Jacobin* is clear from recent work by Nicholas Roe and Paul Magnuson and others on this particular textual/contextual crux. We can be quite certain that Wordsworth and Coleridge knew *The Anti-Jacobin*'s attacks on Coleridge, and read carefully not only its satiric verse and parodies against Coleridge and Southey, but also followed its occasional disquisitions on the proper or best form of poetry for English culture and society.

Southey's poems were *The Anti-Jacobin*'s first and favourite target of parody, and Coleridge's were not far behind, though neither author was *named*: there was some concern about libel laws, and Pitt was nervous that his bright young men would go too far. Southey's knee-jerk liberal poems, such as his "Botany Bay Eclogues," and Coleridge's effusion "To a Young Ass," a democratical effusion dedicated to the proposition that donkeys have rights and feelings too, were the sorts of "Jacobin" poems that made many of *The Anti-Jacobin*'s parodies very easy to write, and some of them hilariously funny. Other frequent targets of attack well within Coleridge and Southey's (and Wordsworth's) ambience were John Thelwall, who tried to join their literary-philosophical "triumverate" in 1797, Erasmus Darwin (his *Loves of the Plants* is satirized in Frere's and Canning's "Loves of the Triangles," perhaps the best of its parodies), William Godwin, Wordsworth's good friend from London, and Thomas Beddoes, Coleridge's Bristol friend (and employer of Humphry Davy at the Pneumatic Institute).

Godwin and Coleridge and Darwin were all attacked under the fictitious name of Mr. William Higgins, an author residing at "St. Mary Axe" (compare Coleridge's own satiric pseudonym, "Nehemiah *Higgin*botham, his birthplace at Ottery St. Mary, and the River Axe running near it). This caricature has well been called a sort of "portmanteau" Jacobin, to whom any kind of Jacobin literary or philosophical excess could be attributed as needed (it has also been taken as a glance toward Mary Wollstonecraft). *The Anti-Jacobin* could always have things both ways with whichever 'Mr. Higgins' it had in mind, as it solicitously explained in a late issue:

we cannot but consider ourselves as the guardians of Mr. Higgins's literary reputation, in respect to every work of his which is conveyed to the world through the medium of our paper (though, what we think of the dangers of his principles we have already sufficiently explained)... (June 11, 1798)

Small wonder that Coleridge, toting up a list of 'Characters for satire' after his return from Germany the following summer, should place 'Canning & the Anti-Jacobins' at the very top of it.

In considering these identifications, we should imagine, as well, Wordsworth's reactions to seeing his new and much-admired friends witheringly and unfairly attacked, nationally, on a weekly basis, throughout the year that we Romanticists often consider an *annus mirabilis*-but that Pitt considered his worst crisis-year to date, marked by the naval mutinies at Nore and Spithead in 1797 and by the Irish rebellions and invasions of 1798. Wordsworth and Coleridge were trying to break back into print in a new, revolutionary, yet anonymous fashion; Pitt & Co. were trying to stay in office in a way that was also new (the *ur*-creation of the modern Conservative party), but determinedly *anti*-revolutionary.

It is not necessary, for the general point of my argument, to establish direct textual connections between *The Anti-Jacobin* and the poetry of Coleridge and Southey and Wordsworth, though the more we can do so the more interesting its conclusions become. Inter-textual methods of cultural criticism allow us more leeway. Nonetheless, in any reading of the poetry sections, one is struck by the intensity, particularity, and familiarity of the attacks on Coleridge and Southey. Running over some of their most closely shared topics, we find, *inter alia,* frequent discussions of correct meter, rhyme, and poetic form, sometimes allowing their targets correct *poetic* principles but ridiculing their content (e.g., No. VI). Chief among *The Anti-Jacobin*'s opponents' supposedly ridiculous subjects were their sympathetic interviews with suffering poor people in the street, as in its send-up of Southey in "The Knife-Grinder and the Friend of Humanity," or its parody of his "Soldier's Wife" as "The Soldier's Friend."

Its very first offering parodied Southey's "Inscription" for Henry Marten, the regicide imprisoned in Chepstow Castle, as an inscription for Mrs. Brownrigg, who was imprisoned in Newgate because "SHE WHIPP'D TWO FEMALE 'PRENTICES TO DEATH, / AND HID THEM IN THE COAL-HOLE." These attacks hit very close to home in Somerset, directly on Southey (who was actually in London for much of the year), but also indirectly on Wordsworth, who was drafting ostensibly very similar poems, such as "The Female Vagrant," "The Tale of Margaret" (or "The Ruined Cottage"), "The Baker's Cart" and others, which he would continue fearlessly into *Lyrical Ballads'* "The Idiot Boy," "The Sailor's Mother," "The Old Cumberland Beggar," and others-all the while trying to distinguish what *his* poems were doing from what Southey's did. (Southey in the meantime having publicly renounced his "Jacobin" phase.) If *The Anti-Jacobin* was parodying Southey, there is a meaningful sense in which Wordsworth's apparently similar poems were parodic re-writings of Southey as well, not just 'serious' treatments of the same subjects (since Southey was nothing if not serious). Furthermore, Wordsworth's rewritings sprang not just from his 'original Romantic genius,' but from his engagement with definitions of the means and ends of poetry that were at once different from, yet not wholly unrelated to, those laid down by *The Anti-Jacobin*.

As for Coleridge, a poem entitled "Lines, Written at the Close of the Year 1797" (No. X; Jan. 15, 1798) can hardly have been written-or read-without conscious reference to his "Lines, written at the close of the Preceding Year" [1796]. Similarly, the "Ode to Jacobinism," by "An English Jacobin," bears close similarities to his "France: An Ode," and others poems he was writing at the time, expressing despair and ambivalence at being caught between Pitt's repression at home and French militarism abroad.

This much is clear. What needs stressing is the seriousness

and cogency of *The Anti-Jacobin*'s arguments for a proper national poetry, and the kind of poet needed to write it. This kind of discussion came to Wordsworth's and Coleridge's eyes precisely at the time they were first hatching their career-defining dream, *not* that they should become the (eventually) world-famous authors of *Lyrical Ballads*, which was viewed simply as a convenient way to make money to pay for their upcoming trip to Germany, *but* that *Wordsworth* should become the epic, prophetic bard of *The Recluse*, with its comprehensive views "on Man, on Nature, and on Human Life."

This was the poem that, as Coleridge said a year later (ca. November 1799), was to be addressed 'to those, who, in consequence of the complete failure of the French Revolution, have thrown up all hopes of the amelioration of mankind, and are sinking into an almost epicurean selfishness, disguising the same under the soft titles of domestic attachment and contempt for visionary *philosophes*.' This was not the same audience *The Anti-Jacobin* sought to address, but it was not completely different, since Canning and Frere, like Pitt himself, had been liberal sympathizers with the early, constitutional phase of the French which they now-like Coleridge here-saw as a 'complete failure.' They were more worried about this 'failure' as a threat (of invasion, for example) than as a disappointment, but they too were concerned to rouse up an erstwhile liberal audience that had fallen into a funk.

(However mistaken local gossips may have been about the purpose of nocturnal rambles between Nether Stowey and Alfoxden, the mission of James Walsh to Somerset was directly related to the government's concerns about a possible French invasion, such as had already occurred in Ireland in 1796 and in England-at Fishguard, in Wales-in February of 1797. The role of the liberal media in 'creating a climate' (as we say) of disaffection-to rise up and embrace the liberating revolutionaries-was every bit as much on the mind of English- and French-authorities as the activities of future partisans marking likely landing spots for the invading troops.)

There are several significant parallels between the language, phrasing, and arguments of *The Anti-Jacobin*'s views on poetry and Wordsworth's 1800 Preface. In considering these parallels, however, we should keep in mind that Wordsworth was likely to have had *The Anti-Jacobin*'s personal political attacks as much in mind-or 'in emotion'-as its more purely literary arguments, when he came to write his famous defence of poetry, a consideration often overlooked by literature professors.

For example, *The Anti-Jacobin* begins its justification for producing yet-another-publication: "some account may reasonably be expected of the views and principles on which it [the journal] founds its pretensions to notice." ("Prospectus," 1). Compare Wordsworth: "It is supposed, that by the act of writing in verse an Author makes a formal engagement that he will grant certain known habits of association" (1800 Preface, para. 5). Such parallels are merely conventional standard practice, but they get closer.

The Anti-Jacobin decries the contemporary over-production of media in language similar to Wordsworth's. "Whatever may be the habits of inquiry and anxiety for information upon subjects of public concern diffused among all ranks of people, the vehicles of intelligence are already multiplied in a proportion nearly equal to this encreased demand". Compare Wordsworth: "the great national events which are daily taking place, and the encreasing accumulation of men in cities, where the uniformity of their occupations produces a craving for extraordinary incident which the rapid communication of intelligence hourly gratifies." And, back to *Anti-Jacobin*: "of the utility of such a purpose, if even tolerably executed, there can be little doubt, among those persons ... who must have found themselves, during the course of the last few years, perplexed by the multiplicity of contradictory accounts of almost every material event that has occurred in the eventful and tremendous period".

In this cultural situation, both *The Anti-Jacobin* and Wordsworth propose to advance on the basis of principles-principles of poetry which, they imply, are intimately related to, if not actually constitutive of, the best powers of the human mind, and hence of society itself. Of course, I am close here to

Wordsworth's well-known statement of this relation: he proposes to produce a kind of poetry "well adapted to interest mankind permanently, and not unimportant in the quality of its moral relations."

He has been urged (he says) by his friends "to prefix a systematic defence of the theory, upon which the poems were written," but he demurs, because "my arguments would require a space wholly disproportionate to the nature of a preface," and because such a theory would require, 1) "a full account of the present state of the public taste in this country," 2) a determination of the "manner [in which] language and the human mind act and react on each other," and 3) a "retracing [of] the revolutions not of literature alone but likewise of society itself."

The Anti-Jacobin also asserts that "it is natural that [readers] should require some profession of our principles as well as of our purposes". But the poetry situation it confronts requires that it proceed with a kind of reverse (parodic) spin-which Wordsworth's preface may be said to re-reverse. After stating that "we have not been able to find one good and true Poet," the journal goes on to make a frank admission: that "the only market where [poetry] is to be had good and ready made [is] that of the *Jacobins*-an expedient full of danger, and not to be used but with the utmost caution and delicacy." It opines that "good Morals, and what we should call good Politics, are inconsistent with the spirit of true Poetry," speculating that this is perhaps because "'*the Muses still with freedom found*' have an aversion to *regular* governments, and require a frame and system of protection less complicated than kings, lords, and commons.'

Be that as it may, the journal will select "such pieces" of Jacobin poetry "as may serve to illustrate some one of the principles on which the poetical as well as the political doctrine of the NEW SCHOOL is established-prefacing each of them ... with a short disquistion on the particular tenet intended to be enforced or insinuated in the production before them".

By this means, though we cannot hope to catch *"the wood-notes wild"* of the Bards of Freedom, we may yet acquire, *by dint of repeating after them,* a more complete knowledge of the secret in which their greatness lies than we could by mere prosaic admiration; and if we cannot become poets ourselves, we at least shall have collected the elements of a *Jacobin* Art of Poetry for the use of those whose genius may be more capable of turning them to advantage." (14; second italics added)

This 'dint of repeating after' its opponents is the key at once to *The Anti-Jacobin*'s genius and to its serious intentions, since it signifies not merely a comic parodic debunking (as in its handling of Southey's poems), but also an effort to, as it were, *mouth* a poetry whose 'greatness' it acknowledges, but whose 'genius' as currently practiced seems to Canning & Co. misplaced, in the sense of not being *turned to advantage.*

This apparently modest, forward-looking pedagogical impulse is also present in Wordsworth's Preface, when he concludes his diatribe against the "gross and violent stimulants" that are debasing the present public taste-"frantic novels, sickly and stupid German Tragedies, and ... idle and extravagant stories in verse"-by saying he has "a deep impression of certain inherent and indestructible qualities of the human mind" [and] "a belief that the time is approaching when the evil will be systematically opposed by men of greater powers and with far more distinguished success."

These 'men of greater powers' have never (so far as I know) been identified, but they must for practical purposes be Wordsworth and Coleridge: the systematic opposition they will mount to the present debased cultural/political situation of the human mind constitutes the 'Jacobin Art of Poetry' facetiously called for by *The Anti-Jacobin*-that is to say, a concept of poetry with revolutionary, liberating powers.

But while Wordsworth would be one of those "Bards of Freedom" who agree that poetry is liberating, in and of itself, *The Anti-Jacobin,* though acknowledging that this "Jacobin" poetry is the best available in England at the time, still proposes to present it "with such precautions as may conduce to the safety of our readers' principles, and to the improvement of our own poetry." Thus both *The Anti-Jacobin* and the Preface to *Lyrical Ballads* present their poetry as contributing to a *future* melioration of a presently debased poetry, politics, and, ultimately, human mind and nature. True, *The Anti-Jacobin* often has its tongue in cheek, but not always, since its poetic parodies are mixed with poems it straightforwardly admires, and occasionally even some "Jacobin" poems that it admires, though prefacing them with the 1790s equivalent of a cultural Surgeon-General's warning.

"It might not be unamusing to trace the springs and principles of this species of poetry, which are to be found, some in the exaggeration, and others in the direct inversion of the sentiments and passions which have in all ages animated the breast of the favourite of the Muses, and distinguished him from the 'vulgar throng'." (This, except for the arch phrase, "not unamusing," would not be out of place in the Preface to *Lyrical Ballads*.)

When the *Anti-Jacobin* specifies the subjects of this new poetry/philosophy/morality, it gives the wartime version of some of Wordsworth's and Southey's commonest peacetime subjects: "we are presented with nothing by contusions and amputations, plundered peasants, and deserted looms. Our poet points the thunder of his blank verse at the head of the recruiting serjeant, or roars in dithyrambics against the lieutenants of pressgangs". It is not far from this to Wordsworth's choice of "low and rustic life [and]... the manners of rural life" (para. 6), nor from his fiercest anti-war diction, in the earliest versions of 'The Female Vagrant,' about she and her children wading 'dog-like' through pools of blood. Indeed, when Wordsworth defends "the language of these men" as "a more permanent and a far more philosophical language than that which is frequently substituted for it by Poets," he may be said to be calling *The Anti-Jacobin*'s bluff, or casting its supercilious assumptions about proper poetry back into its face, in a still more outrageous and challenging way.

We can see the overall unity, intelligence, and seriousness of *The Anti-Jacobin*'s literary attacks throughout the 1797-98 Parliamentary session in many ways, most simply in the congruence between its references to the "New School" and the "New Faith" in its Prospectus and opening issue, and to the "New Morality" in its last. In this respect, "The New Morality" is a poetic recapitulation of the entire year's run (actually 6-7 months), and it is noteworthy that the recapitulation comes *in poetry*, for though poetry and criticism appear in every issue, they usually do not take as much space as the exposure of 'Lies, Misrepresentations, and Mistakes.' (It fell to Gillray's cartoon of the same title broaden the scope of the attack, to include not just the poets and other writers gathered up near the atheistical altar of Larevelliere-Lepaux, the arch high priest of "Theophilanthropy," but the Leviathan train of the Duke of Bedford and Charles James Fox and all other stripes of opposition leaders who-the left-to-right movement of the cartoon suggests-are being *led to* revolutionary atheism by bad poetry, bad morals, and bad political writing.) Just as "The New Morality" is structured as an address to some "bashful [and determindedly *rural*] Genius" to rise up and save his country by poetry, so the whole editorial structure of the journal is that of saving the country from excess by the patient inculcation of better principles.

The Advertisement to *Lyrical Ballads* may have been written by Wordsworth at this time, alone in Bristol, under fire, and separated from Coleridge. Like its successive revisions into the Prefaces of 1800 and 1802, it lacks Coleridge's subtle persuasive powers. It proceeds, in its three main paragraphs, to insult its readers by assuring them that, whatever they may think of poetry in general or these poems in particular, they are most assuredly wrong, either because their taste has been improperly educated or because they have not devoted enough attention to the study of poetry. It speaks with the voice that Wordsworth's friend James Losh complained of, "too earnest and emphatic." But if Wordsworth imagined himself to be answering the editors of *The Anti-Jacobin*, his assertiveness sounds more brave than pompous.

Wordsworth's "Advertisement" may be read as a salvo back in the direction of the "Introduction to the Poetry of *The Anti-Jacobin*," from its very first issue. There, *The Anti-Jacobin* had been spoken with its own lordly authority about the true nature of poetry, and lamented the present cultural situation, in which it seemed "that good Morals, and what We should call good Politics, are inconsistent with the spirit of true Poetry." Hence Wordsworth's reference to Sir Joshua Reynolds, "[who] observed [that "an accurate taste in poetry"] is an acquired talent, which can only be produced by severe thought, and a long continued intercourse with the best models of composition," deliberately invokes the kind of authority that such "readers of superior judgment" would be disposed to accept.

But Wordsworth also made his volume's provocation obvious by imagining the 'scene' (in the sense of scandal) that would be created when these poems appeared, like lower-class intruders barging into a genteel eighteenth-century drawing room: these sneering "readers of superior judgment ... accustomed to the gaudiness and inane phraseology of many modern writers ... will look round for poetry, and will ... enquire by what species of courtesy these attempts can be permitted to assume that *title*." Who are *they*? Who invited *them*?

This view of the poems of *Lyrical Ballads* as fradulent usurpers of proper titles-of proper *poetry*-in this case-glances at the strictures of the *Anti-Jacobin*, and Wordsworth's subsequent attack upon "readers of superior judgment" appears less rhetorically inept (for insulting his readers) if we imagine he is attacking the editors of the *Anti-Jacobin*, who certainly set themselves up as such: "We should bring to the undertaking much less anxiety for success, and should state our claims on public attention with much less boldness, than We are disposed to do in the consciousness of higher purposes, and more beneficial views." As Wordsworth goes on to say rightly, to such readers-"the style in which many of these pieces are executed ... will not exactly suit their taste [and] it will appear to them that ... the author has sometimes descended too low, and that many of his expressions are too familiar, and not of sufficient dignity." (Adv., para 3). But his goals are the same as theirs, only better and higher.

Just as he strenuously argues the *useful purpose* of the poems in *Lyrical Ballads*, so too was it the goal he was setting for his entire career, in announcing his proposed masterwork to his friend James Losh: 'I have written 1300 lines of a poem which I hope to make of *considerable utility;* its title will be *The Recluse or views of Nature, Man, and Society*'.

Was Wordsworth, in effect, responding to *The Anti-Jacobin*'s invitation in "The New Morality" to some "bashful Genius, in some rural cell" to rise up in response to "thy Country's just alarms": "Wield in her cause thy long neglected arms: / Of lofty Satire pour th'indignant strain". The main address of "The New Morality" (like Pope's *Dunciad*) is a call for a strong national poet to rise up and take on the task of moral regeneration which the editors had been preparing for by therapeutic satire. It is a Juvenalian satire, calling for more in the same vein. It is not wholly out of the question that they actually had Wordsworth in mind, and hence protectively did not mention his name. They certainly knew who he was, and they may well have known that he and Francis Wrangham had collaborated on an imitation of Juvenal's Satire VIII in London in 1795, and were still working on it two years later. Their description of this ideal poet has many similarities to his career (and/or Coleridge's) to date:... for who can tell

What bashful Genius, in some rural cell, [Alfoxden?]

As year to year, and day succeeds to day,

In joyless leisure wastes his life away?

In him the flame of early Fancy shone; [*An Evening Walk* and *Descriptive Sketches*? Coleridge's two early volumes?]

His genuine worth his old Companions own; [J.H. Frere, the old Cantab?]

In childhood and in youth their Chief confess'd, [Wordsworth's poetical reputation at Hawkshead and Cambridge? Coleridge's at Christ's Hopsital and Cambridge?]

His Master's pride [William Taylor, Wordsworth's Hawkshead master?], his pattern to the rest.

Now, far aloof retiring from the strife

Of busy talents, and of active life, [London, 1795? Bristol, 1796?]

As, *from the loop-holes of retreat,* he views

[remaining contacts with London friends?]

Our Stage, Verse, Pamphlets, Politics, and News,
[packets of books and newspapers sent to Racedown and Alfoxden?]
He loaths the world, -or with reflection sad
Concludes it irrecoverably mad;
Of Taste, of Learning, Morals, all bereft,
No hope, no prospect to redeem it left.
(55-70; italics added: quoting Cowper, *The Task*)

"Tintern Abbey" may be in part Wordsworth's response to this invitation, adapting it to his different-*but not all that different*-purposes. At the very least, he would have been startled to read lines that hit so close to his own situation. Calls for a great new English poet had been echoing throughout the 1790s, ever since the death of Samuel Johnson in 1784, and Wordsworth's self-creation was, as we see in the linkages between *The Recluse* and the *Lyrical Ballad* prefaces, intimately connected with an idea of his poetry *and* his life forming a model for national regeneration.

Maybe the *Anti-Jacobin* editors had somebody else in mind, but such knowledge of 'Coleridge & Co.' on their part is not at all unlikely. Canning and Frere, when they were not engaged in their semi-clandestine production of *The Anti-Jacobin*, were regularly in contact with the wholly clandestine operations of the government's Secret Service run by William Wickham, John King, and Richard Ford, the latter two of whom had received a full set of reports the previous summer from James Walsh, their top agent, on the disaffected Alfoxden gang, naming Coleridge, and '*Wordsworth*' in particular, as 'a name I [Walsh] think known to Mr. Ford.' John King's brother had tutored Canning's friend George Ellis, a major *Anti-Jacobin* contributor; Frere had overlapped with Wordsworth for three years at Cambridge and with Coleridge for one; and Ford was a close friend of Richard Brinsley Sheridan through their mutual financial interest in the Drury Lane Theater-the same Sheridan who, during this same year, at first encouraged but ultimately rejected the two Somerset poets' first co-operative project, their closely-related plays, *Osorio* and *The Borderers*.

(Wordsworth had been in London to assist the fortunes

of his play in November and December of 1797, when the first five issues of *The Anti-Jacobin* appeared, with their carpet-bombing initial assaults on Southey's knee-jerk liberal effusions.) Despite their differences in political persuasion, the groups of young men who produced *The Anti-Jacobin* and those who produced (or talked about producing) *The Recluse, The Borderers* and *Osorio,* and, eventually, *Lyrical Ballads,* were not very different in class and education, nor in their desires for a moral reform of the country-although they saw its troubles differently-nor in their literary brilliance and ambition.

Young men like Coleridge and Wordsworth and Francis Wrangham had family political backgrounds very much like those of Canning and Frere-rather more conservative than theirs, in fact. Wordsworth in particular had a strong line of connections from his native relations with the Lowthers and the Howards, through his uncles Cookson and Robinson, to Wilberforce and thence right up to Pitt.

"New Morality," a poem widely under-rated in literary history, is one of the last representatives of a grand tradition of verse satire stretching back at least as far as Dryden. The largest target of this satiric tradition had always been excessive zeal or "enthusiasm" in religious and political matters, following the terrible events of the English Civil War. Now these excesses were seen to be rising horribly renewed in a French Revolution which some well-intentioned but misguided young Englishmen seemed to want to bring back home.

In this perspective, *The Anti-Jacobin*'s final appeal to some "bashful Genius, in some rural cell" could have been to the young Wordsworth, putting in public, patriotic terms the appeal to his better, established self that his uncles William Cookson and John Robinson had put to him in personal, familial terms throughout the '90s. Was it a last invitation to come in from the cold, home again, to return to the fold? Instead, he left the country again-but perhaps not before accepting that invitation on some terms, as the payment of nearly 100 pounds to 'Mr. Wordsworth,' recorded in Portland's secret paybook for June 13, 1799, suggests.

But the implications of *that* scene of writing take us away from the culture wars of *The Anti-Jacobin* and *Lyrical Ballads,* and into England's real 'Minister's War' with France, and into the much shadier scenes of suborning and suppressing domestic dissent which Pitt and Portland managed so well by trials, threats, bribes, and punishments throughout the decade of the 1790s. I have no proof that would document the literary connections between these two texts in indisputable terms-other than James Walsh's claim that Richard Ford would recognize the name 'Wordsworth,' and the Duke of Portland's payment to a 'Mr. Wordsworth' who could well be the same man. But in seeking for a closer connection-not to 'expose' Wordsworth but to appreciate the extreme pressures under which he and Coleridge conducted their literary revolution-I have constructed an intertextual argument on principles similar to those enunciated by Simon Schama:

... to have an *inquiry,* whether into the construction of a legend, or the execution of a crime, is surely to require the telling of stories. And so the asking of questions and the relating of narratives need not, I think, be mutually exclusive forms of historical representation.

Coincidentally, Schama's subjects are also 'Romantic': the *legend* of General Wolfe created by Benjamin West's famous painting (1770), and the *crime* of the 1849 murder of George Parkman, uncle to the great Romantic historian of Wolfe's campaign and the opening of the American West, Francis Parkman, Jr. Whether Wordsworth committed a 'crime' in the course of creating his 'legend,' and what exactly that 'crime' was-the real crime (sedition or treason) of supporting revolutionary France or the politically incorrect crime, of bad faith or 'renegadism,' for *not* supporting it-remain matters of speculation. But the connection of both crime and legend to his powerful self-creation as *the* Romantic poet of his generation is not adventitious to his literary development, as is suggested by the close connections of the blunt polemics of the 1798 Advertisement and the 1800 Preface to *Lyrical Ballads* to the equally fierce, if more 'refined' polemics of the 1797-1798 *Anti-Jacobin.*

The Anti-Jacobin's reputation continued long into the nineteenth century, especially its poetry sections, often reprinted as *The Beauties of the Anti-Jacobin*; thirty-four editions have been recorded. Some literary historians might still be disposed to explain this away as the persistence of an 'old' taste for satire, and thus out of step with a new 'Romantic' hegemony. But although *The Anti-Jacobin*'s parody and satire is often very good, it cannot be separated from its subject matter, which also continued to pre-occupy 19th century England: fear of revolution, not only in France in 1830 and 1848, but also in England, in 1819, 1832, and throughout the 1840s. In this respect, the persistence of *The Anti-Jacobin* might be charted alongside-as parody and counter-parody-the slow growth of Wordsworth's reputation from its 'Jacobin' origins-as many critics saw them-in the *Lyrical Ballads* of 1798-1800.

Only by the time of the posthumous publication of *The Prelude* in 1850 was Wordsworth's reputation-by then Poet Laureate-really safe from this imputation, so that this poem, with its chapter-and-verse (but carefully doctored) accounts of his close involvement with several phases and persons of the French Revolution, could be accepted, but dismissively, as part of 'that old business of the French Revolution.' By then, Wordsworth's 'anti-Jacobin' credentials were as well established as his 'Romantic' ones; indeed, by then, he had made the two virtually synonymous-completing a process that began in 1797-98 when he and Coleridge could see, every week, just how far outside the pale of acceptable literary society they were being cast by their opposite numbers, the bright young men of *The Anti-Jacobin*.

Sheila M. Kearns' *Coleridge, Wordsworth, and Romantic Autobiography: Reading Strategies of Self-Representation* is the most recent work in a long series of attempts at interpretating Wordsworth's *The Prelude* and Coleridge's *Biographia Literaria* from an autobiographical point of view. However, Kearns' book stands apart from the previous works on this subject by the extent of her analysis of *The Prelude* and *Biographia Literaria* which is in the best scholarly manner. This is certainly one of the best book to have appeared on the subject of autobiography in relation to Wordsworth and Coleridge for several years; anyone interested in that subject should definitely read it.

Kearns is perfectly aware of the intrinsic difficulty of discussing autobiographical works following the "advet of poststructuralist theories of language and subjectivity". Thus, she devotes her first chapter to a presentation of the current theories, evoking first the 'traditional' notion of autobiography (with references, among others, to Roy Pascal's *Design and Truth in Autobiography* , James Olnes' *Metaphors of the Self*, and Philippe Lejeune's *Le Pacte Autobiographique*). She then moves on to discuss Derrida's important contribution to the genre of autobiography, and discusses briefly Starobinsky's article 'The Style of Autobiography'.

Starobinsky comments that "Every autobiography—even when it limits itself to pure narrative—is a self-interpretation". There is indeed an element of doubt about the veracity of the story which should be borne in mind whenever one reads an autobiography, the story perhaps being fictionalised. The problem that the reader faces is that s/he cannot know whether the story is autobiographical or fictionalised if s/he does not have a preliminary knowledge of the author's life. Although Starobinsky's account contains valuable insights, Kearns mentions the limit(ation)s of Starobinsky's analysis by pointing out that he "examines autobiographical writing so as to try to see through it and to gain a view of the essential subject of the text". John Sturrock argues along the same line as Starobinsky when he declares:

> In autobiography, if anywhere in literature, we are expected to sense that these are texts inhabited by a living person, that an author who was particularly present to himself while he was writing is now present to us as we read.

However, a question arises: how are we to define the author? Indeed, even though it is agreed that it is by comparing the past 'I' with the present 'I' that the autobiography can take place, Benveniste observes that, linguistically speaking, there is no concept such as 'I' and that the 'I' refers to the one who is speaking and that we can identify him/her by the very fact that s/he is speaking. This remark is crucial in the sense that, for a text to be autobiographical, the 'I' has to refer to the author, and if there is no longer an author, a text cannot be autobiographical; the text being only *text* and nothing outside of it.

Of course, one is reminded of Roland Barthes' statement that the author is never more than the instance writing, just as the *I* is nothing other than the instance saying *I* : language knows a 'subject', not a 'person', and this subject, empty outside of the very enunciation which defines it, suffices to make language 'hold together', suffices, that is to say, to exhaust it. Surpringly, Kearns does not mention Roland Barthes in her book, nor even includes him in her bibliography, the only minor flaw in the entire book.

Kearns accurately asserts that the conventional view of autobiographical writings as defined by Starobinsky is challenged by poststructuralist theories of language with regard to the notion of stability in writing and the possibility of recovering an author's past through language. Kearns also discusses Foucault's theory of "author-function" from his essay 'What is an Author?', and rightly retains its main argument for her own analysis of Wordsworth's and Coleridge's works. In fact, one of the very good points of Kearns' study is that she manages to bring into the discussion 'controversial' issues (especially at a time when referring to poststructuralism is certainly not in conformity with the New Historicist approach of the day) and then provides the reader with an in-depth analysis of *The Prelude* and *Biographia Literaria* , thus preventing her study from turning into what Shelley calls "a sort of Asymptote which seems ever to approach & never to arrive".

After her analysis of Vico's *Autobiography* "as an example of the shift in the nature of self-representation that occurs with the developement of print-culture during the Romantic period at the end of the eighteenth century", Kearns gives the reader a challenging reading of Wordsworth's *The Prelude* by demonstrating how Wordsworth's strategy of self-representation within the poem attests his "power to read/ write the text of his life and to set up that model as the guide to be followed by any reader of the poem". She first pays particular attention to Book I to illustrate her argument that Wordsworth defines his reader with regard to the inscription of his life and the relationship to *The Recluse* project. Then, she highlights the way in which Wordsworth represents himself to his readers in Book 4. Kearns' detailed analysis of Wordsworths poem can be seen as exploring to its utmost Hugh Silverman's remark that "In autobiography, the self or subject is written as text. Auto-bio-graphizing is the writing of the self as text".

Moving swiftly to Coleridge, Kearns' *Coleridge, Wordsworth, and Romantic Autobiography* presents the reader with a brilliant analysis of the literary relations between Coleridge and Wordsworth. Although, as Kearns herself acknowledges, recent studies by Lucy Newlyn, Paul Magnuson and Gene Ruoff have focused on this subject, Kearns' account is interesting and different in many ways. By refering to *The Friend* and the poem 'To William Wordsworth', Kearns expands the scope of her analysis and manages to demonstrate how Coleridge appropriates Wordsworth's work in his own writings in order to re-affirm his status as a writer.

Kearns' references to Hazlitt's reviews of *The Stateman's Manual* and the *Biographia Literaria* are cleverly integrated within her discussion of Coleridge's textual and reading strategies as regards Wordsworth. Kearns' account of the public and private exchanges between Coleridge and Wordsworth is well-detailed and definitely thought-provoking. Her reading of *Biographia Literaria* , and in particular the famous Chapter 13, presents Coleridge's own definition of "author-function", and pertinently refers to his *Logic* and his theory of language.

If, as Paul De Man argues, autobiography is "a figure of reading or of understanding that occurs, to some degree, in all texts", there are other texts from the Romantic period which are waiting to be discussed and, no doubt, will be soon in other studies. In the meantime, Kearns' *Coleridge, Wordsworth, and Romantic Autobiography* contains an excellent new reading of two major works famous for their difficulty. Richard Holmes' remark in the introduction to his biography of Percy Bysshe

Shelley remains truer than ever: "What is constantly new is not the past itself, but the way we look back on it".

Casebook, as opposed to textbook, suggests substance. While "textbook" suggests a tissue of received ideas, susceptible to the intemperate breezes of critical discourse, the "case" in "casebook" resonates with case study, associating the term with postmortems and law schools. Casebooks do not necessarily create new knowledge as much create the opportunity to understand how we produce that knowledge in the first place. They can be powerful pedagogical tools, placing before the reader examples of the critical art. However, they can also be a trial for even the most generous minded reader, generating responses of pleasure and dismay because of the choices for inclusion and exclusion.

Placing "new" at the front of "casebook" further amplifies the potential of the genre for annoyance. Does the "new" mean that previous "cases" are now inadequate, fated to be remaindered or pulped? At the same time, the suggestion that a critical method is new also renders the work vulnerable to all the familiar criticisms of novelty. Indeed, if these "new" approaches can now be put forward in a casebook, surely a signal of academic respectability, in what sense are they new?

There are pedagogical reasons, however, for traipsing over old ground, and more especially, there are reasons for collections of "new" approaches to romanticism. The *Coleridge, Keats and Shelley* volume in the Macmillan *New Casebooks* series, edited by Peter J. Kitson, fills a felt need, in providing some examples of new approaches to the eponymous poets. Perhaps the most useful parts of the book, in pedagogical terms, are the introduction and the annotated bibliography. The introduction usefully contextualizes the new approaches to romanticism, dividing the flood of work that appeared after M. H. Abrams' *Natural Supernaturalism* into three streams of "challenges": poststructuralist, historicist, and feminist. Poststructuralism here should really be glossed as the so-called Yale School with a nod towards Lacan.

The lumping of Lacan with deconstructive readings of romanticism, while entirely understandable, is symptomatic of what the editor really takes to be new in romantic studies. All the figures discussed in the section concerning poststructuralism did their major work in the seventies, and the editor doesn't use one of the essays selected as an example of the approach. Kitson therefore gives the impression that deconstruction is an affable uncle of the fraternal twins of historicism and feminism; an influential presence, but one which has been generationally superseded. Understandably, this positioning of the challenges to the idealist reading of romanticism reflects the recent excitement over feminist and historicist readings of romanticism, but whether it reflects the genuine interrelatedness of the movements (Margaret Homans' *Bearing the Word,* for instance, is psychoanalytic as well as feminist, while the (new) historicism is most certainly indebted to the theoretical groundwork of deconstruction) is another question.

The purpose of such introductions, however, is to situate, not exhaust possible avenues of discussion; annotated bibliographies, on the other hand, show how that discussion might be continued. Kitson's inclusion of a thorough and readable bibliography turns what could have been a collection into a casebook. Helpfully, it covers general works on romanticism as well as discussing various recent tendencies in the study of Coleridge, Keats, and Shelley, along with classic starting points for each writer. Kitson's inclusion of a section in bibliography for female romantic poetry is indicative of contemporary concerns, and is a necessary complement for the male centered feminist essays he has selected. Finally, at the end of each essay, Kitson provides an abstract of the writer's argument, a gesture which suggests the provisionality of those arguments. In a sense, they are the first marginal notes in the book.

The most important parts of the collection, however, are the essays themselves. An attentive reading of them will clear away any notion that literary theory comes in nice, neat packages marked "poststructuralist," "feminist," and "historicist," as Kitson's cogent summaries help make clear. Ordered by the author under scrutiny rather than the theory employed, the essays nevertheless construct a narrative of romantic theory. The collection begins with an essay almost new critical in its vocabulary, only to unravel that vocabulary in favour of deconstructive and (literary) political analysis. This move turns out to be a way station for essays as nearly as formalist as the first, but which are hermeneutic (and one might almost say hermetic) in vocabulary.

I submit that one of the reasons for this pattern is that essays are ordered according to degree of difficulty (both for the reader and the writer). Kathleen M. Wheeler's claim for the holistic nature of the Coleridgean imagination seems worlds away from William Ulmer's argument that "*Adonais* never fully accepts the transferential interinvolvement of creation and destabilization, never fully disclaims its metaphysical nostalgia and desire for permanent truths and values." The claims themselves aren't as far apart as they seem (in some ways they describe the same concept seen from opposite perspectives), but Ulmer's depends on a vocabulary and a range of concepts not even dreamed by the latter. The sheer difficulty of the more formalist essays here registers the challenge that the historical (political?) study of literature poses for the aesthetic study.

At first it is hard to see what Kathleen M. Wheeler's "'Kubla Khan' and Eighteenth-Century Aesthetic Theories" is doing in this collection, claiming as it does that "[n]ot only is ... the barren dualism overcome" by the Coleridgean imagination, but in his "distinction between the primary and secondary imagination we see this reconciliation radically pursued and effected". This claim for imaginative wholeness has about it the whiff of Abrams' lamp, but, as Kitson points out, Wheeler's originality is in her reading of "the disruptions and sudden transitions in the poem" as figures for the poet's awareness of the limits of figuration.

This allows her to ally Coleridge with Blake and Shelley as a believer in the radical imagination. It is an ingenious reading, but I find myself more drawn to the less happily divided Coleridge of Susan Eilenberg's "Voice and Ventriloquy in *The Rime of the Ancient Mariner* ." More explicitly indebted to the Yale School, Eilenberg is prepared to recognize that a commitment to ironic procedures entails a commitment to failure, again and again: "The *Rime* , like the Mariner, is obsessed with its need to talk about itself and its relation to speech but never quite manages to name its subject". The result is less New Age holism, and more poetry as possession. The ventriloquism refers to the poem's repetitions and self-quotation; just who is subject to "the strange power of speech"—Mariner or narrator, reader or Wedding guest—becomes abundantly unclear by the end of the poem. One can be forgiven for feeling a bit dizzy when Eilenberg announces the *Rime* is protodeconstructive giving "us imitations, repetitions, representations - but no originals".

Still, both of these essays feel a bit cloistered. Indeed, Eilenberg's concern for originality arises out of her own response of Harold Bloom's hyberbolic assertion that there is but one poem is English literary history. The next three essays, on Coleridge, Keats, and feminism/effeminacy implicitly critique this assumption, by demonstrating how critical history affects interpretation. In "The Debate on the Character of *Christabel* ," Karen Swann examines the treatment of *Christabel* as exemplary of how "feminization" is a "strategy habitually adopted by high culture when defending its privileges". Put off by the sexually charged relationship of Geraldine and Christabel, early reviewers "cast [the poem's] impropriety as *generic* impurity".

Thus, Swann suggests that the criticism of the poem waged a gender war by aesthetic means. Such a claim dovetails nicely with the next essay, "Feminising Keats," by Susan J. Wolfson, whose concerns are "with how the language of gender operates in the literary and social culture in which [Keats] wrote and was reviewed". In this case, the figure of the poet himself cannot be extricated from the poem, as the effeminacy of his writing led to a reading of Keats himself as unmanly. Yet Wolfson does not leave the argument there, noting that this very feminization has allowed for more positive readings - "even to the point of androgyny". Rather Wolfson wishes to historicise the debate itself suggesting that, whatever the value judgment, the debate simply "repeats the problem of reconciling general values with a complex and elusive instance". The reading of Keats' poetry should be an occasion for the examination of those values themselves.

Each of these readings is more about the discourse produced by readers, than the poems themselves, and to a degree, so is Nicholas Roe's "Keats's Lisping Sedition." Yet this essay seeks to examine the critical history in order to set it aside for another interpretation. For this reason, as well as its wit, Roe's essay stands out as the gem of the collection. The wit is best evidenced by the claim to produce, from perhaps the most purely aestheticized romantic, a political poet whose claims for "genius, negative capability, and ideal beauty ... can be seen as developments of a democratic sensibility". These claims might seem fàcile, if they weren't backed up with very patient work at decoding why Keats could be written off as Cockney.

Roe's research reveals a semantic field that underlies the war of words waged by Lockhart and others. I would suggest that this essay, then, places Keats firmly in the romantic literature of subversion, most prominently practiced by Shelley and Godwin. But his method wasn't quite subversive enough. Rather having an afterlife as a radical icon as Shelley did (with *Queen Mab*), the critical reaction was such that Roe suggests Byron was more right than he could have known when he said Keats "had been 'snuffed out by an article'". Instead, Keats's reputation recovered only through his aesthetic deification.

The final two essays on Keats' also take up the relation of aesthetics and history, but they offer a different perspective on the "new" approaches, concerning themselves with recent political readings of the poet that the authors see as overcompensating for that very aesthetic deification (by Bate, Brooks, and others). Like Roe, A. W. Phinney and Andrew Bennett view the poet as more knowing about his relation to history, but their concern is not to replace formal concerns with historical ones, but rather show their implication. Of the two, Phinney's "Keats in the Museum" is more theoretical, using Gadamer to refute excesses of both aesthetics and history.

The occasion for this is the well worn "Ode on A Grecian Urn." In contrast to those who celebrate the poem's perfection, Phinney insists that its persistence is due to its hesitations: "the ode's repeated question, overinsistent repetition, riddling puns and oxymorons, and ambiguous syntax". While Phinney is attentive to these aspects of the poem, his conclusion is at best vague: the poem somehow takes the best of aestheticism and historicism together. What this means, besides another version of the idealization of the poem, is unclear to me. Bennett's "To Autumn" not only surveys history, but specifies it as economic history: "To Autumn": "Figures of reading become, literally, economic figures" as the poem "is an articulation of the politics and economics both of agriculture and of writing".

From this summary, it would seem that Bennett has more in common with Roe. Nevertheless, Bennett adds a twist to his argument that make much more theoretical. For not only is "To Autumn" molested by political and economic overtones, but the very fact that they are so obvious silences a political reading as an egregious "solecism," to use Bennett's term. Surely, the history of readings of "To Autumn" bears out Bennett's point that the political has been repressed by its readers, but it seems overingenuous to suggest that this is a function of the poem's "strategic silencing" of such concerns. Of course, criticism should be nothing if not ingenious; one wouldn't read it, unless one found in it interesting insights. But perhaps the very precariousness of making formal claims about poetry in these days of New Casebooks provokes ingenuity on the part of the critic.

By contrast, the work of Shelley, demands ingenuity, and not merely in the deliberately obscure *Prometheus Unbound* . Ironically, Kitson includes neither a feminist nor a New Historicist reading of his work (though one is defiantly old historicist), as though to suggest only deconstruction, with its complex consideration of troping, passes muster as a new approach. Though I took up Ulmer as representative of the new difficulty in critical style, both his and Frances Ferguson's essays are exemplary instances of poststructuralist readings of romantic poems. Sandwiched between them is Kelvin

Everest's "'Mechanism of a kind yet unattempted': The Dramatic Action of *Prometheus Unbound* ."

Everest's essay is badly placed for my thesis about the book as a whole; hardly at all theoretical, the essay addresses whether an audience could possibly get some of the more recondite imagery "without the assistance of detailed academic commentary". The essay itself is an example of just that, explicating the image of an earth-emitted vapour that plays a large role (according to Everest) in the poem's action. His claim is well-taken, but it seems odd to make such a claim about a poem rhetorically aimed at the "fit though few." More refreshing is his refutation of those who would make the poem a sort of visionary well-wrought urn instead of a composition which is more fragmentary and palimpsestic.

However, Everest's worries about obscurity, as though it necessarily prevents revolutionary impact, are unwarranted, especially in the case of Shelley. In fact, Shelley's obscurity is at times a means of flying under ideological radar - though the case of Leavis' reading demonstrates that this is not a foolproof strategy. What is more curious is this most political of romantic poets attracts the least *engagé* critical school: deconstruction.

Are political readings of Shelley a case of bringing coals to Newcastle? At the same time, Frances Ferguson's "Shelley's *Mont Blanc* : What the Mountain Said" and William Ulmer's "*Adonais* and the Death of Poetry" admirably demonstrate how apt deconstruction is to the reading of Shelley. Indeed, such an affinity shouldn't seem surprising when we remember Shelley's radical conception of language and his concern with the relation of poetry and history. Of the two essays, I prefer Ferguson's, which gets at poststructuralist concerns with a less ornate vocabulary and probably needs no introduction here. In many ways, Ulmer considers the same issues as Phinney and Bennett. If ánything, though, his conclusions about poetry and history are less sanguine. Ulmer offers a more pessimistic reading (in contrast to Jerrold Hogle) of Shelley's use of metalepsis in Adonais. Rather than offering the power to transform history through the lens of the present, by obligating the past to the present, metalepsis renders the past an endlessly reconstructible pawn of contemporary ideologies, with their power to distort the historical record, to forget what deserves remembering. Shelley's reflexive figurations leave cultural continuity unanchored in certain truth.

The reassertion of the sheer contingency of cultural history is a truth that this volume bears witness to, and so it is an appropriate sentiment to end with. Nevertheless, contingency casts a rather awkward light on the project of criticism itself; encountering such thoughts, a student might well think that, on the whole, it's better left undone.

And yet ... Though these are certainly new approaches to the reading of these three poets, Kitson in his introduction and bibliography alludes to other trends that threaten his work with obsolescence. As I mentioned, he includes a separate bibliographic entry for women poets and, in his introduction, he alludes to recent (post)colonialist readings of romantic poetry. He could have added an entry on studies of the romantic novel as well. Though the eighties saw a variety of new approaches, the nineties threaten a reconceptionalization of what is romanticism, in terms of genre and gender. Such contingency is frightening, but also liberating, in that we readily admit there are more things to be read, but that admission suggests that, while there will be new casebooks, the place of Keats, Coleridge, and Shelley (and for that matter, Byron, Blake, and Wordsworth) is not assured.

Notably absent from this volume are pieces more explicitly critical of the poets. As I said, the more formalist essays, in the very elaborateness and qualified nature of their claims, certainly bear the marks of this recent turn in criticism. In a way, this makes pedagogical sense, since demonstrating failure (either poetically or politically) is not a very attractive mode of criticism, but one wonders if this absence makes the collection less representative than it might be. Finally, however, the absence seems to reflect the revved up evolutionary cycle of romantic studies, making it perilous to claim something as new. This *New Casebooks* volume is an admirable and useful attempt, but upon finishing it, I am reminded all too well that romanticism is "ever more about to be."

A Hypertext History of the Transmission of Coleridge's "Christabel," 1800-1816

Chris Koenig-Woodyard

In the touch of this bosom there worketh a spell,
Which is lord of thy utterance, Christabel!

Introduction

An entire epoch of so-called literature... cannot survive a certain technological regime of telecommunications. *Neither can philosophy, or psychoanalysis. Or love letters.*

Jacques Derrida

"What will the critic and theorist of literature do about hypertext?" asks George Landow in *Hyper/Text/Theory*. The answer that Landow offers to his own question—"Write in hypertext itself"—reads as both an abbreviated decree and entreaty. What the literary scholar will *do* about hypertext is *to do hypertext*, is to embrace and apply the medium of hypertext—in its simplest computer form, a system of electronic links and nodes (or units of text)—to their critical and interpretive activities. (Or, as Derrida would have it, lovers will now find themselves writing on-line hypermedia letters, with a requisite rendezvous in a MUD—a Multi-User Dungeon.)

Rising to the occasion of Landow's call to "write in hypertext itself," however, is a task of formidable theoretical and practical complexity. The difficulties of achieving this task is a governing concern among the panellists of the 1996 MLA panel "The Canon and the Web: Reconfiguring Romanticism in the Information Age," and the 1996 NASSR Bruce Graver-led round-table discussion "Electronic Texts and Textuality.

A theme often identified by panellists of both sessions is that the application of hypertext to literary studies necessitates a re-conception of the editorial and critical activities of literary scholars. Their reports of working with hypermedia and hypertext literary projects reveal a new scholarship—an electronic scholarship with a bibliographic concern that centres on textual variation, on how multiple witnesses of a literary work can be presented in an electronic environment. It is in the framework of several of these panellists' comments on treating a multi-versioned literary work that the groundwork can be laid for a discussion of how the application of hypertext technology (re)shapes scholarly activities—particularly the study of the transmission of a literary work.

A hypertext history of the transmission of Samuel Coleridge's "Christabel" (1816) from 1800 to 1816 serves as a model with which to explore the theoretical and practical issues at stake in working with a multi-versioned literary work in hypertext form.

Chapter 8

The Ancient Mariner and Parody

An ancient literary practice often aligned with satire, parody "comes of age as a major comic expression during the Romantic period," as Marilyn Gaull has observed, the same era that celebrated and became known for the literary virtues of sincerity, authenticity, and originality. Significant recent anthologies of Romantic-period parodies make the sheer bulk and topical range of such imitative works available for readers and critics for the first time, providing ample evidence for the prominence of the form. The weight of evidence in these collections should also put to rest the widespread assumption that parody is inevitably "comic" or gentler than satire, that it is essentially in good fun.

At least during the politically volatile Romantic period, as Linda Hutcheon has asserted, parody "is almost always aligned with satire; that is to say, parody is the literary shape taken by social satire." The very act of imitation implies a closeness and familiarity rather than a mere dismissal of the target. This is why many parodies have historically been seen as a form of flattery, tributes to their originals.

As Hutcheon says elsewhere, parody is "imitation with a critical ironic distance, whose irony can cut both ways," producing in some cases "scornful ridicule" and in others what looks like "reverential homage." Nonetheless, Romantic-period parody often served as a powerful mode of topical satire—a particularly galling and intimate way of ridiculing a target by stealing and distorting one's very voice.

It is often observed that, considered etymologically, "parody" can mean either "beside" or "against" another poem, and that parodies can serve either to pay tribute to or to ridicule the targeted work. Samuel Taylor Coleridge approached the same matter from a slightly different direction in the following epigram for anonymous inclusion in Robert Southey's *Omniana*:

> Parodies on new poems are read as satires; on old ones, (the soliloquy of Hamlet for instance) as compliments. A man of genius may securely laugh at a mode of attack, by which his reviler in half a century or less, becomes his encomiast.

This way of putting it helpfully focuses on historical context as necessary to any interpretation of a parody's tone and purpose; but it is important to notice that it also emphasizes by implication *the canonical status* of the targeted work. The difference between parodic "satire" and parodic "compliment" is time, according to Coleridge, the distance traveled from a "new" to an "old" poem. But the chosen example of an old poem is telling; in 1812, when Coleridge wrote the passage, Shakespeare had begun to stand at the head of an English vernacular canon.

The kind of old poem that both survives the test of time and is at the end still considered worthy of parody is likely to be a work of recognized "genius," which is to say, a canonical work. Coleridge's gnomic and ironic remark suggests that whether a parody counts as satire or compliment depends in part upon the process of canonization, a process in turn dependent upon the kind of critical judgments offered by parody. Such parodic judgments identify the works worthy of being remembered and taken seriously enough to be parodied in the first place, and help to define the qualities of those works that make them worthy of (even negative) attention.

There is a double circularity at work in this scheme: parody helps to shape the context that partly determines the effect of other parodies; and, in a kind of poetic Doctrine of the Elect, only the man of genius can rest securm in eventual victory, in the promise that his satiric "attackers" will eventually, in the due course of cultural change, be transformed into his encomiasts. The canonical have the last laugh. But whether a work is worthy of such canonization only becomes known when the work is no longer "new" but still considered significant, literally imitable. In most cases, true security is only certain after the death of the author. Coleridge's parable speaks to the dialectical relationship of satire and poetic expression in literary history. Parody and satiric commentary not only help to cull and determine the works that remain in the field, sometimes they help through their overall contributions to its critical reception to shape a paradigm-setting, movement-defining major work even after the fact of its publication—as in the case of Coleridge's *Rime of the Ancient Mariner*.

This essay looks through the lens of parody at one of Coleridge's most characteristically "romantic" works, his famous ballad of the supernatural, *The Rime of the Ancient Mariner*. Along with the other so-called "Mystery Poems"—"Christabel" and "Kubla Khan"—this is among his most significant generic contributions to the developing idea of Romanticism, the kind of work that comes through a kind of synecdoche to stand for the whole movement as it was conceived. According to his own statement of intentions, these poems most clearly represent his "supernatural, or at least romantic" mode that was to serve as a pendant to Wordsworth's "natural," rustic simplicity in the *Lyrical Ballads* project. In what follows I will place the *Rime* in the context of Coleridge's changing conception of the work and his own satiric practice, including his propensity for self-parody and the parody of his fellow-poets.

In the late 1790s Coleridge joined a literary trend, producing supernatural works always on the verge of self-parody. Over the course of the following three decades he attempted to distance himself from the more fashionably romantic works of the same generic family—and from those qualities in his own works, representing them as part of a more metaphysical kind, constructing a philosophically coherent corpus fit for a place in the canon. Parody, broadly conceived, plays a role at every stage of this process.

Chapter 9

The Ancient Mariner and the Romantic Canon

My choice of poem is no accident. *The Rime of the Ancient Mariner* is rooted in Coleridge's most "romantic" early works (as the term was understood at the time) but is also the exemplary Romantic poem (in the canonical sense). Wordsworth's and Coleridge's own accounts of the composition and publication history of the ballad make up one of the founding myths of English Romanticism, beginning with their attempts to collaborate on it and publish it in the *Monthly Magazine,* a way to pay the expenses of a walking tour.

Coleridge quickly took over the composition, but was then caught up in the larger plan for a volume of poems on rustic and supernatural subjects. In the event, the *Rime* was the first poem readers encountered in the first edition of *Lyrical Ballads* in 1798. It was also one of the works in that collection that contemporary readers would have immediately recognized as fashionably "romantic" in the German style, a kind of gothic horror ballad then popular in the magazines. As an anonymous reviewer looking back from twenty years later noted, *The Rime of the Ancient Mariner* appeared at a time when, to use a bold but just expression, with reference to our literary taste, '*Hell made holiday,*' and '*Raw heads and bloody-bones*' were the only fashionable entertainment for man or woman. Then Germany was poured forth into England, in all her flood of sculls and numsculls: then the romancing novelist ran raving about with midnight torches, to shew death's heads on horseback, and to frighten full-grown children with mysteries and band-boxes, hidden behind curtains in bedrooms .... This reviewer is essentially correct about the origins of the *Rime:* it began as a romantic horror ballad in the popular sense, and only later was made over into the quintessentially Romantic poem. When it first appeared, it was in a self-consciously archaic form, and in these terms Wordsworth's brief Advertisement to *Lyrical Ballads* offered a kind of pre-emptive apology for it, saying that it was "professedly written in imitation of the style, as well as of the spirit of the elder poets."

Privately, Wordsworth said that he believed it had "upon the whole been an injury to the volume," that "the old words and the strangeness of it have deterred readers from going on;" he wrote an apologetic note for its appearance, near the back of the collection, in the 1800 edition. Between 1798 and 1817, Coleridge continued to revise the poem, producing a number of different versions, but by far the most significant version is the one he prepared for publication in his own *Sibylline Leaves* of 1817.

During the intervening years the poem and its author became famous. Coleridge's brother-in-law, Robert Southey, wrote one of the earliest reviews of the *Lyrical Ballads*, a scathing attack satirizing the *Ancient Mariner* as a "Dutch attempt at German sublimity;" another friend, Charles Lamb, strongly disagreed at the time, saying that it was on the contrary a successful attempt to "dethrone German sublimity," and confessing elsewhere that he "was never so affected with any human Tale."

Even some critics who could on occasion be highly acerbic towards Lake School poetry professed admiration for the ballad, most notably John Gibson Lockhart, who said that this "most wonderful" of the poems in *Sibylline Leaves* was the most Coleridgean: "From it alone, we are inclined to think an idea of the whole poetical genius of Mr. Coleridge might be gathered, such as could scarcely receive any important addition either of extent or distinctness, from a perusal of the whole of his other works."

The anonymous *Monthly Review* writer cited above, while attacking the German influence and lurid poetry of the ballad, quotes other passages with approval, specifically avoiding what he calls "the horrors of the poem." In *The Spirit of the Age* William Hazlitt summed up the positive view of the ballad and located its place in Coleridge's oeuvre:

> Of all Mr. Coleridge's productions, the Ancient Mariner is the only one that we could with confidence put into any person's hands, on whom we wished to impress a favourable idea of his extraordinary powers. Let whatever other objections be made to it, it is unquestionably a work of genius—of wild, irregular, overwhelming imagination, and has that rich, varied movement in the verse, which gives a distant idea of the lofty of changeful tones of Mr. Coleridge's voice.

Hazlitt describes the poem in terms that would later be seen as essentially Romantic ("a work of genius—of wild, irregular, overwhelming imagination") and associates it with the author's name and voice, the authority under which it is to enter the canon. Notice as well how his terms of sometimes equivocal praise—"wild, irregular ... rich, varied movement"—anticipate, acknowledge, and answer the very kind of criticism (those "other objections") Southey and others made of the poem. Hazlitt's description participates in making the poem into what Coleridge called it (recorded in *Table Talk*): "a work of ... pure imagination." Among the so-called younger generation of Romantics the poem became a touchstone of themes and techniques, narrative and lyrical. In the nineteenth and twentieth centuries it has retained a place of preeminence in the canon and has entered the public consciousness and the culture at large, producing its own extensive academic Midrash of critical commentary and a long chain of multiple editions, versions, imitations, and parodies.

That process of commentary and canonization was begun by Coleridge himself in collaboration with the poem's audiences, even before he revised it for publication in 1817. In that decisive, authoritative version he added as a kind of integrated paratext the famous marginal gloss, as if in the hand of some later (but still "antique") hermeneut. By doing so, as well as through his own critical remarks in the *Biographia Literaria* and elsewhere, he in effect collaborated with readers, critics, and parodists in determining the form in which it would be handed on to the canon and literary history. The gloss, itself a parody of academic or monkish interpretation, has proven to be a continuous source of hermeneutic questions about the poem and about hermeneutics in general.

It is by now a critical commonplace that the gloss offers a kind of enfolded dialectical or ironic perspective on the main text of the ballad, though critical disagreement persists as to how to read the precise tone of the marginal text. For my purposes, it is enough to acknowledge that there are places in the text where the gloss opens up an ironic counter-voice on the main action of the ballad, in effect anticipating the poem's inevitable parodies. This may be discerned as early as the use of the word "Gallants" adjacent to the first stanza; but it is a clearer possibility in stanzas 9-10:

The bride hath paced into the hall,
Red as a rose is she;
Nodding their heads before her goes
The merry minstrelsy.
The Wedding-Guest he beat his breast,
Yet he can not chuse but hear;
And thus spake on that ancient man,
The bright-eyed Mariner.

The gloss merely says in deadpan fashion: "The wedding-guest heareth the bridal music; but the mariner continueth his tale." The simple discrepancy in tone between the agony of the Guest and the gloss-writer's imperturbability is potentially parodic, whatever Coleridge's specific intentions. Elsewhere, specific moral-theological judgments are offered, or quirky, seemingly personal, and sometimes over-obvious reactions are recorded. When the poem describes the ghastly appearance of Life-in-Death and her mate (III.10-11), the glossist simply observes, "Like vessel, like crew!"

In other instances, the key discrepancy is between the pace of the ballad meter and of the glossist's terse remarks, as when the moon rises and two-hundred sailors one by one silently curse the Mariner and drop dead, told by the ballad in four full stanzas (the first of which is extra long at nine lines);

synchronized with the slow motion of the "star-dogged Moon" (III.16), their souls fly away. The gloss, by contrast, moves quickly through three phrases: "At the rising of the Moon,... One after another,... His shipmates drop down dead." the parody here is a matter of style: a play between "scholarly" understatement and sentimental overstatement.

It is difficult to separate intended from unintended ironic effects in the interpenetrating texts of gloss and ballad, but the possibility of parody—in the full range of its senses, from iterative tribute to allusive appropriation to satiric mimicry—is at least anticipated and subsumed in the structure of Coleridge's dialogic text of 1817. This merely brings to an initial climax (but does not end) a process of effusion and parody that was intimately bound up with the composition, revision, and reception of this most "romantic" of Romantic works.

Two parodies: 1819, 1989

What is it about the Ancient Mariner that parodists continue to find imitable and risible? Many of the work's parodies target the *Ancient Mariner*'s family ties to the gothic ballad tradition, which persisted despite Coleridge's attempts to turn the poem into something of a higher kind. Especially after 1817, parodies offer a satiric perspective on the whole process of revising the poem, and thus on the making of Romanticism itself out of "romantic" elements in popular and fashionable literature. Looking at the poem through parodists' eyes is a useful dialectical exercise, and one that provides a counterweight to the institutionalized academic readings of the poem as a central text in the High Romantic canon.

From the many possible examples of parodies by others I select two representative works widely separated by era and cultural context—a poetic imitation from 1819 and a comic book adaptation from 1989. These serve first to dramatize the persistence of the poem's cultural capital into the late twentieth-century—and well outside the academy—but also to demonstrate the specific ways in which both parodies make much of what Coleridge had already provided in the way of dialogic and parodic openings, openings he himself responded to with revisionary moves even as he was creating them. Already in 1819 the *Ancient Mariner*—though a "new" poem still in terms of Coleridge's dichotomy—had achieved the kind of fame that turned the "satire" of any parody into something of a "compliment." The work's reception and legacy was shaped by the interaction of such canonizing compliment and satiric commentary.

I. 1819

Less than two years after the publication of *Sibylline Leaves* and only months before Lockhart's praise of *The Ancient Mariner* appeared in *Blackwood's*, an anonymous parody was printed whose title suggests a satire on Wordsworth along with Coleridge, "The Rime of the Auncient Waggonere."

Its author, David Macbeth Moir, would in quick succession also publish a parody of *Christabel*, purporting to complete the fragment. The effect of this parody is based on verbal mimicry and on various substitutions for elements in the original, but also on exploiting the discrepancies between gloss and main text.

IT is an auncient Waggonere,
And he stoppeth one of nine:—
"Now wherefore dost thou grip me soe
With that horny fist of thine?
"The bridegroom's doors are opened wide,
And thither I must walke;
Soe, by your leave, I muste be gone,
I have noe time for talke!"
Hee holds him with his horny fist—
"There was a wain," quothe hee,
"Hold offe, thou raggamouffine tykke,"
Eftsoones his fist dropped hee.

The gloss to the second stanza merely reads: "The waggonere in mood for chate, and admits of no excuse." So far this is very much like the effect in the 1817 original of discrepant tones and ironic understatement, but with coarser Northern slang in place of Coleridge's vaguely medieval or Renaissance language. At times this effect takes the form of slapstick bathos—though again, the original had provided the example and pointed the way:

"The wain is fulle, the horses pulle,
Merrilye did we trotte
Alonge the bridge, alonge the road,
A jolly crewe, I wotte:"—
And here the tailore smotte his breaste,
He smelte the cabbage potte!

The gloss merely repeats the event in a mindless refrain, with something of the pedantic long-windedness of the original: "The appetite of the Tailore whetted by the smell of cabbage." ("Tailore" is likely a pun on Taylor.) Coleridge's ethereal wedding music is brought down to the level of the cabbage (and the baser sense of smell), the social class of the wedding party is made clear, and the parody mocks the intrusion of quotidian details—and the body—into the melodramatic action and supernatural or psychological effects of the original ballad.

The main joke, emphasized by this play of gloss against text, turns out to be the blatant physical violence of the Waggonere, which satirizes the Mariner's violent act against the Albatross, but also generally punctures the metaphysical pretensions of the original. Coleridge's first version and what survives in 1817 of the gothic horror ballad decorum—whose conventions can compass ghost ships, waking corpses, and slimy things—are satirically debunked by the direct knockabout of the parody, as the Waggonere proves himself the kind of low ruffian who might be expected by *Blackwood's* readers to appear in a ballad.

"At lengthe we spied a goode grey goose,
Thorough the snow it came;
And with the butte ende of my whippe,
I hailed it in Goddhis name.
"It staggered as it had been drunke,
So dexterous was it hitte;
Of broken boughs we made a fire,
Thomme Loncheone roasted itte."—

Signaling that it is subtle enough to mimic Coleridge's

archaic diction ("thorough"), the parody remains otherwise deliberately crude, thus taking aim at the whole Lake School's favourite poetic virtue of "simplicity." The power of the Waggonere to hold the Tailore as an audience begins to look increasingly like thuggish intimidation.

In "Part Second,"as the Waggonere rides away, conventional balladic questions, including for a moment an allusion to the Albatross ("a foreigne bird"), come to a mundane anticlimax. As the gloss says: "Various hypotheses on the subject, frome which the passengers draw wronge conclusions."

"Some saide itte was ane apple tree,
Laden with goodlye fruite,
Some swore itte was ane foreigne birde,
Some said it was ane brute;
Alas! It was ane bumbailiffe,
Riding in pursuite!

Not surprisingly, the Waggonere "complimenteth the bumbailiffe with ane Mendoza" (a special boxing blow): "Why star'st thoue soe?—With one goode blow, / I felled the bumbailiffe." So it is with less metaphysical than physical dread (what the gloss names "Corporal Feare") that this interlocutor says,

"I feare thee, auncient waggonere,
I fear thy hornye fist,
For itte is stained with gooses gore,
And bailiffe's blood, I wist.

The parody ends by tacking on an explicitly labeled, clumsy "Morale," thus going right to the heart of what was and remained perhaps the key interpretive question of Coleridge's poem, from the legendary comments of Anna Barbauld and for the next two hundred years. Making fun of the moralizing stanzas of the *Rime,* the parody's moral is rendered bluntly explicit. It simply cautions "foolish men" to avoid "bade companye," implying again the danger of treating too seriously ill-mannered low-life rustics like the Waggonere, demonstrating why it is better to avoid than indulge "simple" strangers on the road. Instead of a narrative of increasing mystery and wonder, the Waggonere tells an all-too mundane story of quotidian rough behaviour. In the same way the whole parody demystifies with a vengeance (by caricaturing and domesticating) the exotic, "wild" atmosphere and machinery of the 1817 original, reducing the sublime to the ridiculous—with a brickbat.

Moir reads even the 1817 text as pretentiously romantic in its mystified supernaturalism; and he is aware of and willing to capitalize on the ironic openings provided by Coleridge's dialogic gloss. This revision was precisely the device through which Coleridge also enhanced the ballad's susceptibility to "Romantic" interpretations—as a metaphysically transcendent and aesthetically symbolic text. The parody returns to the half-buried ur-romantic qualities of the ballad, which persist despite Coleridge's attempts to revise them away; in fact it calls attention to how the layered revisions of the poem work to dress up the simple narrative events, thus encoding the shifting senses of "r/Romantic" as they apply to—indeed as they are in part defined by—Coleridge's poetry.

II. 1989

We find similar demystifications of the poem everywhere in the so-called "underground"—really only extra-academic—tradition of continuing parodies, illustrations, and popular adaptations of *The Rime of the Ancient Mariner*. One striking example is Hunt Emerson's 1989 comic-book version, which includes Coleridge's text in word bubbles and panel captions, according to comic book conventions, but also supplements it with additional speeches and parodies the text through its illustrations. Emerson's no-holds-barred lampoon style originates in the underground comics of the early 1970s, and makes use of a conventional repertoire of psychedelic distortions, hallucinatory and surrealistic fantasies, and gleeful bodily humour, including puns and slapstick jokes of questionable taste.

Within those conventions—in fact I would argue because it is within them—it offers a remarkable parodic tribute and satiric commentary on Coleridge's ballad, and on its long reputation and vast store of accumulated cultural capital. The comic's astute commentary is evident from the start in the frontispiece to the book, a brilliantly grotesque full-page representation of a textual passage in the 1797 version of the poem, later deleted by Coleridge as too luridly "German," in which the living-dead sailors raise their arms to burn as lurid torches:

A little distance from the prow
Those dark-red shadows were;
But soon I saw that my own flesh
Was red as in a glare.
I turn'd my head in fear and dread,
And by the holy rood,
The bodies had advanc'd, and now
Before the mast they stood.
They lifted up their stiff right arms,
They held them strait and tight;
And each right-arm burnt like a torch,
A torch that's borne upright.
Their stony eye-balls glitter'd on
In the red and smoky light.
nbsp; (1798; VI.485-98)

Emerson cannily chooses to restore this deleted passage to his overall "text" by way of this silent image, thus foregrounding the kinship of the original poem to his own metier and form.

The panel could almost be an illustration of the nineteenth-century review quoted above, with its "*Raw heads and bloody-bones*" entertainments. Uncaptioned and wordless (except for the T-shirt on one of the figures), the image reminds us of the "silenced" text Coleridge deleted and in effect declares it as a measure of what is to follow, establishing the spirit and tone of the rest of Emerson's parody.

It shows a line of five zombie sailors on the deck, with eyeless skulls, rotting flesh, protruding bones, and grotesque entrails, but the effect of horror is undercut with numerous broadly comic details—an airhorn, opium pipe, chicken bone, aged cheese, and a dead bird—extending out of the skulls/

brains, held aloft by extra hands, repeating the image of the burning fists.

One holds what appears to be a frog, one a flaming cigarette lighter, the universal signal calling for an encore at rock concerts, and wears a ratty T-shirt reading "Bob Dylan World Tour 1795." In the centre of the composition, the Albatross itself pecks angrily at a sailor's silly animal slippers. The slapstick anachronisms are licensed by the irreverence of the comic book form and by the mode of parody itself (and implicitly by the theme of the undead). In fact, the flouting of historical boundaries is only one way the parody targets the stuffy academic ownership of this text. As if in anticipatory defiance of conventional distaste, one of the sailors thumbs his nose at us in the frontispiece tableau.

In his playful treatment of the grotesque and macabre, as if in a dream or drug-induced hallucination, Emerson exploits the distant family resemblance between this counter-cultural art form and Coleridge's own opium-induced variations on the gothic. The mixture of horror and humour is also profoundly true to the contradictory effects of Coleridge's ballad from the start—but especially after the gloss was added for the 1817 version—effects of which Moir's 1819 parody is well aware. The exaggerated sensibility and "supernatural" and sublime pyrotechnics of late eighteenth-century gothic balladry, novels, and theater already, at their inception, opened themselves up to the possibility of caricature and parody by their very nature.

By design, at least among the artists who began at the time systematically to use these effects for the purposes of art, they were self-consciously in excess—sentimental, passionate, lurid and wild in their imaginative intensity—in a word, "romantic." Defining themselves as "against" or "beside" conventional morality and decorum, such expressions come into being as part of a "parodic" relationship to the status quo, which is easily enough turned back upon them, reversed in actual parody. These "outsider" qualities, still present in fossil form within the long history of the Rime's reception, are brought out by the historically distant and yet generically consonant, exaggerated and distorted psychedelic exuberance, of Emerson's comic-book style.

Emerson places Coleridge's gloss as an "argument" at the beginning of each part of the poem, but he also "glosses" the text himself in various ways, first of course in the images, which often comment on the text, but also in additional speeches put in the mouths of the characters, and finally in completely new interpolated sequences, bits of comic business that comment on the "real" plot like theatrical asides or Aristophanic *parabases* to the audience, as if improvised by actors performing a well-known script.

One of the funniest of these is his depiction of the poem's early plot crisis—the actual shooting of the Albatross. Emerson has the Mariner use his cross bow but with a suction-cup tipped arrow. He repeatedly fires at the bird and misses in a series of snapshot images, panel by panel. When he is finally hit, the Albatross hams it up, reeling and staggering around the deck, one panel at a time, overacting a burlesque-melodramatic dying scene, the arrow protruding ridiculously from its head.

The staring sailors form a stone-faced audience to this performance at first, listening to the moral-mongering speech in word balloons ("martyred to man's dominion!... DEAD!"), but finally grow frustrated, until the Mariner silently and grimly returns with a large gun and blasts the bird in the final panel. The comic timing, using rhythmic transitions between the closely-articulated panels, is impeccable. But what is so successfully parodic about this interlude is the way it targets the tropes of sensibility inherited by Coleridge with his chosen form.

From the poem's initial reception through much of twentieth-century criticism, it has been clear to readers that the "bird of ill-omen" has to bear an inordinate weight of emotional significance in the narrative. The "dying" of Emerson's Albatross is a pop cliché straight out of Tex Avery's animated cartoons, for example, but ultimately derived from the same kind of sentimental melodrama that was popular in the 1790s. The comic-book bird is both a sentimental hero and its own long-winded exegete; in one sense the gun-toting Mariner acts on behalf of countless readers, frustrated with the sententiousness of the critical tradition and the seemingly disproportionate significance attached to the poem's ornithological protagonist. A wicked satiric relief results from watching the feathers fly from this most famous Coleridgean symbol.

Similarly, at the poem's strange climax ("Part Fourth"), Emerson parodies the famous blessing of living things by the Mariner. The Albatross is very much alive again ("Aw—give us a break, boss—there aren't many good parts in literature for albatrosses," it pleads), hanging around the Mariner's neck. Emerson indulges in an outrageous visual pun on "spring of love" (the Mariner's heart protrudes from his chest on a spring), and a punning reply to sneezing water snakes ("bless you"). At the conclusion of the poem, Emerson further demonstrates his awareness of the poem's history of interpretation. First, there is an extraordinary sequence of twenty-one separate panels across two pages in which the Mariner recites as if onstage the famous lines summarizing the purported moral of the poem ("O Sweeter than the marriage-feast.

He prayeth well who loveth well ..."). Then, Emerson provides another silent graphic interlude. The Wedding Guest—obviously sadder and wiser, in fact looking properly "stunned"—wanders along the road until he is tapped from behind by the revivified Albatross, still wearing the suction-cup arrow but now carrying a beggar's tin cup. The Wedding Guest drops two coins into the cup, then watches as the bird walks away, presumably to join his nemesis the Mariner on the road, both itinerant opportunities for hapless charitable interlocutors. The final two stanzas of the poem, in which the Mariner turns and goes on his way, are illustrated in a 1/3-page borderless panel by Emerson's caricature of Coleridge himself, quill in hand, completing the poem in a state of laudanum-intoxication.

The poet's wicked grin suggests a conspiracy of satire with the comic book artist, and in fact Emerson seems to have caricatured himself, as well, making a cameo appearance earlier in the text as the drunken Hermit. It is as if the narrative's lurid gothic effects, arcane symbolism, and narrative ambiguities were all part of a plan of self-parodic poetic effects that were merely imitated, illustrated, and exaggerated by Emerson.

The reception of a canonical work is ultimately an uncontrollable process. A work like *The Rime of the Ancient Mariner* (or, to name another example—and one inspired by the *Rime*—Mary Shelley's *Frankenstein*) possesses a sort of super-canonical status, claimed by popular or even mass culture as well as elite intellectual culture, that allows its reception to far exceed its official interpretations by academic critics, the contemporary clerisy. Knowledge of such a work—often through a diverse array of versions and adaptations in various media—functions as a marker of cultural capital for a wide range of readers. Hunt Emerson's parody is aimed at this kind of wide audience, and is enjoyable on a number of levels.

Though he includes the gloss and uses the basic text from 1817, he also makes good use of variants from earlier versions, and, as I have been suggesting, highlights the general gothic tone descended from the 1798 version. In this sense Emerson's comic book is a parody of the composite artifact we might call the vulgate *Rime of the Ancient Mariner*. One of the reasons his parody works so well is that there is a happy consonance between the lurid effects of underground comic book art and the lurid effects of gothic horror balladry, the "gross and violent stimulants" Wordsworth denounced in the culture of his time and which found their way into Coleridge's ballad at its inception. Emerson brings out in high relief precisely those qualities of the *Rime* that Coleridge partly effaced in revision, but which still mark its family resemblance to Bürger's ballads or the plays of Kotzebue, the very qualities that most opened it up to parody in the first place, as Coleridge was well aware.

The Roots of the *Ancient Mariner*: Mystery and Parody

Since John Livingston Lowes' exhaustive study, *The Road to Xanadu*, the question of the sources of the *Ancient Mariner* has become a singularly uninteresting topic, taken on its own.

In this case, however, I am interested in a particular kind of source, exemplified in Gottfried Bürger's "Lenore," which almost everyone agrees was an inspiration for Coleridge's ballad. I am interested less in the private imagination of Coleridge during composition, or in specific intertextual echoes (though they exist, particularly with the translations by Walter Scott), than in the generic family to which the two ballads belong and what this family tie tells us about how the "romantic" qualities of Coleridge's poem would have been perceived by his contemporary audience.

"Lenore" was translated by Thomas Taylor and published in the *Monthly Magazine* for March 1796 (as "Lenora"), whence it "awakened a native strain of 'spook' balladry," in England, as it has been pointed out, "at a time when an interest in gothic horror had reached a peak in both the novel and the drama." The ballad had been imitated in the first place in 1773 from a Scottish original. Walter Scott translated it and reportedly said it inspired him to turn to poetry; it clearly helped to inspire his *Minstrelsy of the Scottish Border* (1803), and reinforced the widespread influence of Percy's *Reliques* and the ballad as a form.

Among a more limited circle of influential writers, "Lenore" was a decisive text. An excited Charles Lamb called it to Coleridge's attention in a letter of 6 July 1796. In the same issue of the *Monthly Magazine* in which his translation appeared Taylor published a note arguing that Bürger's poetry was "singularly fitted to become national popular song" because of his "impetuous diction," and praised his style in terms now recognizably Romantic:

> Bürger is every where distinguished for manly sentiment and force of style. His extraordinary powers of language are founded on a rejection of the conventional phraseology of regular poetry, in favour of popular forms of expression, caught by the listening artist from the voice of agitated nature.

Note that the gothic subjects of Bürger's works are never mentioned here. Instead Taylor stresses the vehicle of his vernacular style in terms that align him with the literature of sensibility—"manly sentiment" expressed in "the voice of agitated nature." Lenore foresees her lover's death in "frightful dreams"and he eventually does return as a revenant to take her away with him. Thinking him dead, she then falls into "furious despair" when he fails to return home from the crusades:

"Go out, go out, my lamp of life;
In endless darkness die:
Without him I must loathe the earth,
Without him scorne the skye."
And so despaire did rave and rage
Athwarte her boiling veins;
Against the Providence of God
She hurlde her impious strains.
She bet her breaste, and wrung her hands,
And rollde her tearlesse eye,
From rise of morne, till the pale stars
Again did freeke the skye.
(sts. 21-23)

The melodramatic passions of horror ballads, like those expressed in this passage, would have been for many contemporary critics subsumed in the larger vogue for sentimental effusions, and both would have been seen as the result of a new dominance in literature of the popular taste.

Coleridge seems to have seen it this way, and to have been deeply ambivalent about the degree to which his own work was implicated in such taste. A February 1797 review of M.G. Lewis's *The Monk* attributed to Coleridge opens by declaring that "The horrible and preternatural have usually seized on the popular taste, at the rise and decline of literature."

Most powerful stimulants, they can never be required except by the torpor of an unawakened, or the languor of an exhausted, appetite. The same phaenomenon, therefore, which we hail as a favourable omen in the *belles lettres* of Germany, impresses a degree of gloom in the compositions of our countrymen. We trust, however, that satiety will banish what good sense should have prevented; and that, wearied with fiends, incomprehensible characters, with shrieks, murders, and subterraneous dungeons, the public will learn, by the multitude of the manufacturers, with how little expense of thought or imagination this species of composition is manufactured. But, cheaply as we estimate romances in general, we acknowledge, in the work before us, the offspring of no common genius.

Though he decries the proliferation of such "powerful stimulants" (foreshadowing Wordsworth's attack in the Preface to *Lyrical Ballads*) and suggests they represent a decline in taste in England, he values this movement more highly in the German context, perhaps even hinting that it is the novelistic form—"romances in general"—that he particularly regrets; poetry may be another matter. And Coleridge goes on to praise *The Monk*, including its embedded gothic tale of the bleeding nun and the character of the Wandering Jew—extremely romantic devices. Coleridge's own professed weariness with gothic conventions cannot be taken at face value as his final or unambivalent judgment on the value of sentimental and romantic writing, but he did profess such weariness. One month after this review appeared, he wrote to William Lisle Bowles:

indeed I am almost weary of the Terrible, having been an hireling in the Critical Review for these last six or eight months—I have been lately reviewing the Monk, the Italian, Hubert de Sevrac & &c & &c—in all of which dungeons, and old castles, & solitary Houses by the Sea Side, & Caverns, & Woods, & extraordinary characters, & all the tribe of Horror & Mystery, have crowded on me—even to surfeiting.—

If Coleridge was indeed becoming surfeited with "Horror and Mystery" in early 1797, it is likely because he had been devouring it over the past year—in order to prepare the reviews, as he implies in this letter, but also in pursuit of his own taste. A self-protective irony seems during these months to accompany a submersion in popular romantic literature, so decisive to the production of his so-called Mystery Poems. Here is a chronology of significant events: Bürger's "Lenore" appears (translated by Taylor) in March 1796 and Lamb and Coleridge correspond about it; less than one year later Coleridge writes the review and letter quoted above. Shortly thereafter (within months) he composes *The Rime of the Ancient Mariner* and begins to conceive of the *Lyrical Ballads* collection with Wordsworth.

In fact, during this same time Coleridge published a collection of sentimental effusions (as sonnets were seen at the time) by himself, Lamb, and Lloyd, and then, shortly thereafter, parodied this very form himself in the *Monthly Magazine*, the same venue in which such sentimental poetry was often printed, and in which "Lenore" had appeared the previous spring. In the letter to Joseph Cottle (ca. November 1797) in which he first reveals that he has written *The Rime of the Ancient Mariner*—"a ballad of about 300 lines"—he also says that he sent to the *Monthly Magazine* three mock Sonnets in ridicule of my own, & Charles Lloyd's, & Lamb's, &c &c—in ridicule of that affectation of unaffectedness, of jumping & misplaced accent on common-place epithets, flat lines forced into poetry by Italics (signifying how well & *mouthis[h]ly* the Author could read them, puny pathos &c &c—the instances are almost all taken from mine & Lloyd's poems—-I signed them Nehemiah Higginbottom. I think they may do good to our young Bards.—

These three "Sonnets, attempted in the Manner of Contemporary Writers" are apt parodies of the exaggerated simplicity and sentimental effusion that had recently been so much in vogue in Coleridge's own circle. It has been pointed out that the first poem works best as a self-parody.

PENSIVE at eve on the hard world I mused,
And my poor heart was sad; so at the MOON
I gazed, and sighed, and sighed; for ah how soon
Eve saddens into night! mine eyes perused
With tearful vacancy the dampy grass
That wept and glitter'd in the paly ray:
And I did pause me on my lonely way
And mused me on the wretched ones that pass
Oe'r the bleak heath of sorrow. But alas!
Most of myself I thought! when it befel,
That the soothe spirit of the breezy wood
Breath'd in mine ear: "All this is very well,

But much of ONE thing, is for NO thing good."
Oh my poor heart's INEXPLICABLE SWELL!

This is funny in several ways, beginning with the "mouthish" italics which Coleridge explicitly called attention to. The limp surprise of "myself" in line 10, the sententiousness with which cliché is dispensed as if from the oracle in the quoted passage in lines 12-13, all contribute to a sharp satire on the gloomy narcissism, "breezy" pantheism, melodramatic sentiment, and exaggerated treatment of trivial things common in this poetry of romantic sensibility.

In the *Biographia Literaria* Coleridge cited these self-parodies as if in self-defence, in the midst of a discussion of what makes Milton's or Shakespeare's texts "*essential poetry*". He admits that he had earlier "adopted a laborious and florid diction," but implies that he has now moved beyond such youthful romantic excess:

Every reform, however necessary, will by weak minds be carried to an excess, that itself will need reforming. The reader will excuse me for noticing, that I myself was the first to expose *risu honesto* [with honest laughter] the three sins of poetry, one or the other of which is the most likely to beset a young writer. So long ago as the publication of the second number of the Monthly Magazine, under the name of NEHEMIAH HIGGINBOTTOM I contributed three sonnets, the first of which had for its object to excite a good-natured laugh at the spirit of *doleful egotism*, and at the recurrence of favourite phrases, with the double defect of being at once trite, and licentious....

He then reprints the sonnets so the reader can see the evidence of his own skill at parody. "I myself was the first," Coleridge here claims, thus situating himself as the premiere parodist of the youthful romanticism so many had found so risible. This amounts to revisionist literary history in the guise of autobiography, a pre-emptive or talismanic self-parody protecting him against other parodies, then and now. In yet another such gesture, he appends an anecdote to the note containing the parodic sonnets, telling of an amateur versifier who claimed to have written a "severe epigram" on the *Ancient*

Mariner. The joke is on the foolish would-be parodist, however, when Coleridge reveals to his readers that "to my no less surprise than amusement, it proved to be one which I had myself some time before written and inserted in the *Morning Post*."

To the Author of the Ancient Mariner.
Your poem must eternal be,
'Dear sir! it cannot fail,
'For 'tis incomprehensible
'And without head or tail.
(I, 28)

The act of telling the story is itself satiric, and reclaiming his authorship of the epigram returns the advantage to Coleridge of course, but this is nothing compared to the original act of writing the parodies. This footnote uses the press for the purposes of public relations, a parody of the puffery then common, in which authors or their literary agents would write the early reviews of their own works. Even in this small way satirizing himself in public only enhances Coleridge's reputation as someone worth satirizing. Most significantly, the humorous focus of the epigram is on the canonical status of the poem in question—which is linked (however humorously) to its opaque and incomprehensible qualities.

The *Biographia* is a self-promotional work, but it is also a self-parodic purge in the pursuit of a more mature style and reputation. By reprinting the sonnets and his own satiric epigram—then staking the claim to have been the first to parody his own youthful indiscretions—Coleridge places himself in 1817 on a plane far above such flaws of sentimentality. In fact, "doleful egotism" and excess in diction were charges that continued to be leveled against Coleridge's poetry, as was incomprehensibility. The revisionism of these passage works by exaggerating the differences between then and now, the 1796-98 and 1817, in order to elevate the latter as a new era giving rise to a new species of poetry in Coleridge's oeuvre.

The Rime of the Ancient Mariner was open to the same sort of charges Coleridge leveled at the sonnets. There is a general consensus by about 1817 that the romantic excesses of the Lake School as a group consisted in "sickly sentimentality," the tendency "to invest trifling subjects with an air and expression of great importance and interest," and to use vernacular language in exaggerated ways, "expressions which are merely vulgar or ridiculous"—all these terms come from an 1817 review of *The Rime of the Ancient Mariner* as it appeared in *Sibylline Leaves*. From his self-parodic stance, Coleridge is well aware of all this. I would argue that even in 1797 he was writing romantic poetry with an ironic edge, a self-conscious hint of the self-parodic tendencies of such writings. The Higginbottom sonnets attest to this, but it is also discernible *from within* Coleridge's romantic poetry, as the reviewer quoted above seems half-consciously to recognize. Speaking of the *Rime of the Ancient Mariner*, he says that it "has always appeared to us in the light of a very good caricature of the genius of its author."

> It displays, in fact, all the strength and all the weakness, all the extravagances and eccentricities, all the bold features, and peculiar grimace, if we may so express ourselves, of his intellectual physiognomy, and in forming an opinion respecting the talents which he possesses, this composition may serve the very same purpose which an overcharged drawing of a countenance could answer ....

The Nehemiah Higginbottom sonnets merely reveal the degree to which Coleridge was prepared to parody before being parodied, even while producing his highly caricaturable romantic poetry of 1797-1800. This tendency to self-parody as a self-protective—but also canon-forming—gesture was perhaps most systematically pursued in the strategic self-representations of 1816-17, which culminated in the revisions and revisionist self-editing of *Sibylline Leaves* and the *Biographia Literaria*. The revisions of *The Rime of the Ancient Mariner* substitute what is really a new poem—with a number of revisions including the added gloss and its layered effects, and in a new context as an independent poem published as the work of S. T. Coleridge—for the German-influenced horror ballad published in the 1798 collection. In each case satiric and parodic modes come to the aid of revisionist taste-making, helping Coleridge (and he hopes his readers) to make canon-defining distinctions.

It is as if Coleridge first moved into and found himself occupying the same cultural niche as Bürger, Southey, the "minor" Wordsworth—the Nehemiah Higginbottoms of the period's fashionably sentimental literature—and then set about destroying the competition, exaggerating distinctions in order in effect to define a new species of poetic achievement to dominate that romantic niche: eventually, this species of poetry came to be identified as Coleridgean Romanticism. Purged through self-parody and the parody of others of weaker strains, elevated through theory and a ubiquitous layered hermeneutic contextualization, this is romantic writing more philosophical, transcendent, self-aware, serious—in a word, more worthy of the canon than mere popular "'spook' balladry" could ever hope to be. It remains resilient and thus dominant in part through a self-generated openness to parody from within and without, which, as Coleridge himself pointed out, in the due course of time and canonization, is one way to turn satire into encomium.

Chapter 10

Aftermaths of Classicism in Wordsworth and Coleridge

In *Romantic Aversions*, J. Douglas Kneale argues with an engaging combination of learning and rhetorical pyrotechnics that 'there is a deep strain of classicism in ... the very origins of Romanticism itself.' For Kneale, 'aftermaths' of the classical tradition are traceable not only in such work as Wordsworth's 'Laodamia' or in the Romantic Hellenism of second-generation poets, but in a pervasive 'textual attitude toward classicism and neoclassicism'—and especially toward the classical rhetorical tradition—that 'at once incorporates repetition and difference, occupation and aversion, in a mutually assured contestation.'

Romantic turnings away from classical rhetoric are read here as 'double gestures' in which the essential characteristic of repression (in Freud's terms, a 'turning something away' that also 'keeps' the thing at a distance) is figured rhetorically in an *aversio* (or apostrophe), a 'turning from' that is also an *occupatio*, or a dwelling upon.

Classical rhetoric is the 'other' that 'Romanticism at once turns to and away from,' an 'other' that hangs around in the poetry of Wordsworth and Coleridge in what Kneale wittily calls 'haunted figures.' Kneale's method of flushing these haunted figures from their hiding places is deeply indebted to Geoffrey Hartman, as is acknowledged early and late in the book.

The preface says that, if the book has a *genius loci*, it is Hartman. The last chapter is a reprint of Kneale's 1996 *homage*,

'Gentle Hearts and Hands: Reading Wordsworth after Geoffrey Hartman' (published in *Studies in Romanticism*). In that essay, an exhilarating reading of Wordsworth's 'Nutting,' Kneale gives an exemplary performance of what he calls his 'quest-romance' style of interpretation.

'Close readers,' he writes, 'know the "lucky words" in a text, the ones that, when the critical imagination double-clicks on them, open an interpretive window or"'magic casement" onto literary history.' Tracking 'intertextual nodes from poem to poem,' along a 'tantalizing but tenuous' pathway through Milton, Spenser, Dante, Virgil, and Ariosto, Kneale's prose crackles with the thrill of the chase, as when he pauses to wonder whether his interpretation threatens to 'make more ado about "Nutting"' than has been made before.

For Kneale, the key questions are not 'what is this text about?' or 'what does this text do?' but 'what else is this poem like? What is that a repetition-with-a-difference of?' In the remaining seven chapters of the book, three of which have previously been published, Kneale's questioning quest leads him into some fascinating places. Two essays reconsider Wordsworth's use of key figures. In Chapter One—'Apostrophe Reconsidered'—Kneale combines an historically informed corrective to Jonathan Culler's confusion about the nature of apostrophe—it is not simply address, but movement or shift of address that constitutes apostrophe—with a brilliant reading of Wordsworth's 'There Was a Boy.' The essay gives new rhetorical legs to Hartman's well-known statement that 'the life of Wordsworth's lines is often uneasy as if somewhere else.'

Kneale shows how—and how frequently—Wordsworth's voice travels by apostrophe, arguing convincingly that 'voice in Wordsworth cannot be ... halted in one place for long; it is always on the move.' In Chapter 3, a reconsideration of Wordsworth's supposed rejection of prosopopoeia, the focus is Book 2 of the *Prelude* and Wordsworth's humanizing of nature in compensation for the early loss of his mother. Reading these passages as 'pitched against an eighteenth-century literary fashion,' Kneale sees Wordsworth reclaiming prosopopoeia by giving 'a human shape to a *rhetoric*, and not just an abstraction, that had become mechanical'.

Three more chapters also focus on Wordsworth. Chapter 5, 'Transport and Persuasion in Longinus and Wordsworth,' like Chapter 1, is valuable for its clarification of an often confused set of terms in the rhetorical tradition as well as for its treatment of Wordsworth's place in that tradition. In it, Kneale makes playful use of the distinction between rhetorical persuasion and sublime 'transport' in reading Wordsworth's sonnet against one kind of 'transport[ation]'—'On the Projected Kendal and Windermere Railway.' Chapter 6 discusses the place of Wordsworth's largely overlooked 1833 tour poems on the Isle of Man as explorations of the relationship of genre and geography, situating these late poems 'as topoi—that is, both literal places and figural commonplaces' in Wordsworth's 'imaginative itinerary.'

In another particularly strong essay, Kneale describes in Chapter 7 the rhetorical operation of the binary trope of 'symptom' and 'scene' developed by Freud in 'The Aetiology of Hysteria' to show how Freud and Wordsworth 'use and put into question the binary oppositions on which their analytic model,' whether therapeutic or autobiographical, depends. In a close reading of the 'slow-moving boat' simile (*Prelude* 4.256-72) focusing especially on that passage's use of chiasmus, Kneale shows that for Wordsworth, as for Freud, the interpretation of the surface—of symptom or sign—when traced along a figural path toward its psychical ground or scene, 'always keeps reaching what looks like a limit.' Here Paul de Man, the *genius loci* of Kneale's earlier book, *Monumental Writing* (1988), comes to the fore: 'You never actually reach a limit, however; the ground or bottom repeatedly falls away so that even the final or primal scene is rendered textually.' The scene, then, like its symptom, 'is always a scene of reading.'

The chapter uses such insights to question Alan Liu's positing of a vertical relation of history, nature, and self, in which history is the 'rock bottom' or 'base,' and the 'nature' and 'self' of Wordsworth's journey of self discovery are the symptoms of history's denial (*Wordsworth: The Sense of History* [1989]). Kneale asks, what if Wordsworth's hermeneutic were less a journey of discovery, seeking the ground of interpretation, than a tour? What if we were to read Wordsworth not according to the archeologically based, vertically binary assumptions of surface and depth that 'discovery' implies, but according to an 'economy of difference' and a hermeneutic in which all is 'surface and not depth,' a scene of constant crossing and re-crossing of scene and symptom, event and sign? 'If the hermeneutic in Wordsworth's poetry *is* a voyage of discovery,' Kneale argues, 'it is a discovery that discovers it is really a tour, and Wordsworth forever the tourist, the *spectator ab extra*.'

Both of the chapters on Coleridge are essays published here for the first time. Chapter 2 explores the generic betweenness of the 'Effusion' in Coleridge's *Poems on Various Subjects* (1796), showing how these peculiar works, precursors of the 'conversation poem,' map out a territory between poetry and oratory, between the private and public voice. In 'Coleridge's Emergent Occasion: "To the Autumnal Moon"' (Chapter 4), Kneale explores the 'rhetorical enthusiasm' of Coleridge's early poetry, and especially such moments of exclamatory 'puffing' as are on display in 'Effusion XVIII'—'Mild Splendour of the various-vested Night! / Mother of wildly-working visions! hail!' Under Kneale's analysis, such passages turn out to contain 'something quite original.' They are moments of 'rhetorical *invention* or *heuresis*,' in which the reader has a 'sense of poetic genius breaking through the 'swell and glitter' of conventional rhetoric to wonder at itself and itself be wondered at.' In such moments of discovery, or self-discovery, 'invention becomes its own topos.' We watch as Coleridge 'bares the device' and 'shows us a mind in the act of finding what rhetoric will suffice.'

The Coleridge chapters are good enough to make one wish for more. The disproportion in the treatment of the two poets—only two of eight chapters on one of the two poets given equal billing in the sub-title—is the only real disappointment of Kneale's book. It would be especially valuable to have much more consideration of exactly those points on which Wordsworth and Coleridge might be seen as diverging in their relation to rhetorical traditions, or of specific moments of aversion, (pre)occupation, and rhetorical haunting in each poet's intertextual relation with the other. But surely a writer as well-versed in rhetoric as is Kneale knows that there are worse things than leaving readers wanting more.

Chris Koenig-Woodyard

The pictographic arrangement of "text" and "sex" in the title of this article embodies my critical focus as well as my methodology. The typographic intersection of "text" and "sex" emblematises my bibliographic reading of the friction between sexuality and textuality in contemporary parodies of Coleridge's "Christabel" (1816). Where sex and text cross paths, a fruitful scene of interpretation emerges. In this critical space, sexuality is an arena of interpretive conflict between two groups of readers: contemporary parodists and the Coleridge family. The former attempts to more closely align the supernatural and sexual poles of the poem, while the latter endeavours to textually and editorially robe the sexually suggestive elements of "Christabel."

The friction between sexuality and textuality is the result of the rub—the contact—between the poem's oral and textual transmission and the corpus of criticism that has attended "Christabel" for more than 180 years.

From William Hazlitt in 1816 to Camille Paglia in the 1980s to Laura Adams in 1998, readers of "Christabel" have been alternately intrigued and aggrieved by the sexual and gothic representations of the Christabel-Geraldine relationship. There is "something disgusting at the bottom of [Coleridge's] subject," Hazlitt declares; while Paglia reprimands humanistic scholarship for its failure to engage what she sees as the poem's "blatant lesbian pornography." And in her novel *Christabel*, Adams transports Coleridge's poem to the late twentieth century, exploring the gradual evolution of the love affair between Christabel and Dina (Geraldine).

But to suggest that there has been a point of contact between textual study of the poem and the near-200 year corpus of commentary over-states the case. Critics have invested little energy in consideration of the connections between the poem's transmission and reception history and various textual witnesses' depictions of the Christabel-Geraldine relationship. In unpacking the sexual and gothic elements of "Christabel," critics have been largely silent about the relationship between the poem's textual history and sexual interpretations.

This inattention is problematic; the result is that a significant element of the poem's textual and critical history has been neglected: Coleridge's attempts to counter and suppress the sexual (even lesbian) code of "Christabel" that contemporary parodists expose and ridicule.

Chapter 11

The "Christabel" Parodies

Between 1816 and 1832, no less than seven verse parodies of "Christabel" were published. The parodies, considered in combination with the 15 "Christabel" continuations published between 1815 and 1909, position the poem as one of Coleridge's most often emulated works in the nineteenth century. The appeal of Coleridge's poem is its incompletion: only two of a projected five Parts were written. The poem's frustrated entelechy hampers interpretation but invites speculation and continuation.

The conventions of the gothic romance allow us to conjecture the future course of the three unwritten Parts: a "fairy tale" resolution may be proposed—the disruptive, supernatural Geraldine is exposed and expelled, for instance, and a moral, Christian, heterosexual order is restored to the world of Langdale Hall. Christabel and "her lover that's far away" reunite and marry. This, of course, matters little to the parodists.

"Christabel" parodists follow few, if any, rules and conventions, which is the very point of parody. Literary parody is not simply parasitic—as the common image of the mechanisms of parody leads us to believe. As a negotiating metaphor of parody, the parasitic is of limited value. In the case of "Christabel," the full structure of the trope (a parasite connected to and dependent upon a host text) misconstrues parody's invasive power. Parodies of "Christabel" operate on a molecular level, entering into and intermingling with the flesh and bone of the poem.

Of the "Christabel" parodies, the first is the most

incisive. The anonymous *Christabess* appeared soon after "Christabel" in 1816, and the volume's title page provides a telling glimpse into the anonymous parodist's handling of Coleridge's poem. The title *Christabess* brings to mind the ophidian imagery of "Christabel"—Bard Bracy's dream of a snake coiled around the neck of a dove, as well as Geraldine's snake-like eyes. The onomatopoeic ending of the suffix "bess" also recalls Christabel's snake-like hissing in Part II: she "drew in her breath with a hissing sound" and "Shudder'd aloud, with a hissing sound".

But "bess" also deflates the aristocratic substructure that informs the poem's gothic conventions, perhaps cutting up the religious title "Abess," just as it brings to mind milk maids—who were, by 1816 in the history of English literature, commonly named "Bess." Christabess, unlike Christabel, is not the daughter of a noble-man: *Christabess* transforms Sir Leoline into "Tom Bottomly, the Tinker Fat". Too, as a short form of "Elizabeth," the suffix puts Queen Elizabeth and prostitutes into the same breath; both were colloquially referred to as "Bess."

The ironically derogatory subtitle—"a right Woeful Poem, Translated from the Doggerel by Sir Vinegar Sponge"—is also noteworthy. The Old English typeface of "Woeful Poem" bibliographically ridicules Coleridge's poem, exaggerating the Cloister Black typeface of the half title page of the 1816 "Christabel." Moreover, the exaggerated and embellished Old English typeface of "Woeful Poem" lampoons Christabel's "woes" (190, 233, 317). The phrase recalls Wordsworth's emphasis on the "woe" (the "rueful woes") of "Christabel" in *The Prelude*. In *Christabess*, content and typography intersect—the physical appearance of the typeface (with its air of antiquity) intimates the medieval setting of "Christabel" while "woeful" hints at the recurring gothic atmosphere of distress in Coleridge's poem.

Christabess displays a heightened awareness of the physical appearance of the 1816 "Christabel" volume, parodying not only the typography but also the poem's larger section divisions (preface, two Parts, and two Conclusions) as well as more minute details of diction and imagery. The preface, for example, closely copies Coleridge's. Christabess maintains Coleridge's pre-emptive strike against anticipated charges of plagiarism, while the historical and geographical circumstances of composition are altered for comic effect. Coleridge's comments on the originality of "Christabel" are exaggerated, presenting the poet as boastfully self-important—even, as unwittingly courting hubris:

> I have now only to insist that the metre of Christabess is perfectly regular, although I am aware not one of my readers will find it so; but they will instantly attribute it to their own shallowness of intellect, when they are informed that I have, out of my profundity of genius, entirely created a new system of my own.

The indented lines in the opening of the Conclusion to Part I (a recapitulation of the Part I scene of Christabel praying beneath the oak tree)—

It was a lovely sight to see
The lady Christabel, when she
Was praying at the old oak tree.
Amid the jagged shadows
Of mossy leafless boughs,
Kneeling in the moonlight,
To make her gentle vows;
Her slender palms together prest;
Heaving sometimes on her breast. (279-87)

—are reproduced in Christabess, while Coleridge's verse is collapsed into bathetic half-rhymes:

O goodly sight! I fancy yet
I see the lovely Christa' sit
Beneath the tree to rest a bit,
And see her head recline
Upon her little fist,
And see the moon-beams shine
Upon her heaving breast
O gentle sighs that swell her breast,
And almost seem her sash to burst!

The references to nudity in these lines may also be

explained—and more clearly historically grounded—by the title page of Christabess. The presence of the publisher's name—"J. Duncombe"—hints at the Christabess parodist's risqué treatment of "Christabel." The London publisher John Duncombe was known as "a purveyor of middle-class erotica." Duncombe's catalogue includes many collections of bawdy and sexually charged bar-room songs. Christabess fits right in. The parody is a physically and sexually graphic reworking of the Christabel (Christabess) and Geraldine (Adelaide) relationship.

Christabess charges the bedroom scene of "Christabel" with a voyeuristic sexual electricity. The parody freights the scene of Geraldine embracing Christabel in Part I with sexually suggestive terms and imagery:

And, lo! the worker of the spell
Hugs the maid, and sleepest well;
Sleepest—or else she seems to sleep,
Like a Ram beside a Sheep.

Combined, the em dash hesitant syntax of the line "Sleepest—or else she seems to sleep" and the simile "like a Ram beside a Sheep" convey sexual activity. The simile recalls Iago's comment about Desdemona to her father, Barbantio, early in Othello, when Iago describes Othello as "an old black ram... tupping your white ewe.". Adelaide's hair, it is worth noting, is "black and long," and "coal black"; Christabess's legs are "snow white".

The innuendo of Christabess quickly turns into voyeuristic romp, as Christabess watches Adelaide undress:

...she sat upon her bum,
And peep'd behind the curtain sly;
And in the corner of the room,
There she saw the maid untie
A piece of hempen cord, that bound
her alabaster belly round!
Down dropt her shift, and——O dear me!
She's naked!—naked!!—naked!!!—see!—
But, reader, turn away your view,
She's not to sleep with me or you.

Christabess apes Coleridge's technique of indirect description in "Christabel," by instructing the reader to "turn away." In the 1816 "Christabel," readers are not given a view of Geraldine undressing; rather,

Her silken robe, and inner vest,
Dropt to her feet, and full in view,
Behold! her bosom and half her side—
—A sight to dream of, not to tell!
And she is to sleep by Christabel.

Voyeurism in Christabess soon leads to sexual interaction. Echoing Geraldine's spell—"In the touch of this bosom there worketh a spell" —Adelaide casts one of her own: "In the tip of this titty there dwelleth a charm". The two women fall asleep, and dreaming, Christabess'

eye in anguish roves,
Like a little Gipsey witch,
With her lover in a ditch,
Who cries thro' fear of what she loves.
And if she lay there quietly,
Perchance it is because that he,
Having been there with her before,
Cannot fright her any more.

The language is that of sexual violation, but the narrator of Christabess anticipates and plays with such a sexual interpretation:

Was this the fate of her I sing?
O gentle reader, no such thing!
Think'st thou she bent to lawless will?
No, reader, she's a virgin still.

The handling of the bedroom scene of "Christabel" in Christabess is characteristic of the parody's brand of satire—a facetious manipulation of the events and figures of "Christabel" and of Colèridge's language. For example, after several drams of gin (the "wild flower wine" of "Christabel" comically distilled in Christabess), Adelaide sinks by the bed-post: "Oh she was lovely, sweet, and plump, / Egad—and such a noble rump!". The author of Christabess ironically ascribes to Adelaide a physical characteristic more suited to

Christabess, given her last name of "Bottomly." And Bard Bracy's dream descends into the ridiculous, as "Billy Brown" tells of a snake "wound" around the neck of a "dying duck" under an old oak tree. Unable to separate the snake and duck, the "snake, duck, and all sunk in the ground." Billy recounts that, then, there "came a voice" that told him "to mark the spot where stood my foot" by the oak tree; he comments that while "I thought I mark'd the spot," he, upon waking, "found I'd mark'd the bed".

Similarly absurd is the treatment of Coleridge's Conclusion to Part II. Christabess is unique among "Christabel" parodies in offering a full parody of the Conclusion. Coleridge's "little child, a limber elf, / Singing, dancing to itself" (656-57) is transformed into

A little chubby, funny brat,
Bellowing after this and that—
A plaguesome thing with blubber'd cheeks
That always gabbles—never speaks;
And while it makes its mother glad,
Drives its father almost mad,
That he enraged in language keen,
Vents threats which he can never mean.
"Hah—hold your tongue, and waddle off,
"Or else I'll cut your doodle off,"
Perhaps, sometimes, a pretty maid,
If hid from view, is not afraid
To dally, play, and feel a charm
In little things that do no harm;
It may, perhaps, be very pretty,
To tickle fancy with a whim,
To figure Love, or fancy Pity,
Until the eyes in tear-drops swim.
But, ah! such hearts are seldom seen—
Such pretty giddiness is gone;
Each only feels for number one,
Not even that, except in pain.

Christabess seeks to clarify the Conclusion to Part II with

a reading that highlights domestic and parental themes. In the case of Christabess, however, the lines offer a literal rendition of the paradoxically violent language of parental affection—"A very metaphysical account of Fathers calling their children rogues, rascals, & little varlets— —&tc— —," as Coleridge describes it. It is difficult to say if Coleridge was aware of Christabess and the "little chubby, funny brat." Walter Hamilton suggests that Coleridge "quoted [Christabess] as an admirable parody," but there is no evidence to support such a claim. More than likely, Hamilton may be confusing Christabess with a parody that appeared in Blackwood's in 1819.

Two other parodies of "Christabel" appeared in 1816. Unlike the unknown Christabess author, James Hogg offers more tonally subdued parodies of "Christabel" in The Poetic Mirror. As an anonymous reviewer in the Augustan Review remarks, Hogg's "The Cherub" and "Isabelle" tackle "the raving doggerel and wretched prose of 'Christabel,' and the glitter and rapturous fancies of the early poetry of the author."

The resemblances between "Christabel" and "The Cherub" are stylistic—and, generally, minor. Modelled upon Coleridge's largely anapestic tetrameter, "The Cherub" presents a female angel who physically resembles Christabel. Like "Christabel", the Cherub is "beauteous," and the Cherub's hair ("ringlets of wavy gold") recalls Christabel's "ringlet curl".

"Isabelle," on the other hand, draws heavily upon "Christabel." Structurally, it resembles a Part and Conclusion of "Christabel"—in Hogg's case, 138 lines. The parody is characterised by a shifting, even wandering, narrative perspective. At one point, for example, the events of the poem seem to be glimpsed through the eyes of the deceased, and, at another, through the eyes of a dog. Where *Christabess* satirically and sexually excoriates "Christabel," "Isabelle" is more tonally restrained—preferring a less sarcastic approach that apes yet gently mocks Coleridge's style.

Coleridge's "mastiff bitch," for example, becomes a "cut-tail'd whelp":

What ails that little cut-tail'd whelp,

That it continues to yelp, yelp?
Yelp, yelp, and it turns its eye
Up to the tree and half to the sky,
Half to the sky, and full to the ground.

Hogg displays an interest in Coleridge's portrayal of the supernatural, and particularly of the perception of the presence of the supernatural in the natural world, by focussing on the process of question and answer that strives phenomenologically to draw readers into the poem's events as they unfold (a topic that I shall return to). In "Isabelle," as in "Christabel," gothic atmosphere, suspense, and mystery are generated through a series of questions and answers:

Can there be a moon in the heaven to-night,
That the hill and the grey cloud seem so light?
The air is whitened by some spell,
For there is no moon, I know it well.

Hogg applies this technique more generally in "Isabelle," as well, demonstrating an interest in Coleridge's construction of simile and its relationship to the development of setting. Describing a cloud, for example, Hogg enacts the process of matching the cloud with a like object:

There is a cloud that seems to hover,
By western hill the church-yard over,
What is it like?—'Tis like a whale;
'Tis like a shark with half a tail,
Not half, but third or more,
Now 'tis a wolf, and now a boar.

Here, Hogg apes Hamlet. Following the player's rehearsal, the scene closes with a brief exchange between Polonius and Hamlet, as the madness-feigning prince stalls Polonius's message from Gertrude for an immediate interview:

Hamlet. Do you see yonder cloud that's almost in the shape of a camel?

Polonius. By th' mass and 'tis—like a camel indeed

Hamlet. Methinks it is like a weasel.

Polonius. It is backed like a weasel.

Hamlet. Or like a whale.

Polonius. Very like a whale.

Hamlet. Then I will come to my mother by and by. (III.II.376-83)

Hogg figures Coleridge as Polonius—an unimaginative fool, easily swayed. The passage is typical of Hogg's style throughout "Isabelle"—as he pokes fun at, rather than scourges "Christabel" and Coleridge.

A more sarcastic treatment of "Christabel" appeared in the June 1819 issue of Blackwood's. "Christabel, Part Third" is signed "Morgan O'Doherty," the regular Blackwood's pseudonym of the Irish journalist and poet William Maginn (although the name was an occasional aegis for other Blackwood's writers). "Christabel, Part Third" is not by Maginn, however, but by the Musselburgh physician and writer David Macbeth Moir.

Coleridge found "Christabel, Part Third" funny—as Thomas Allsop records:

I laughed heartily at the continuation in Blackwood, which I have been told is by Maginn: it is in appearance and in appearance only, a good imitation; I do not doubt but that it gave more pleasure, and to a greater number, than a continuation by myself in the spirit of the first two cantos.

Coleridge conveys as much to William Blackwood in a letter of 30 June 1819. Prompted by reports that the parody displeased him, Coleridge was eager to set the record straight:

A very slight personal acquaintance with me would have enabled the Editor to take for granted that I should not be offended with the droll Christabelliad. None of Mr O'Doherty's readers will peruse it with less pain, few with greater pleasure. I should indeed be wanting both to myself and to common-sense if I did not regard it as a compliment, and that of no ordinary kind, for, not to mention the names with which my own stands in juxtaposition, it would be strange if a man of O'Doherty's undoubted genius should have employed so much wit, humour, and general power of mind on a work wholly without worth or character.

Let only no poison of personal moral calumny be inserted, and a good laugh is a good thing; and I should be sorry by making a wry face, to transfer it from the Lady Christabel to myself. An appreciative response by Moir to Coleridge's letter appeared in the July issue of Blackwood's. This congenial atmosphere is surprising, given Moir's caustic handling of Coleridge and "Christabel," and given Blackwood's opinions of "Christabel" after 1819. A 1821 Blackwood's piece, for example, again by "Morgan O'Doherty," included a proleptic obituary of "Christabel" that called for Coleridge to write his friends of the death of "Christabel": "he must, without delay,scribble four dozen of letters, inviting his friends to her funeral,—let him employ a patent coffin, as she is a restless and unruly subject."

For Moir, Coleridge is equally a "restless and unruly subject." Coleridge is a deranged poet and philosopher capable of composing only when dreaming:

Listen! ye know that I am mad,
And ye will listen!—wizard dreams
Were with me!—all is true that seems!—
From dreams alone can truth be had—
In dreams divinest lore is taught,
For the eye, no more distraught,
Rests most calmly, and the ear,
Of sound unconscious, may apply
Its attributes unknown, to hear
The music of philosophy!
Thus I am wisest in my sleep,
For thoughts and things, which day-light brings,
Come to the spirit sad and single,
But verse and prose, and joys and woes
Inextricably mingle,
When the hushed frame is silent in repose!

In the background of Moir's comments on dreams are the preface to "Kubla Khan," and Biographia Literaria—the latter published two years before "Christabel, Part Third," and reviewed unfavourably in Blackwood's. In his critique of Bertram in chapter 23 of Biographia Literaria, Coleridge discusses the power of the poet to open readers to "dramatic possibilit[ies]"—that is, to the fantastical and the supernatural, to "the wildest tales of ghosts, wizards, genii, and secret talisman." Coleridge writes that "the poet does not require us to be awake and believe; he solicits us only to yield to a dream; and this too with our eyes open."

Here, dreaming furnishes Coleridge with a metaphor to describe the phenomenological process by which readers can be drawn into the fictive and linguistic worlds of literature. The dream metaphor (and Coleridge's more general use of dreaming as an explanatory metaphor in Biographia Literaria) informs Moir's sardonic attitude toward Coleridge's claims for compositions like "Kubla Khan" that came to him while sleeping. A result of such dream-inspired composition is that Coleridge's writings are indecipherable, mixing prose and poetry unsuccessfully and "inextricably."

"Christabel" is similarly disparaged by Moir. He scores the gothic opening of "Christabel" as a Babel-like cacophony that moves from the antiphonal exchange of tolling clock and clamouring animals to a lone lowing cow:

One—Two—Three—Four—Five—Six—Seven—Eight—Nine—Ten—Eleven!—

Tempest or calm—moonshine or shower,
The castle clock still tolls the hour,
And the cock awakens, and echoes the sound,
And is answered by the owls around—
And at every measured tone
You may hear the old baron grunt and groan;
'Tis a thing of wonder, and fright, and fear,
The mastiff-bitch's moans to hear—
And the aged cow in her stall that stands
And is milked each morning by female hands
(That the baron's breakfast of milk and bread
May be brought betimes to the old man's bed
Who often gives, while he is dressing,
His Christabel a father's blessing.)
That aged cow, as each stroke sounds slow,
Answers it with a plaintive low!

Moir deflates the gothic atmosphere (the "fright" and "fear") that opens "Christabel" with innocuous imagery: a dairy cow, and a parenthetical glimpse into the daily domestic routine of Langdale Hall. It is a strategy typical of "Christabel, Part Third" as Moir derides the mystery and suspense of Coleridge's poem by grounding the supernatural elements of "Christabel" in the banal and the ordinary.

But Moir's treatment of "Christabel" is also lascivious. There is a strong current of sexual scandal, as Christabel is impregnated by Geraldine (who, we learn, is a man in disguise):

As she wandered down the dell
None said 'twas the lady Christabel.—
Some thought 'twas a weird and ugsome elf,
Some deemed 'twas the sick old Baron himself,
(For his shape below was wide to see
All bloated with the hydropsie.)
Thy cheek is pale, thy locks are wild—
Ah, think, how big thou art with child!—
For who that saw that child of thine
Pale Christabel, who could divine
That its sire was the Ladie Geraldine?

Ironically, in presenting Christabel as pregnant, Moir situates "Christabel" as a thematic (yet chronologically antecedent) rejoinder to one of the literary works that Coleridge's poem influenced: John Polidori's The Vampyre—first published in the New Monthly Magazine in 1819. The impregnation of "Christabel" recalls Lord Strongmore's seduction of Miss Aubrey. After "gain[ing] her affections," the vampire Strongmore reminds Aubrey's brother—who attempts to thwart the marriage between Strongmore and his sister—that "your sister is dishonoured." The portrait of Christabel impregnated by a man marks the extreme of Moir's spoof of "Christabel."

The events of "Christabel, Part Third"—ranging from the domestic and innocuous to the sexually and supernaturally shocking—are governed by a narrative of gothic distress, and in particular by the tale of Christabel, a damsel in distress, as she wanders the woods late at night. Moir stands "Christabel" upon its head, closing the parody with a ghost-like Christabel:

Does thou wander to the field of graves

Where the elder its spectral branches waves?
And will thy hurried footsteps halt
Where thy mother sleeps in the silent vault?
Thither go not, or I deem almost
That thou wilt frighten thy mother's ghost!

Where the parodic energy of Moir's "Christabel, Part Third" concentrates on an ironic deflation of the gothic figure of the damsel in distress, William Frederick Deacon targets the supernatural. A London journalist and poet, Deacon published two parodies of "Christabel." The first, "The Baron Rich.—Part II. By S. T. C." appeared twice in 1820, and was reprinted in 1825. The second parody, "The Dream, A Psychological Curiosity" appeared in Deacon's 1824 volume Warreniana, with Notes, Critical, Explanatory, by the Editor of the Quarterly Review.

Physical violence and the supernatural as a disruptive force characterise Deacon's parodies. Indeed, the action of "The Baron Rich" is governed by these elements. The parody divides into two sections: a protracted view of the natural world in a state of disarray (as humans and animals wake in the night, their sleep having been disturbed by the tolling clock and calling animals), and the appearance of Satan. (The sections are separated by the "Song of the Old Bitch.") Throughout both sections, Deacon pays little attention to the original context of Coleridge's language. For example, the scene of Christabel "moan[ing] and leap[ing]" as she sleeps in Part I of "Christabel" is applied to the mastiff bitch who "in her sleep / ...begins to 'moan and leap'". "Bard Bracey," following his attempt to silence the mastiff bitch barking in the middle of the night, ...swears as often as he can;

And like a 'little limber elf,'
Singeth and danceth to himself.

Here Deacon combines the "one red leaf" of Part I—"The one red leaf, the last of its clan, / That dances as often as dance it can"—with the Conclusion to Part II—"A little child, a limber elf, / Singing, dancing to itself," (656-57). His interest in Coleridge's language is casual, presenting a loose allusional framework in which the diction of "Christabel" provides general points of reference for readers. Deacon's focus on Coleridge's language is more global than local. His interest in the figures of "Christabel," however, is more highly refined.

As he exaggerates the opening scene of "Christabel," Deacon offers an extended fight scene between the mastiff Bitch and Bard Bracey, who has been ordered outdoors to quiet the dog:

The bard came forth in his night-cap he,
And he was as skinny as bard mote be
And away he went with a hem and a haw!
To make the old mastiff lie still in her straw.
He kick'd her once—he kick'd her twice,
But the old bitch snapp'd at his fingers thrice;
Then Bracey kick'd her again, times four,
But the old bitch snapp'd at his fingers the more.

The scene continues, ending with Bracey bitten by the dog, and the dog revealing itself as an agent of evil in its brief "Song of the Old Bitch":

"There's a cloud in the sky,
And it's wandering by,
And in it I'll lump,
With a hop, ship, and jump,
For I'm a warlock of evil, I trow—"
(Here the bitch ended with, bow—wow—wow.)

The mastiff bitch is a central figure of Deacon's "The Baron Rich." Deacon's extended treatment of the dog brings to mind Hazlitt's comments in his Examiner of "Christabel" review that

We wonder that Mr. Murray, who has an eye, should suffer this 'mastiff bitch' to come into his shop. Is she a sort of Cerebus to fright away the critics? But—gentleman, she is toothless.

The seemingly minor and "toothless" dog is pivotal to the physical action of "The Baron Rich." Deacon playfully promotes a minor figure into a major one in the face of critics' derision toward the "mastiff bitch." The dog is the vehicle with which Coleridge's treatment of the supernatural is satirised. In "Christabel," the dog serves as a barometer of the supernatural—its growling while it sleeps functioning as a gauge of the potential presence of the otherworldly (the ghost of Christabel's deceased mother). In "The Baron Rich," the dog is itself otherworldly. Following the "Song of the Old Bitch," the dog "vanish'd" and re-appeared as Satan:

In popp'd father Satan in shape of a cat.
And he skipp'd thro' the key-hole with terrible pother,
A match in one hand, and his tail in the other;
And said to the Baron, with funeral glee,
'Come, leap thro' the window, and fly with me;
For I'm the mastiff that kick'd up a rout,
And my broomstick is waiting to carry you out.'

The devil and the Baron travel to hell, arriving "at five o'clock, just in time for dinner." The "Baron Rich" ends with a retrospective view of the Baron's encounter with the devil: five years after his encounter with the devil, the Baron is still "tormented" by his experience.

Deacon equals his satire of Satan and the supernatural in "The Baron Rich" with his second parody, "The Dream," which, again, sees the supernatural and violence as guiding thematic principles. The "Advertisement to the Reader" of "The Dream" recalls Moir's "Christabel, Part Third." Like Moir, Deacon is sceptical of Coleridge's comments on visionary versification—on poetry that comes to a poet while dreaming:

Dreams... are to be estimated solely in proportion to their wildness... A friend of mine, who is a most magnificent dreamer, imagined but the other night that he had invited a flock of sheep to a musical party. Such a flocci, nauci, nihili absurdity will, I am afraid, puzzle even our transcendental philosophers to explain, although Kant, in his treatise on the Phænomena of Dreams, is of opinion that the lens or focus of intestinal light ascending the œsophagus at right angles, so that the nucleus of the diaphragm reflecting on the cerebellum the prismatic visions of the pilorous, is made to produce that marvellous operation of mind upon matter better known by the name of dreaming.

Deacon's critique of Coleridge's comments on the creative process (and of his syntactically complex prose style) is fuelled by the nonsensical, rendered in terms that mock the language and philosophical foundations of one of Coleridge's chief metaphysical influences, Immanuel Kant. By 1824, Coleridge had been frequently and unfavourably criticised for the Kantian elements of his work. Deacon mocks the process by which the substance of everyday life creeps into poetry; in this case, the boxing match "between Cribb and Molineaux" that the author had been reading about in the newspaper furnishes Deacon with an organisational structure for part of his parody.

The first half of "The Dream" is dominated by the supernatural as Deacon extends the opening scenes of Part I of "Christabel" into an interview between Warren—"the manufacturer rich"—and a "spirit"; the second, by a round-by-round commentary on a boxing match between the devil and Warren.

Deacon revisits familiar terrain in "The Dream," reworking the appearance of the devil in "The Baron Rich":

Beside his counter, with tail in hand,
[Warren] saw a spirit of darkness stand;
I guess 'twas frightful there to see
A lady so scantily clad as she
Ugly and old exceedingly.

Deacon inverts the figure of Geraldine, who Coleridge describes as

...a damsel bright
Drest in a silken robe of white,
That shadowy in the moonlight shone:
The neck that made that white robe wan,
Her stately neck, and arms were bare;
Her blue-veined feet unsandal'd were,
And wildly glittered here and there
The gems entangled in her hair.
I guess, 'twas fearful there to see
A lady so richly clad as she—
Beautiful exceedingly!

The description continues, echoing Coleridge's "Ancient Mariner." The "spirits of darkness"—referred to as the "old mother Nightmare-life-death"—is:

In height her figure was six feet two,

In breadth exactly two foot six,
One eye as summer skies was blue,
The other black as the waves of the Styx,
Her bloodless lips did aught but pair,
For one was brown and one was fair,
And clattered like maid in hysteric fit.

Like Moir, Deacon presents the supernatural as absurd. "Old Mrs. Life-in-death" and Warren travel to hell, where, upon meeting Satan, Warren and Satan argue about boot blacking. In the early nineteenth century, Robert Warren was the manufacturer of a popular and well advertised boot blacking.

Satan challenges Warren that
...though brilliant your blacking, the water of Styx
Is blacker by far, and can throw, as it suits,
A handsomer gloss o'er our shoes and boots.—

Warren disagrees, and after a heated exchange, he and Satan agree to a fist fight—of which Deacon jests:

Gentles, who fondly peruse these lays,
Wild as a colt o'er the moorland strays,
Who thrill at each wondrous rede I tell,
As fancy roams o'er the floor of hell,
Now list ye kindness, the whiles I rehearse
In shapely pugilistic verse.

After five rounds of boxing, one in which Satan receives a bloody nose ("the blood from his peepers, went drip, drip, drip)," Warren wins. During Warren's victory celebration, Satan leads "the shadowless spectres" in a chorus of "Buy Warren's Blacking." "The Dream" ends where it began in the "advertisement," with mention of dreams and sleep. In the closing stanza of the parody, the bard is awakened by "the voice of the crowing cock" and "the toll of Saint Dunstan's clock." The events of "The Dream" were themselves part of a dream, and "the bard hath awoke from the 'Pains of Sleep'".

Deacon's parodies mark the supernatural pole of "Christabel" parodies, while Christabess and "Christabel, Part Third" mark the sexual. The five other parodies fall between. The parodists' strategy—as my molecular metaphor early in this article suggested—is that of penetrating the atomic structure of "Christabel"—diction, tone, image, metaphor, atmosphere, as well as typography and layout. Parody, however, also operates on a subatomic level—on the level of rhetoric and descriptive technique. It is here that we witness parody's trespass of literary property and propriety—jumping the fence late at night to steal a skinny dip in someone else's pool, and leaving without closing the gate.

"And must she sleep by Christabel?":
Sex, Hypophora, and the Supernatural

Language is the fuel that feeds literary parody's satirical fire. Yet to study the parodic imitation of a writer's diction is to observe the mimetic operative mode of parody functioning on a microscopic level. To do justice to such a study requires examination of the macroscopic as well. In the case of "Christabel," Arthur Nethercot offers just such a macroscopic study in The Road to Tryermaine, where he delineates a tripartite paradigm of the thematic concerns, and aesthetic, ideological and historical focuses of "Christabel" parodies and completions. Parodists follow one or all of three avenues of approach: scandal (sexual), the supernatural, and the moral and didactic.

While Nethercot's model offers a fruitful global view of parodist's general handling of "Christabel," it is at the expense of a detailed consideration of the relationship between the macro- and micro-, and the global and local. (And even then, as a macroscopic study, Nethercot's consideration of the impact that genre, biography, and the history of the poem's transmission and reception has upon the parodists, is inadequate.) The parodists focus simultaneously on the relationship between the diction of "Christabel," the poem's reception and transmission, the gothic genre, and Coleridge. The poem as Coleridge composed it, the poem as it is perceived in popular culture, and the poet himself blur together, forming a common subject for the parodists.

If language is the fuel of parody, its consumption is characterised by adoption and alteration for comic effect. Coleridge's onomatopoeic hooting owl, for example, is a favourite subject of the parodists. In Christabess, the hooting owl becomes a braying donkey: "And the donkey hath waken'd the girl up stairs; / Ee—eau!——Ee—eau!". In "Isabelle," Hogg transforms the owl into a "Rail"—"harping, harping in the brake, / Craik, craik——Craik, craik". In Deacon's "The Dream," a crowing cock calls: "Cock-a-doodle-doo, / Cock-a-doodle-doo"; and, the mastiff bitch "barketh a chorus of bow wow, wow". In the "Baron Rich" the cock sounds (illogically) like Coleridge's owl: "the crowing cock his shrill clarion blew, / To whit! to whoo!"—confounding even further the disarray of the natural world. It is Gerald Griffin, however, who takes the parody of Coleridge's owl to its extreme:

Did you not read the sonnet to an owl, No. II?
Not a whit of thy tuwhoo,
Thee to woo to thy tuwhit,
Thee to woo to thy tuwhit,
With a lengthen'd loud halloo,
Tuwhoo, tuwhit, tuwhit, tuwhoo—o—o!

The parodists reduce the owl of "Christabel" to the acoustic playfulness and simplicity of a children's song—language that is seemingly non-sensical, as it aspires to a level of verisimilitude, emulating phonetically and sonically the calls of animals.

But the "Christabel" parodists' manipulation of Coleridge's language also speaks of a more refined critique of Coleridge's handling of gothic conventions. The manipulation of religious language in "Christabel," for example, demonstrates the parodists' attempt to debase the pious Christabel. This is, in turn, part of the larger parodic programme of undermining the poem's gothic elements.

"Jesu Maria, shield us well," a distinctive epithet of "Christabel" (and one echoed by Scott in theLay of the Last Minstrel), stands as a call for divine protection, and for the return of a natural and Christian order to the world. In the mouth of the narrator, the phrase conveys an exasperated and disbelieving fear of the poem's events: "Hush, beating heart of Christabel! / Jesu, Maria, shield her well!" and Geraldine "look'd askance at Christabel—/—Jesu, Maria, shield her well!". (Indeed, the invocation to Jesus is used, generally, in "Christabel" as an appeal to divine authority—to the order of a Christian world. In swearing "by the wounds in Jesu's side", Leoline demonstrates the seriousness and conviction of his pledge to punish Geraldine's captors.)

In Deacon's "The Dream" "Jesu Maria" is altered to "Miserere Maria"—a cry of despair by Warren that causes the "spirit of darkness" to draw back momentarily. Warren continues with the prayer "For Mary, sweet Mary, hath power to fright, / And palsy the souls of the dæmon of night" in an effort to protect himself from "Mrs. Life-in-death". Christabess corrupts the phrase further: Christabess, frightened that the moaning she hears near the old oak tree may be "some rogue," cries "O gemini"—a vulgarisation of Jesu domine. This vulgarisation continues in Christabess with Christabess asking Adelaide, upon discovering her by the oak tree, "Lud-a-mercy! who are you?". "Lud" is a crude reduction of Lord, a comic version of the title of legal officials, and the aristocracy.

The parodists' vulgarisation of the religious language of "Christabel" is emblematic of their larger project of perverting (in both the religious and sexual senses of to debase, and to lead astray) the gothic genre and the Christabel-Geraldine relationship. In its simplest form, parody attempts to hobble the rhetorical elements of "Christabel" that contribute to the development of gothic tension, mystery, and suspense. Deacon, for example, parodies Coleridge's use of the rhetorical figure of antimetabole—a chiastic figure in which a phrase is repeated, but, in the second instance, in reverse order.

In "Christabel," antimetabole unites content and form, advancing the gothic atmosphere of the poem, as well as developing character. The figure appears several times, one of which occurs in Part II, as Geraldine's spell—"Which is lord of thy utterance, Christabel!"—takes effect:

...Christabel awoke and spied
The same who lay down by her side—
O rather say, the same whom she
Rais'd up beneath the old oak tree!

Nay, fairer yet! and yet more fair!

The phrase "Nay, fairer yet! and yet more fair" enacts the spell through repetition as it assumes control of Christabel's thoughts. Another instance is found in Part I, as Christabel and Geraldine enter Christabel's dark bedroom:

The silver lamp burns dead and dim;
But Christabel the lamp will trim.
She trimm'd the lamp, and made it bright.

Here antimetabole contributes to the gothic atmosphere of "Christabel," underscored by the incantatory rhythm of Coleridge's stressed-based anapestic tetrameter metre. The final example of antimetabole in "Christabel" serves several purposes. In Part II, Coleridge writes of Sir Leoline, following Christabel's request to have Geraldine removed from Langdale Hall:

Within the Baron's heart and brain
If thoughts, like these, had any share,
They only swell'd his rage and pain,
And did but work confusion there.
His heart was cleft with pain and rage.

And in the closing line of the Conclusion to Part II, Coleridge writes:

And what, if in a world of sin
(O sorrow and shame should this be true!)
Such giddiness of heart and brain
Comes seldom save from rage and pain,
So talks as it's most used to do.

The double antimetabole of "rage and pain"—dispersed across the two passages—highlights the disintegration of Leoline's psyche, and further underscores his bellicose nature. But the lines also serve a more formal function as they rhetorically connect the Conclusion to Part II with the rest of the poem.

The collapse of Coleridge's antimetabolic phrase by Deacon affects the disintegration of a controlling rhetorical component of "Christabel." In "The Baron Rich," Deacon writes of the "old mother Nightmare-life-death" that "In height her figure was six feet two, / In breadth exactly two foot six";

and, in "The Dream":

The Baron has put on his night-gown and cap,
To know the reason of this mishap;
The Baron has put on his cap and night-gown.

The second instance is deliberately non-sensical. Although lacking the comic absurdity of the description of "old mother Nightmare-life-death," the repeated phrase deadens the gothic rhetoric and spell-like metre of "Christabel."

To parody antimetabole is to begin to parody the more subtle and complex rhetorical elements of Coleridge's writing. It represents in miniature the parodists' more refined parodic targeting of the figurative and descriptive techniques that Coleridge employs in "Christabel"—not just his choice of words but how he uses them. But the "Christabel" parodists are also influenced by the poem's reception history—by the poem as Coleridge wrote it and as it was perceived and circulated. The parodists' transformation of Coleridge's language from the formal, aristocratic, proper, and religious, to the colloquial, vulgar, and secular, as well as their efforts to defuse the poem's rhetorically-loaded gothic conventions, manifests itself more subtly in the parody of Coleridge's hypophoric method and self-conscious narration.

Hypophora—the rhetorical figure of asking and immediately answering a question—provides an apt rubric with which to discuss the series of questions and responses in "Christabel." In "Christabel," as in the "Ancient Mariner," sequences of questions and answers fuel the self-aware quality of both poems. In both poems, the questions focus on the supernatural, and participate in the process of question and answer that phenomenologically draws readers into the supernatural events of "Christabel" as they unfold. The First Voice in Part VI of the "Ancient Mariner," for example, asks:

But tell me, tell me! speak again,
Thy soft response renewing—
What makes that ship drive on so fast?
What is the ocean doing?

When these questions are left unanswered, the First Voice reiterates: "But why drives on that ship so fast, / Without wave or wind?" The First voice sounds like a reader who is unwilling to suspend disbelief, to possess "poetic faith." The First Voice, to use Coleridge's metaphor from Biographia Literaria, is a reader who does not "yield to a dream" depicted in literature.

In Chapter 14 of Biographia Literaria, Coleridge writes of the original intention of the 1800 Lyrical Ballads that my endeavours should be directed to persons and characters supernatural, or at least romantic; yet so as transfer from our inward nature a human interest and a semblance of truth sufficient to procure for these shadows of imagination that willing suspension of disbelief for the moment, which constitutes poetic faith.

Through the First Voice in the "Ancient Mariner," Coleridge questions this method of "transfer." He interrogates the supernatural at the level of representation. The First Voice questions the logic of the supernatural. What is the nature of the "roaring wind" that appears but "did not come anear," that "never reached the ship"? What made "the ship [move] on? "Yet never a breeze up-blew... / Yet never a breeze did breathe". Although Coleridge eventually answers these questions with the addition of a marginal gloss, the questions lead to a paradoxical treatment of the supernatural. The insistent questioning of a supernatural occurrence scrutinises the logic of gothic conventions even as it advances an atmosphere of suspense and mystery.

Like the First Voice of the "Ancient Mariner," the narrator of "Christabel" also questions the poem's gothic logic. In the case of "Christabel," however, Coleridge leads the reader to suspend disbelief as he works his way through an increasingly unstable hypophoric sequence:

Is the night chilly and dark?
The night is chilly but not dark.
The lovely lady, Christabel,
Whom her father loves so well,
What makes her in the wood so late,
A furlong from the castle gate?
She had dreams all yesternight
Of her betrothed knight;

Dreams, that made her moan and leap,
As on her bed she lay in sleep;
And she in the midnight wood will pray
For the weal of her lover that's far away.
Is it the wind that moaneth bleak?
There is not wind enough in the air
To move away the ringlet curl
From the lovely lady's cheek—
[Christabel] folded her arms beneath her cloak,
And she stole to the other side of the oak.
What sees she there?
There she sees a damsel bright....
Mary mother, save me now!
(Said Christabel,) And who art thou?
The lady strange [Geraldine] made answer meet,
And her voice was faint and sweet:—
Have pity on my sore distress,
I can scarce speak for weariness.
Stretch forth thy hand, and have no fear,
Said Christabel, How cam'st thou here?
And the lady, whose voice was faint and sweet,
Did thus pursue her answer meet:—

Geraldine's failure to answer the question "who art thou?" marks a shift in Coleridge's employment of an interrogative mode in "Christabel." He collapses the hypophoric series of questions and answers, revealing what Susan Wolfson refers to as "the dark potency of questioning":

the dark potency of questioning—not a sly plot by the mind but a possession of the mind by indecipherable mystery—is the imaginative core of Coleridge's two great narrative poems, "The Rime of the Ancient Mariner" and 'Christabel'.

Coleridge broadens the function of his gothic hypophora as the questions progress. As the questions accumulate in the disintegrating hypophoric sequence, their function shifts from being "a sly plot by the mind" to being an attempt to possess "the mind by indecipherable mystery." Coleridge gains readers' sympathies for "the wildest tales of ghosts, wizards, genii, and secret talisman." Thus, these questions reflect on the representation of the supernatural as a topos of the poem.

The first four questions of Part I of "Christabel" simultaneously present and interrogate setting, character, plot, atmosphere, and an indication that something is amiss in both the natural world and in Christabel's world. It is midnight but it is not dark, and why is Christabel in the forest at midnight? The final two questions mark a distinct shift from a narrative or authorial inquisitor to a voice internal to the poem—Christabel. No longer does an authorial presence ask and promptly answer questions for the reader; rather, Christabel and the readers are left to find their own answers. But there is an increasing informational distance between Christabel's questions and their answers, and it is in this gap that Coleridge attempts to phenomenologically draw readers into the process of telling the poem's story.

The final two questions present not only the "sly plot of the mind" of Coleridge, but an attempt to "possess the mind," laying the groundwork for Geraldine's possession of Christabel—first, through her tale of abduction, and then through a magic spell. In turn, readers are to be similarly possessed by the gradual disclosure of the poem's plot. Because answers to the final two questions are not as factually simple or direct as the first four, readers—by continuing to read the poem, and by seeking answers to these final questions—display what Coleridge deems the "willing suspension of disbelief for the moment," evincing a "poetic faith" that answers are forthcoming.

The gothic hypophora of "Christabel" is subverted and perverted by the parodists. It occasions buffoonery. In Christabess, for example, the narrator asks "Does it rain to-night?—are you asleep?" and immediately and illogically answers "It does not rain, but I'm asleep". Similarly, Deacon writes in "The Baron Rich": "Am I asleep or am I awake? / In very truth I oft mistake, / ...that I were asleep".

But the parodist's subversion of Coleridge's hypophoric technique is also motivated by a more licentious impulse than merely achieving a good laugh. Christabess and "Christabel,

Part Third," in particular, appropriate the self-reflective infrastructure of "Christabel"—Coleridge's hypophoric execution of supernatural and gothic conventions, and the poem's self-conscious narrator. Both become the means by which the parodists sexualise the Christabel-Geraldine relationship.

From her earliest appearances in Christabess, we see in Christabess a sexually charged doppelganger of Christabel. Wandering the woods at night, the Christabess narrator asks:

That Blooming sphinx, Miss Christabess,
Whom her daddy loves to kiss,
Hath she not yet come home to bed?—
What whim is in the numbscull's head?
She dreamt, last night, some stuff, perhap,
About the gawky soldier chap,
Something that made her kick and leap,
And hug the bolster in her sleep;
And that's what keeps her up so late, I think,
For love I wot won't let her sleep a wink.

Christabess appears as a sexualised and demonised version of Christabel. There is the suggestion of incest in the colloquial and snide remark "Whom her daddy loves to kiss"—changed from Coleridge's more formal "whom her father loves so well". The image of Christabess hugging her "bolster," her pillow, is similarly suggestive. She does so because her dreams "about the gawky soldier chap" "made her kick and leap." Christabess' actions recall Christabel's, who

...had dreams all yesternight
Of her own betrothed knight;
Dreams, that made her moan and leap,
As on her bed she lay in sleep.

Coleridge seems to have perceived the "moan and leap" lines as too sexually suggestive. He excised the last two lines in the above passage from all versions of "Christabel" published after 1816. Coleridge also took steps to suppress the lines in existing copies of the 1816 volume, cancelling them by hand in dedication copies to James Gillman, David Hinves, and an unknown recipient at Ramsgate.

The sexualisation of "Christabel" in Christabess extends to Adelaide as well. Upon meeting Christabess for the first time, she is wearing "nothing save her chemise":

With heaving breasts, and tearful eyes,
And shift but half way down her thighs;
Oh! had the finder been a he!
Gentle reader, you, or me!—
Vexing; an't it—"damnably."

The self-aware narrator of Christabess is also keenly aware of readers, anticipating and subverting their horizons of expectation that we are about to witness a sexual scene. But the potential for such a scene is frustrated by gender; the narrator expects a heterosexual encounter only—"Oh! had the finder been a he!"

The expectation of graphic nudity and a heterosexual encounter continues in Christabess with a parody of the bedroom scene of Part I of "Christabel." Adelaide speaks to Christabess about their preparations for retiring to bed—hinting at anticipated sexual activity:

And then she smiled, and thus she spake
To lovely Christa' Bottomly:
"My pretty little virgin bright,
"I love you for your kindness sake
"And, Oh! how we will hug to night.
"With all the skill I have I'll try
"To yield your little heart delight,
"And I'll unlace your stays, she said,
"For I'm in haste to be in bed."

Adelaide helps Christabess undress—unlacing her "stays," her under-bodice—and a naked Christabess "nimbly 'twixt the sheets jumpt she". Adelaide, however, hesitates. She is no longer "in haste" to retire for the night. Instead, Adelaide

...tore a song,
To curl her hair so black and long;
Nor did she seem, as first she said,
So much in haste to come to bed;
And Christabess almost began
To fancy t'other was a man.

Again we are reminded of the expectation of a heterosexual encounter—an expectation that Christabess only flirts with but that Moir enthusiastically develops with delight in "Christabel, Part Third":

For who that saw that child of thine
Pale Christabel, who could divine
That its sire was the Lady Geraldine?

"Christabel, Part Third" is thus transformed from a parody of the poem as Coleridge penned it to a parody of a poetic entity comprised of layers of cultural accretion. Lingering in the background of the portrayal of the sexualised (and pregnant) Christabel in Christabess and "Christabel, Part Third" is a rumour that Coleridge believed Hazlitt circulated about "Christabel"—that Geraldine is a man in disguise.

Coleridge did not let the rumour go un-checked. But what is significant about Coleridge's complaint against Hazlitt is that he recorded it in the flyleaf of the 1816 edition—in a dedication copy to his son Derwent. Bibliographically, the 1816 volume participates in the transmission and reception of "Christabel," serving as a vehicle of complaint:

I still cherish the hope of finishing the poem... I hope to finish it in the course of the present year. Enough at present to assure you, that Geraldine is not a Witch, in any proper sense of that word. That she is a man in disguise is a wicked rumour sent abroad with malice prepense, and against his own belief and knowledge, by poor Hazlitt. Unhappy man! I understand that when one of his Faction had declared in a pamphlet ("Hypocrisy Unveiled") the Christabel "the most obscene poem in the English language" he shrugged himself up with a sort of sensual orgasm of enjoyment, and exclaimed—How he'll stare (i.e. meaning me) Curse him! I hate him.

Coleridge's venom is not surprising. Hazlitt's Examiner review clearly spells out his opinion of Coleridge and of "Christabel."

Hazlitt felt that Coleridge was trying to hide, if not to silence, elements of "Christabel." To substantiate his accusation that there is "something disgusting at the bottom of

[Coleridge's] subject," Hazlitt provides enticing evidence—another version of "Christabel":

Christabel's dread of [Geraldine] arises from her discovering... [that Geraldine is a "witch"], which is told in a single line, which line, from an exquisite refinement in efficiency is here omitted. When the unknown lady gets to Christabel's chamber, and is going to undress, it is said:

Behold! Her bosom and half her side
A sight to dream of, not to tell
And she is to sleep by Christabel!
The manuscript runs thus, or nearly thus:
Behold her bosom and half her side—
Hideous, deformed and pale of hue.

The manuscript Hazlitt refers to is one of two transcripts made by Sarah Stoddart in 1805. Hazlitt came into possession of Stoddart's copy after their 1808 marriage. Significantly, Hazlitt misquotes (or mis-remembers) both Coleridge's published version and Stoddart's transcript. In Coleridge's, he alters the punctuation, changing a period to an exclamation mark in line 248: "And she is to sleep by Christabel." The change heightens the anxiety and impropriety of the scene, suggestively investing the verb "sleep" with a stronger sexual sense.

As well, Hazlitt alters the line "Are lean and old and foul of Hue" in the Stoddart manuscript to "Hideous, deformed, and pale of hue." The line, Hazlitt argues, "is necessary to make common sense of the first and second part. 'it is the keystone that makes up the arch'."The altered lines commingle the monstrous and the sexual. A naked but horrifically scarred and discoloured Geraldine stands before Christabel. The exposure of Geraldine on both fronts does not sit well with Coleridge.

Following the release of "Christabel" in 1816, Coleridge's editorial management of the poem corroborates Hazlitt's insinuation that he is trying to silence "something disgusting." The bedroom scene is frequently revised, although the revisions are not as wide-sweeping as those of, say, "The Rime of the Ancient Mariner" or "Dejection: An Ode." Of the lines that Coleridge repeatedly returned to in "Christabel," one in particular speaks of his attempts to silence the poem's sexuality—line 248 of the 1816 edition, "And she is to sleep by Christabel."

In the 1800 holograph, the line reads "And she is to sleep with Christabel." "With" becomes "by" in 1816. Both words denote proximity—a relative nearness. "With," however, connotes a greater degree of physical involvement, of interaction or participation. "With" is more hands on than "by." Unlike "by," which indicates a defined location, "with" implies mutual even simultaneous or overlapping co-existence. "With" conveys the sense of relative nearness that "by" denotes, but also suggests an intermingling that "by" does not.

So the "with" of 1800 becomes "by" in 1816, and the shift gestures at Coleridge's attempt to physically separate Geraldine and Christabel as they share the same bed. But Coleridge questions the 1816 configuration—whether the two women should even be in the same bed at all. In a dedication copy of the 1816 edition to David Hinves, Coleridge strikes out the line "And she is to sleep by Christabel." In its place he pencils in "And must she sleep by Christabel?" The italicised "she" calls attention to its antecedent—Geraldine—and returns us to the Champion reviewer's list of questions:

What is it all about? What is the idea? Is Lady Geraldine a sorceress? or a vampire? or a man? or what is she, or he, or it?

Coleridge only adds to the list—and must Geraldine sleep by Christabel? Coleridge's further revisions of the line answers the question: he is uncertain. In the Hinves copy, Coleridge deletes his own emendation, striking the line out—"And must she sleep by Christabel?" These accreted changes provide a glimpse not so much of the creative process, as they do of self-censorship in process—of Coleridge silencing the potential sexuality of "Christabel." In this case, the silence remains; Coleridge does not replace the omitted line in the Hinves copy. Nor does he return to the line "And she is to sleep by [or, with] Christabel" in editions after 1816.

Even there, it is suppressed: Coleridge deleted the line in

dedication copies to James Gillman, Joseph Green, Ludwig Tieck, and to an anonymous recipient of Ramsgate. Unlike the Hinves dedication copy, in these copies Coleridge deletes the line and replaces it with the line "O shield her! Shield sweet Christabel!" With this new line, Coleridge diffuses the sexual and supernatural threat posed by Geraldine into a more general unknown, anxious terror that Christabel needs to be protected from. But Coleridge's efforts—as the parodists demonstrate—come too late: the 1816 edition provided ample sexual fodder, and Coleridge's revisions are not lastingly committed to print until the 1828, 1829, and 1834 Poetical Works.

Following Coleridge's death in 1834, the Coleridge family inherited the post of protecting "Christabel" from those who would reveal the poem as a homo- and hetero- sexual work. In their various editorial and creative endeavours, successive generations of the Coleridge family undertake a project that can be described through reference to Geraldine's spell in Part I:

In the touch of this bosom there worketh a spell,
Which is lord of thy utterance, Christabel!

In the case of "Christabel," members of the Coleridge family stand as lords of the poem's utterance—a poem they see as supernatural and moral, not as sexual.

Coleridge's son-in-law Henry Nelson Coleridge, for example, has a guiding editorial hand in the 1834 Poetical Works. Moreover, he champions and defends Coleridge's genius and the originality of "Christabel" in a Quarterly review of the 1834 Poetical Works, and in his edition of Coleridge's Table Talk (1835). Other family editors follow suit: Derwent and Sarah edit Coleridge's poetry, and an 1870 edition contains a note by Derwent that explains the poem as a moral exemplum, as a tale of vicarious suffering. Ernest Hartley Coleridge also stresses the supernatural and moral, as well as genre in a number of editions of the poem in the early twentieth century.

The Coleridge family editors are matched by family poets. Coleridge's son Hartley writes of the incompletion of

"Christabel" in "To Christabel Rose Coleridge." He closes his verse tribute to his daughter with the question, "Who of Christabel can close the story?" Hartley answers his own question in another poem, "Ada of Grasmere"—a story of the supernatural, and a never realised heterosexual romance. Derwent's Wife, Mary, emphasises the supernatural in her poem "The Witch"—a portrait of a Geraldine-like figure, the ghost of a dead witch wandering the earth. Sara Coleridge's *Phantasmion, A Fairy Tale* reveals the thematic and imagistic influence of "Christabel," opening with a scene of a "young boy," Phantasmion, "laughing and talking to himself." And Ernest Hartley Coleridge continues "Christabel" in his poem "Christabel, Part III, or (haply) Part I." The poem offers a glimpse into the background of Geraldine's supernatural character and ends on a hopeful note. Christabel's "lover that's far away" has returned, and, we are left to conjecture, will expose Geraldine, marry Christabel, and restore a heterosexual, Christian order to Langdale Hall.

Coleridge's Discursive "Monody on the Death of Chatterton"

Prompted, in part, by a wide-spread skepticism with maps of totalizing history, literary historians now focus on particular material conditions of production, publication, and authorship. They have turned their attention from schools and families of writers traced in a genealogical descent in the long sweep of literary history to local knowledge and particular circumstances for several reasons. Particulars seem less vulnerable to skeptical inquiry than general accounts of historical movements and can stand as the ground for a materialist criticism.

The significance of a literary work appears stabilized by being fixed to historical facts, the moment of creation, the means of production, and organs of reception. For some critics, a materialist criticism of particulars thus aims to install history and society at a work's origin and to anchor it in such a way that its boundaries are not violated and its figuration is not dispersed among the codes of language.

The focus on historical specificity is evident in a number

of critical methods. Jerome McGann has outlined the topics for a historical criticism: the "originary textual *moment*" of authorship and collaborative authorship; the "secondary *moments* of textual production and reproduction," the reprinting of works; and "the immediate *moment* of textual criticism," its reception by reviewers whose tendentious purposes enter into the account. Jack Stillinger, along with other editors of Romantic literature, has called for a theory of versions of a work. Since many authors revised their works in republication, a poem may exist in many versions.

No one version, Stillinger argues, can be preferred over another, not a first nor a final version supervised in the author's lifetime: "I suggest ... that we drop the concept of an ideal single text fulfilling an author's intentions and put our money instead on some theory of versions." More recently, James Chandler has argued that the turn to history in literary studies is a return to "dated specificity." He describes literature "concerned with its place *in* England in 1819—concerned, that is, with a national operation of self-dating, or -redating, that is meant to count as a national self-making, or -remaking." I have recently offered another approach to historical and textual specificity by practicing a criticism that reads a version of a work in the paratextual frame of its original publication, which links the Romantic lyric to public debates and the discourse of politics, morality, law, and aesthetics.

Historical specificity, however, raises a number of problems. Locating a work in relation to its printing, its versions, its date, or its paratext determines its significance, and that determination severely limits significance, since a work is reprinted with different contexts, dates, and paratexts. Poems are republished and therefore repeated in different locations; dated contexts are not repeatable. Poems are iterable; dates are not. Strict historical specificity limits a work's significance in practical criticism, so that one date or version provides one meaning. As Kelvin Everest argued at the 1998 Coleridge Conference, "Some texts plainly also live both independently of this context, as it might be in the modern classroom, study, beach, fireside, or aeroplane."

We must acknowledge that a work worth rereading is always in excess of its historical moment. To practice a critical method that relies exclusively on an originary moment, version, date, or paratext is to entomb a work in a paratextual memorial. Some editors of poetry place two dates after each poem. On the left, the date of composition, or birth; on the right, the date of publication, or death. The most important dates for poems, as for people, then become those on a tombstone. Locating a work within its originating context may explain its field of reference or its illocutionary force, but as Everest argues, has little to say about its formal properties or its affective power.

Everest also argues that "if the meaning of a text lies in its lost unity" with an originating context, "then the reconstitution of that lost unity" requires the reconstitution of an original textual form." Historical meaning depends on unique versions, and different meanings depend on differing versions. Everest concludes this "implies a very narrow view of poetic meaning." And so it does, if the originary moment is conceived as a stable unity of context and version. Originary moments, however, are often neither unitary nor stable. Both creative and productive moments contain contrary impulses obscured by our historical distance from them. As an example of the instability of origins, I will explore the originary moment of Coleridge's "Monody on the Death of Chatterton" as it was printed in *Poems* (1796).

The originary moment for the "Monody" in 1796 is not the date of its composition. It could have been written any time from October 1794 to early 1796. The moment of its origin is March 1796 when Coleridge composed the volume and wrote the notes. Coleridge constructed a paratext for "Monody on the Death of Chatterton" to encourage the reader to read it as his personal expression of melancholy. At the same time, however, he wrote, and then canceled, a note for the poem, which, had it been published, would have changed the "Monody" from an effusion of melancholy to a bitter denunciation of class, wealth, and ecclesiastical power. The complex paratext of the originary moment does not determine a single or stable reading. Differing readings, based upon the differing illocutonary acts involved in publication, are present from the very beginning.

The text's instability resides, not primarily in questions of meaning or representation, but in the utterance as illocutionary act. Coleridge's "Monody" is either an individual effusion of Coleridge's sensibility, as in a traditional reading of Romantic lyrics; or it is a discursive utterance, alluding, echoing, and responding to other utterances and entering public debates. In this instance a historical method that locates a work by version, date, and paratext does not limit the text to a single meaning or affect. I will first describe the paratext of the "Monody" and then turn to readings of the poem as it actually appeared to contrast that reading with the issues raised in the canceled note.

Published as the first work in *Poems on Various Subjects* (1796) "Monody on the Death of Chatterton" followed a Preface, which justified the poems' emotional egotism. The "Monody" is a self-portrait of the melancholy poet in which Coleridge identifies himself with Chatterton. James Averill has commented that Coleridge introduced later volumes with poetic self-portraits: the political prophet in "Ode on the Departing Year" in *Poems* (1797) and the imaginative prophet in "The Ancient Mariner" in *Lyrical Ballads* (1798). If one reads the poem with the paratext as finally printed in the 1796 volume, the "Monody" is primarily an expression of Coleridge's identification with Chatterton and a protest against society's neglect of poets and literature, which serves Coleridge's own search for financial support.

On the title page of the volume, Coleridge printed a quotation from Statius as a motto:

Felix curarum, cui non Heliconia cordi
Serta, nec imbelles Parnassi e vertice laurus !
Sed viget ingenium, et magnos accinctus in usus
Fert animus quascunque vices.—Nos tristia vitae
Solamur cantu.

["Happy thou in thy labours, who carest not for the chaplets of Helicon nor for the unwarlike bays from Parnassus' summit, but thy intellect is keen and thy mind girt up for mighty deeds endures whatever may befall; we beguile a melancholy life with song"]

When Coleridge quotes for mottoes, epigraphs, and the like, he often changes or adapts the original, as he does here. Statius had written that the poet beguiles a "leisured life," *otia vitae,* which Coleridge changed to a "melancholy life," *tristia vitae.* Coleridge wished to avoid the class associations implied by the *otia vitae* at a time when he felt the financial pressure of supporting a growing family and the political pressure of increasing intolerance of dissent. A motto on the title page is a form of signature, as the word "motto" originally indicated writing on a scroll or heraldic device that identified the bearer. Coleridge changes the quotation to deny his association with a leisured life. His title on the title page is "S. T. Coleridge, Late of Jesus College, Cambridge."

Although the volume includes the political "Sonnets on Eminent Characters" and "Religious Musings," Coleridge's Preface echoes the motto's rejection of the higher genres of poetry for the expression of individual feeling:

Compositions resembling those of the present volume are not unfrequently condemned for their querulous egotism. But egotism is to be condemned then only when it offends against time and place, as in an History or an Epic Poem. To censure it in a Monody or Sonnet is almost as absurd as to dislike a circle for being round. Why then write Sonnets or Monodies? Because they give me pleasure when perhaps nothing else could. After the more violent emotions of Sorrow, the mind demands solace and can find it in employment alone; but full of its late sufferings it can endure no employment not connected with those sufferings.

The "Monody" expresses Coleridge's private melancholy. The public is no more than an aggregate of sympathetic individuals: "how are the Public interested in your sorrows or your description?... What is the Public but a term for a number of scattered individuals of whom as many will be interested in these sorrows as have experienced the same or similar?" Coleridge chose the title "Monody" rather than ode, although as I. A. Gordon points out, the first, 1790 version is an "irregular Pindaric." In Greek the word "monody" defined a lyric spoken by a single voice, as opposed to a choral ode. Coleridge's choice of "monody," rather than elegy or ode, emphasizes his personal reaction to Chatterton's death.

With the motto, preface, and title indicating that the poem is an effusion of individual melancholy, and with Coleridge's later classification of it as a "juvenile poem," one is tempted to read it as a youthful imitation of the literature of sensibility, an exercise in a style Coleridge soon abandoned and to read its rhetoric as reminiscent of the odes of Collings and Gray. The "Monody" is a highly allusive poem, but its allusions and quotations are not random appropriations from a pool of poetic conventions.

They are commentaries on their original contexts. By including some in quotation marks, Coleridge indicates that the poem should be read through its references. The "Monody" challenges eighteenth-century progress poetry and issues a counter-statement. Gray's "Progress of Poetry" and Thomson's "Liberty," for examples, argued that liberty and literature originated in Greece, but migrated through Europe to England, although Gray's poem raises some doubt that his contemporary writers were the equal of their Greek and earlier English originals. Similarly, while Gray's "The Bard" relates the legend of an English King killing Welsh bards, it concludes with the prophecy of a Welsh monarch ascending to the British throne.

For Coleridge, liberty and literature cannot reside in repressive English culture. England has neglected its writers, and the only recourse is emigration, to leave England for America, a point Coleridge announced in the Preface: "Some of the verses allude to an intended emigration to America on the scheme of an abandonment of individual property." The 1796 version of the "Monody" adds a Miltonic turn from the melancholy of Chatterton's death. "Hence, gloomy thoughts," echoes "Hence loathed melancholy," which opens Milton's "L'Allegro." The turn introduces the octave of a sonnet sent to Southey September 8, 1794:

Hence, gloomy thoughts ! no more my soul shall dwell
On joys that were ! No more endure to weigh
The shame and anguish of the evil day,
Wisely forgetful ! O'er the ocean swell
Sublime of Hope I seek the cottag'd dell
Where Virtue calm with careless step may stray;
And, dancing to the moon-light roundelay,
The Wizard passions weave an holy spell!

The poem concludes with a fantasy of Chatterton's joining them in America where "we, at sobre eve, would round thee throng, / Hanging, enraptur'd on thy stately song! / And greet with smiles the young-eyed Poesy / All deftly mask'd, as hoar Antiquity" (ll. 130-33). Coleridge's gesture toward emigration, in 1796 no more than dream of an ideal state, since the pantisocracy plan ended in August 1795 with his break with Southey, echoes Berkeley's "Verses on the Prospect of Planting Arts and Learning in America" (1752): "There shall be sung another golden age, / The rise of empire and of arts ... Westward the course of empire takes its way" (ll. 13-14, 21). It also echoes the conclusion of Goldsmith's "Deserted Village" (1770) where the "rural virtues leave the land" (l. 398) and "sweet Poetry ... Still first to fly where sensual joys invade" (ll. 407-408) leaves for the Americas to avoid sensuality and the "rage of gain".

The long central section of the poem (ll. 23-117), which places Chatterton in a tradition of neglected poets who commit suicide or die in poverty, opens with an allusion to Warton's "The Suicide. An Ode." Coleridge asks

Is this the land of song-ennobled line?
Is this the land, where Genius ne'er in vain
Pour'd forth his lofty strain? (ll. 23-25)

Warton at first sympathized with the poet who committed suicide:

"Is this," mistaken Scorn will cry,
"Is this the youth, whose genius high
Could build the genuine rhyme?" (ll. 37-39)

Yet Warton's poem ends with a warning against excessive sympathy with the religious guilt of suicide, yet still retains some feeling for the poet. Coleridge forsakes a conventional moral stance and blames, not the poet, but the culture that neglected Chatterton and, as legend had it, permitted Spenser to die of hunger. Otway suffered a similar fate: "While 'mid the pelting of that merciless storm,' / Sunk to the cold earth Otway's famished form!" (ll. 31-32). Coleridge's quotation marks call attention to *King Lear*: "Poor naked wretches, wheresoe'er you are / That bide the pelting of this pitiless storm" (III, iv, 27-28) and to Charles Churchill's "The Prophecy of Famine" (1763): "Safe from the pelting of this perilous storm" (l. 345).

Coleridge was reading Churchill in 1796, since he quoted him in the Preface to *Poems* (1796). *Lear* is a closer verbal source, since the 1794 version of the "Monody" had "pitiless storm" for the later "merciless storm." Shakespeare's storm is the natural parallel to the storm within Lear, while Churchill's storm, which confines Scottish shepherds to their cave, is the storm of poverty and hunger. Churchill's phrase is thus closer to Coleridge's use of the storm for Otway, who died, as Theophilus Cibber reported, of hunger, dunned by creditors, and starved by indifferent patrons: "From the example of Mr. Otway, succeeding poets should learn not to place any confidence in the promises of patrons," precisely Chatterton's error.

Coleridge portrays Chatterton as a patriotic poet, who sings of Ella's battles with the Danish. Yet Coleridge redefines Chatterton's patriotism as sympathy with the oppressed. Chatterton "Pours the bright blaze of Freedom's noon-tide ray: / And now, indignant, 'grasps the patriot steel,' / And her own iron rod he makes Oppression feel." Coleridge quotes Collings's "Ode to Fear" where Collings praises the fear defined in Aristotle's *Poetics,* just as his "Ode to Pity" praises Aristotle's pity. Collings cites Aeschylus as a patriot who fought against the Persians at Marathon and Salamis. "Patriot," in the 1790's, came to mean "revolutionary," and Coleridge enlists Chatterton in the ranks of democrats and Jacobins. He similarly transforms Collings' dramatic emotions of pity and fear into the social sympathies of benevolence, charity, and philanthropy. Toward the end of the 1794 version, Coleridge invokes Gray. Coleridge describes the Avon near Bristol as Chatterton's haunt: "Ye woods! that wave o'er Avon's rocky steep, / To fancy's ear sweet is your murm'ring deep!" (ll. 92-93), which alludes to Gray's "The Progress of Poetry": "Woods that wave o'er Delphi's steep, / Isles that crown the Aegean deep" (ll. 66-67). Gray's lines, however, introduce the silence of corrupt Greece and the muses' safe harbor in England:

the sad Nine in Greece's evil hour
Left their Parnassus for the Latian plains.
Alike they scorn the pomp of tyrant-power,
And coward Vice that revels in her chains.
When Latium had her lofty spirit lost,
They sought, oh Albion! next thy sea-encircled coast. (ll. 77-82)

Chatterton assumes the position of the prophet in Gray's "The Bard": he "upon some rough rock's fearful brow / Would pause abrupt—and gaze upon the waves below," which echoes Gray's

On a rock, whose haughty brow
Frowns o'er cold Conway's foaming flood,
Robed in the sable garb of woe,
With haggard eyes the poet stood; (ll. 15-18)

Having prophesied civil chaos following Edward I's invasion of Wales and the murder of the bards, the bard also prophesies the reign of Tudor kings and English grandeur. No such consolation is available to Chatterton. His gazing on the waters below recalls the suicide of Gray's bard and foretells his own.

Yet even with Coleridge's criticisms of England's neglect of poets, the "Monody," as printed in 1796, remains a personal expression of sorrow, a work of the literature of sensibility, which takes its place among other complaints of impoverished poets. Thelwall thought Coleridge's versification typical of the "Della Crusca school which blurs almost every one of your poems—I mean the frequent accent upon adjectives and weak words—'Escap'd the *sore* wounds' [l. 11]—'Sunk to the *cold* earth' [l. 32]—'Love glittering, thro' the *high* tree branching wide' [l. 99]—'When most the *big* soul feels' [l. 101]—'Anon upon some *rough* rock's fearful brow' [l. 106]—'But dare no longer on the *sad theme* muse' [l. 112]—all occur in the first 8 pages." Coleridge admitted that Thelwall's criticisms were just: "Your remarks on the Della-crusca place of Emphasis are just in part—where we wish to point out the *thing*, & the *quality* is mentioned merely as a decoration, this mode of emphasis is indeed absurd—therefore I very patiently give up to critical vengeance *high* tree, *sore* wounds and *rough* rock" (*CL* 1, 216). Both versification and allusions link Coleridge's "Monody" to the literature of sensibility.

Shortly before publication of the volume, Coleridge composed a long note to the "Monody," which for political reasons he and Cottle finally canceled. The note changes the "Monody" from an individual effusion to a public poem on England's cultural state. The note was set in print for pages 177-78, revised to exclude the more incendiary comments, and finally canceled. In transcribing the note, I have included in brackets those passages that Coleridge deleted and two spelling corrections he made before the cancellation of the entire note:

Poor Chatterton! Herbert Croft has written with feeling concerning him; and Vicesimus Knox has *attempted* to write with feeling.—Hayley [who (so future Antiquarians will inform our posterity) has written sundry things in the reign of King George the Third,] describes [the death of] Chatterton in his Essay on Poetry—as *tearing the strings of his lyre in the agonies of death*! !—By far the best poem on this subject is "Neglected Genius or Tributary Stanzas to the Memory of the unfortunate Chatterton," written by Rushton, a blind Sailor.

Walpole writes thus. "All the house of Forgery are relations. Although it be but just to Chatterton's memory to say, that his poverty never made him claim kindred with the more enriching branches yet he who could so ingeniously counterfeit styles and (the asserter believes) hands, might easily have been led to the more facile imitation of prose promissory notes!"—[O ye, who honour the name of Man, rejoice that this Walpole is called a Lord!]

Miles [corrected to Milles] too, the Editor of his Poems—a Priest who though only a Dean, in dullness and malignity was most *episcopally* eminent, fouly [corrected to foully] calumniated him—

An Owl mangling a poor dead Nightingale!—
Most inspired Bard!
To him alone in this benighted age
Was that divine Inspiration given,
Which glows in Milton's and in Shakespeare's page,
The pomp and prodigality of heaven.

Cottle informed Coleridge that a Captain Blake, the son-in-law of Dean Milles, was a member of the Bristol Corporation: " 'What,' said Mr. Coleridge, 'the man with the great sword?' 'The same,' I answered. 'Then,' said Mr. C. with an assumed gravity, 'I will suppress this note to Chatterton; the fellow might have my head off before I am aware!'" With this note, Coleridge's "Monody" becomes one utterance among many, one voice in the discourse over Chatterton's memory; the place of literature in society; and the problems of class, the established church, morality, money, and patronage. In short, the "Monody" becomes a discursive utterance. The paratextual variations, the product of both Coleridge's and Cottle's intentions, lead, not to a single, limited, and reductive historical reading of the poem, but rather to a complex play of multiple meanings, affects, and illocutionary intentions.

The latest possible date for Coleridge's writing the note is late March 1796 when he wrote to Cottle that "I will write out the whole of the notes & Preface." The volume was published April 16, 1796 and the notes reflect Coleridge's political and social views of late 1795 and early 1796, when he was on a tour to the Midlands to collect subscribers for the *Watchman*, and when he was completing the text and notes of "Religious Musings." The note addresses two major issues. The is first Chatterton's character, his reputation, not as the author of the Rowley poems, but as the freethinking libertine of the satires.

This Chatterton is not the marvelous boy but the partisan of patriots of the 1770s and the literary heir of Charles

Churchill. The second is the question of class and patronage. Without leisure and education could Chatterton aspire to become a poet without patronage? The issue of the authenticity of the Rowley poems is, in the discourse cited by Coleridge's note, secondary; both the note and the poem assume that Chatterton himself is the author.

Coleridge's note relies heavily on Edward Rushton's *Neglected Genius: or, Tributary Stanzas to the Memory of the Unfortunate Chatterton* (1787), printed for J. Phillips in London. I have been able to locate only two copies: one in the Library of Congress and the other, without boards, in the British Library. It was reprinted as "To the Memory of the Unfortunate Chatterton" in Rushton's *Poems* (1806), but the later version was greatly toned down. It is certain that Coleridge saw the 1787 version and more than likely that he had a copy at hand in composing his own note. Coleridge's quotation from Walpole comes almost exactly from a two-page preface to Rushton's 1787 poem, which was omitted in the 1806 version.

While Coleridge's quotation is very close to the Preface, both his quotation and the Preface differ significantly from Walpole's actual prose. Rushton's Preface also states, "A Croft, A Hayley, and a Knox have moistened many an Eye on this subject," and Coleridge mentions the same three as sympathetic to Chatterton, although he has some disparaging comments on Hayley. Coleridge also copied Rushton's closing comment in the Preface: "Here then, ye sobre scholars, or rather ye formal owls, who have thus fallen upon a poor dead Nightingale, and with the sharp Talons of Invective have endeavour'd to mangle him in so cruel a manner."

In addition, there are three stanzas omitted in the 1806 version that attack Walpole, Wharton, and Milles. The fifth stanza of the 1787 version interrogates Walpole for belittling Chatterton's forgeries when his *Castle of Otranto* was a forgery:

Compassion, o'er thy much-lov'd Clay,
Shall duly drop the briny tear;
Shall duly brush the Weeds away
Which Pride and Envy scatter there:
Say, Walpole, Honourable Sage!

What Right hadst thou to brand the Page?
Why reprobate the great Design?
Was not Otranto's Forgery thine?
But, tell me, what wouldst thou have thought,
Had some rude Soul, with Venom fraught,
For that Offence attack'd thy Name, and cry'd
Beware the Felon's Fate, All Forgeries are ally'd.

The sixth stanza dismisses the Bristol patrons and targets Wharton: "Ye Bristol Patrons! but the Muse / Disdains to brand a petty Train; / Disdains such Pigmies to accuse, / While Giant Wharton claims the Strain." Rushton's footnote complains of Wharton's calling Chatterton "*unprincipled*." Finally the seventh stanza is a more resentful outburst against Milles:

Thou, too, with antiquarian Eyes,
Illiberal Critic, proudly mean;
Thou Pattern for unjust Surmise,
Thou harsh, uncharitable Dean:
Great Judge of Diction Obsolete,
Say, could'st not thou of Rowley treat,
And lift his various Beauties high
Without traducing Bristol's Boy?
Why fling thy sacerdotal Dirt
On him who never did thee Hurt?
On him, who spurn'd a World where Scoffs abound,
Where Genius often droops, whilst Dulness lords it round.

The 1806 version, without the preface and these three stanzas, is a much milder poem although a few barbs against unnamed unsympathetic patrons remain. Most of Rushton's poem is a gothic staging of the suicide in which the figure of Suicide persuades Chatterton:

"Sweet bard—ah why does thou remain.
"On this vile orb, this scene of pain?
"Art not thou steeped in blackest woe?
"Hast thou a single patron? no.
"Or can thy sweetly sounding lyre,
"Make stern necessity retire?
"If not, be firm, these sordid reptiles spurn,
"(Oh Phoebus glowing son !) and to thy sire return."

In 1782 Jeremiah Milles, Dean of Exeter, defended the authenticity of the Rowley poems on the grounds that the uneducated and rebellious Chatterton could not have conceived of the noble sentiments in the Rowley poems. His edition of *Poems, Supposed to have been Written at Bristol, in the Fifteenth Century by Thomas Rowley, Priest, &c. With a Commentary, in which the Antiquity of them is Considered and Defended* (1782) is a response to Thomas Tyrwhitt's third edition of 1778, which included "*an Appendix, Containing some Observations upon the Language of these Poems; Tending to Prove, that They Were Written, Not by any Ancient Author, but Entirely by Thomas Chatterton.*"

Coleridge borrowed Milles's edition from the Jesus College Library from January to May 1793, and since he did not quote from it in 1796, he may not have seen it again when he attacked Milles, following Rushton's Preface, which described Milles as "a Preacher of that Mild Religion which censures all Uncharitableness," who "has taken every opportunity to stigmatise him as an illiterate Charity Boy, dissolute, profligate, and licentious." Milles's Preface noted that Rowley has "rectitude and purity in all his sentiments" and argued that Chatterton knew nothing of the "pleasures of virtue" or "rewards of religion". Milles asked

Could a youth, thus estranged from the pure principles of religion and morality, enslaved to his passions, stung with disappointment, disgusted both with himself and mankind, (could he, I say) recommend those precepts of benevolence, morality, and religion, which abound in these poems, unmixed with any indelicate sentiment or expression, which might wound the chastest ear, or offend the most religious heart?

Milles might have in mind Chatterton's "Happiness," published in Croft's *Love and Madness* (1780), which opens with the creed of the libertine and freethinker.

Since Happiness was not ordained for Man
Let's make ourselves as easy as we can
Possesst with Fame or Fortune Friend or Whore
But think it Happiness we want no more
Hail Revelation Sphere-envelop'd Dame

To some Divinity to most a Name
Reason's dark Lanthorn Superstition's Sun
Who Cause mysterious and Effect are one
From thee Ideal Bliss we only trace
Fair as Ambitions' dream or Beauty's face
But in reality as Shadowy found
As seeming Truth in twisted Mysterys bound

On Chatterton's political views, Milles may have had in mind "Resignation," a topical political satire on the resignation of Grafton, the first four hundred lines of which were published in the *Freeholder's Magazine* in April and May 1770, shortly before Chatterton's suicide. The published lines echo Churchill's "Prophecy of Famine" and its patriot attack upon Bute:

Hail Resignation, 'tis from thee we trace
The various Villanys of Power and Place.
When Rascals once but Infamy and Rags
Rich with a Nations ruin swell their bags
Purchase a Title, and a royal Smile
And pay to be distinguishably vile
When big with self-importance thus they shine
Contented with their gleanings they resign. (Chatterton 1, 468, 2, 1046-47)

Coleridge's reference to Milles as a priest resonates with the notes to "Religious Musings." A note to line 235, which equates "Warriors, and Lords, and Priests", defines priest: "a name, after which any other term of abhorrence would appear an anti-climax. By a Priest I mean a man who holding the scourge of power in his right hand and a bible (translated by authority) in his left, doth necessarily cause the bible and the scourge to be associated ideas, and so produces that temper of mind that leads to Infidelity." At the end of this note Coleridge refers the reader to " 'Address to the People,' Page 57," a reference to his *Conciones ad Populum* where he notes that all the bishops but one had voted for war because religion was at stake. Coleridge responded:

Not the Religion of Peace, my Bretheren, not the Religion of the meek and lowly Jesus, which forbids to his Disciples all alliance with the powers of this World—but the Religion of Mitres and Mysteries, the Religion of Pluralities and Persecution, the Eighteen-Thousand-Pound-a-Year Religion of Episcopacy.

For a reader willing to follow the direction of Coleridge's notes, the references to Milles as a priest who was "*episcopally* eminent" located Milles's abuse of Chatterton in a discourse on the established church. Coleridge's position of 1795 and 1796 is, like that of Priestley and other dissenters, opposed to the unity of church and state and in favour of a return to primitive Christianity before the unholy alliance of Christianity with secular power. In the 1796 volume, Milles' abuse of Chatterton is merely one example of the abuse of episcopal power. It is difficult to see Coleridge in sympathy with the libertine and freethinking Chatterton, but Milles's criticisms offered Coleridge a chance to attack the alliance of church and state.

The second issue in Coleridge's note is patronage. Walpole's *Letter to the Editor of the Miscellanies of Thomas Chatterton* (1779) defends himself against the accusations of the *Miscellanies* editor, John Broughton. Walpole cites Broughton's Preface:

One of his [Chatterton's] first efforts to emerge from a situation so irksome* to him, was an application to a gentleman well known in the republic of letters: which, unfortunately for the public and himself, met with a very cold reception: and which the disappointed author always spoke of with high degree of acrimony, whenever it was mentioned to him.

Walpole's note also quotes Broughton's Preface:

* He was bound apprentice to a lawyer, and "possessed," says the preface, "all the vices and irregularities of youth, and his profligacy was at least as conspicuous as his abilities. Although he was of a profession which might be said to accelerate his pursuits in antiquities, yet so averse was he to that profession that he could never overcome it."

Walpole was particularly offended at Broughton's statement that Chatterton was treated with "neglect and contempt."

First, Walpole dismisses Chatterton's version of his application for patronage: "It is very seriously that I must ask you, whether it was the part of a wise man to credit the tales of an acrimonious and disappointed youth, and whose profligacy, you say, was so conspicuous?" Walpole's narrative of the events is simple:

A lad at Bristol, whom I never saw then, before, or since, sends me two or three copies of verses in old English, which he tells me had been found there, and were lent to him by another person; acquaints me that he is clerk to an attorney, but, having more inclination to poetry; wishes that I would procure him a place that would enable him to follow his propensity; I suspect the poetry to be modern; he is angry, re-demands it; I return it—and two years after, the youth is found dead ...

On March 25, 1769 Chatterton first sent Walpole writing on English painting, which Chatterton claimed were by Rowley, to which Walpole politely responded. When Chatterton responded on March 30, he probably informed Walpole of his poverty and apprenticeship along with a request for a government position. In an early April letter, now lost, Walpole advised Chatterton to stick to his apprenticeship and "that when he should have made a fortune, he might unbend himself with the studies consonant to his inclinations" (*Chatterton* 2, 770). Chatterton responded on April 8 that "I am obliged to you, sir, for your advice, and will go a little beyond it, by destroying all my useless lumber of literature, and never using my pen again but in the law" (*Chatterton* 1, 271).

To Walpole the cultivation of literature is the occupation of the *otia vitae* and for Chatterton and Coleridge it is the consolation of the *tristia vitae*. The final sentence on Walpole in Coleridge's note, "O ye, who honour the name of Man rejoice that this Walpole is called a Lord," was marked for deletion before the cancellation of the note. Coleridge quoted Walpole's equation of literary and financial forgery in which Walpole implies that Chatterton's claim for literary legitimacy is as fraudulent as his claim for financial support: "All the house of Forgery are relations."

Rosemary Ashton has aptly summarized Coleridge's own financial concerns at the time he composed the note to the "Monody": "Lack of money became an acute problem in the spring of 1796. Coleridge found himself responsible not only for his pregnant wife, but also for Mrs. Fricker and her son George, and for George Burnett too." To add to his financial worries Mrs. Fricker was thought to be terminally ill, although she lived until 1809. Coleridge's letters in the late spring of 1796 make plain his financial needs and the results of the failure of the *Watchman*. He received aid from a number of sources. Cottle gave him thirty pounds for *Poems* (1796), when London publishers offered only five.

Thomas Poole and the Rev. J. P. Estlin gathered seven or eight friends to promise Coleridge thirty-five to forty pounds a year (*CL* 1, 210). George Dyer made him a substantial grant for which he thanked him: "How deeply I am affected by your kindness, you will conceive better than I can express.—You have already sent a sum amply sufficient to extricate me from my difficulties" (*CL* 1, 218).

Probably through Dyer's assistance Coleridge received a grant from the Royal Literary Fund, recorded on its books as "a donation of ten guineas ... to the author of a volume of poems, and several pieces in prose, on his being represented to the Committee as in a very distressed situation." Finally, through the efforts of John Fellows of Nottingham, about twenty subscribers sent Coleridge a guinea each to compensate him for the failure of the *Watchman*. One of Coleridge's purposes in printing his "Monody" as the first poem in the volume was to publicize his quest for income.

C. G. Martin ponders Coleridge's sarcastic tone on Hayley: "It is not immediately clear why Coleridge thought Hayley's lines on Chatterton so bad." Hayley's *Essay on Epic Poetry* anticipates Coleridge's complaint about England's neglect of writers. Hayley denies that literature and liberty are safe in England:

If changing times suggest the pleasing hope,
That Bards no more with adverse fortune cope;
That in this alter'd clime, where Arts increase,

And make our polished Isle a second Greece ...
look on Chatterton's disastrous end.

Martin explains that Coleridge's attitude results from Hayley's lack of "any quality of sympathetic *feeling*" (Martin 397). However, Hayley attributes Chatterton's death to a vague "malignant fate," and "pressing Want's calamitous controul, / And Pride, the fever of the ardent soul," not the failure of patronage. Coleridge's note associates Hayley with aristocracy as a poet who "has written sundry things in the reign of King George the Third," a phrase that was deleted in proof as being excessively offensive. Hayley lived on an independent income and was offered, in 1790, the laureateship, although he declined it. It was not so much Hayley's lack of sympathy as it was his living the *otia vitae* among the ranks of wealthy patrons and poets acceptable to the crown that prompted Coleridge's sarcasm.

Those whom Coleridge cites approvingly, Croft, Knox, and Rushton, answer the charges against Chatterton's freethinking and libertinism and deplore the contempt for Chatterton's class and poverty. Croft acknowledges Chatterton's profligacy, celebrates his genius, and is sharply critical of Walpole's social attitude. Croft says that when Chatterton requested that Walpole return manuscripts, considerable time elapsed before Walpole returned them, and then reports that Chatterton complained that Walpole "would not have *dared* to use him so ill, if he had not acquainted him with the narrowness of his circumstances."

Croft relates Walpole's reply: "This Mr. W. calls '*singularly impertinent*.' Let me ask what treatment Mr. W. would expect from an *equal* to whom he should tacitly refuse to return something which had been lent?" Similarly Vicesimus Knox acknowledged Chatterton's poems as "the most remarkable productions in modern poetry and complained of the neglect of patrons:

There seems to be a general and inveterate dislike to the boy, exclusively of the poet; a dislike which many will be ready to impute, and, indeed, not without the appearance of reason, to that insolence and envy of the little great, which cannot bear to acknowledge so transcendent and commanding a superiority in the humble child of want and obscurity ...

The originary moment of the "Monody" in 1796 is not its first version of 1790, nor even the probable date of its composition, which may be as early as September 1794. The moment is late March 1796 when its paratext was composed, the notes written, and the note to the "Monody" canceled. In 1796 the poem is both the private utterance of sorrow over Chatterton's death and England's neglect of poets and the public and discursive expression of Coleridge's political stand. As a private effusion of sympathy, it recognizes the common plight of impoverished genius. The Preface justifies the expression of personal sorrow on the grounds that others share it.

The illocutionary force of private grief is to arouse sympathy for Chatterton and to earn patronage for Coleridge. The canceled note, on the other hand, defines the impoverished poet as a member of a class suppressed by ecclesiastical power and aristocratic pride. The reader is asked to share Coleridge's indignation at the abuse of those who wish to aspire beyond their station. The affective range from sympathy to indignation typifies much protest poetry in the 1790's. The historical specificity of the moment transforms Chatterton's patriotism. Shortly before his death, Chatterton published a letter to the Princess Dowager in the *Middlesex Journal* supporting Wilkes: "Mr. Wilkes stands now at the head of this opposition: in him you find an enemy, as long as you are an enemy to the constitution of this country; his enmity extends no further; it has nothing meanly personal" (*Chatterton* 1, 568).

Coleridge's opposition to government is, in 1796, more precisely focused on church and state and more ideologically motivated. He changes Chatterton's patriotism from that associated with Churchill and Wilkes of the 1770s to that connected with Unitarian and Jacobin causes.

At stake in the paratextual complexity of the originary moment is more than the conflicting self presentations of the private and public selves, the textual instability, and the affective complexity. The poem in 1796 is not confined by a rigid paratextual frame because as paratext the note can be located in the volume but it cannot be bound by the volume. Its use of allusion and quotation extends the note to a discourse of the 1770s and 1780s, which the note transforms into the ideological battles of 1796. It is not a case of one paratext determining one limited meaning. The "Monody" exemplifies expressive practices and illocutionary intentions conditioned by the economics of patronage, ecclesiastical and aristocratic power, and legal trials as well as a literary tradition.

The Multeity of Coleridgean Apostasy

Charles Mahoney, University of Connecticut

...for definite terms are unmanageable things. (Coleridge, 1802)

"Once a Jacobin always a Jacobin," Coleridge maintained in 1802. And 1809. And 1818. In itself, the recurrence of this adage might appear to be nothing more than a piece of journalistic ephemera, a detail rightly relegated to the footnotes by various editors of the *Collected Works*. But the near-pathological obsession Coleridge's writing belies regarding this curious formulation—repeating or alluding to it, claiming its originality while disclaiming its implications, not once or twice but on numerous occasions between its original appearance in the *Morning Post* in 1802 and its *n*th revivification in *The Friend* in 1818—suggests that it is more than merely a successfully catchy slogan for (or is it against?) the revolutionary politics of the day.

In league with its heretical relation, "apostate," "Jacobin" emerges in Coleridge's treatment as a word to watch with skepticism and vigilance. Indeed, the entire phrase, and the implicit ideological indictment it contains, presents us with a prism through which we can observe the numerous refractions not only of Coleridge's personal politics of the 1790s but also, increasingly, of his transmogrifications of politics into metaphysics in the 1810s.

With its converse insight into the modality of romantic apostasy, this volatile epigram is nothing less than the fulcrum with which we can gain sufficient purchase to negotiate the critical conversions of Coleridgean recantation, from the odes of the 1790s through the desultory journalism of the 1800s and

1810s to the "Logosophia" of 1817 and after. These six words summarize the tortuously circuitous "logic" of Coleridge's notoriously lax "foundational principles." Indeed, as we shall see, they epitomize in an altogether perverse fashion the "consistency" of political principle that he regularly claimed for himself, as eloquently as (and far more succinctly than) such habitual sites of interrogation as the Bristol lectures of 1795, numerous articles written for the *Morning Post,* and Chapter 10 of the *Biographia.*

By examining the putative logic of (as well as the spell cast by) this enigmatic adage, we can obtain a far more nuanced understanding of the critical question pertaining to Coleridge's politics: not was he (once) a Jacobin, but was he (always) an apostate?

Concentrating on this adage can provide us with an answer that will be at once more discriminating and more comprehensive than would be possible through looking at either the revolutionary Coleridge of the "*Conciones ad Populum*" or the reactionary Coleridge of the *Statesman's Manual*—or even (à la Hazlitt, Thelwall and others) through repeatedly juxtaposing the two *personae* with the intent to expose either their chaotic inconsistency or their fundamental consistency. For there may in fact be an unanticipated consistency to Coleridge's political reasoning, albeit not what either his apologists or his detractors have claimed, one better described as "hypostatic" than as apostatic; that is, closer to an under-standing than a standing-away (*hypo*-under; *apo*-away; *stasis*-standing).

"To hypostasize" is in fact a Coleridgean neologism, one concocted to denominate the recognition of a substance (or power or person) as self-existent; thus, to speak of a hypostatic Coleridge is to acknowledge an abiding sub-stance between the "Jacobin" of the 1790s and the "Tory" of the 1810s. To postulate a hypostatic union at the outset serves to underline the temporal dimensions of any inquiry into the question of Coleridge's apostasy. How long does Coleridge have to stand for his standing to count as such? What does it mean for "He Hath Stood" to make a stand? That is to say: what is the time of apostasy? As we shall see, the operations of the term "apostasy" are fundamentally uncontrollable. Whenever put in play (or even merely conjured, as above), "apostasy" elides any attempt to fix the terms according to which it might be managed. While, etymologically, "apostasy" may signify a standing-off or -away, it repeatedly figures a standing so precarious as finally to be indistinguishable from a falling—and not an isolated fall at that, but an always- or always-already falling that can be seen to occur with reference not merely to political principle but, far more unpredictably, literary language.

The unmanageability of the term is such that any definition of apostasy as merely a standing off postulates a limit to which, in its seemingly inevitable performance of falling, it cannot be held. In this sense, apostasy is an exemplary *mot glissant*—or, as Coleridge would have it, it is a word with a *multeity* (i.e. multitude) of registers.

If there is a logic to Coleridge's politics, it is not one of principle so much as of figure, of apostasy considered as a trope according to which a standing converts or *turns into* a falling. This disruptive interruption is an operation of irony, of irony considered as the undoing of any narrative of apostasy. To represent apostasy narratively entails an attempt to render the movement of standing away (the stepping from one stasis to the next) both consistent and stable, in order that the subject might be understood to have maintained a coherence of self in the interim. When the discourse of romantic apostasy shifts to represent the standing-away of apostasy as something other than simply another stand—as something more akin to a turn, which in turn raises the possibility of a fall—the register of apostasy must be reconfigured to accommodate this new, tropological attention to inconsistency and inversion.

Irony, then, can be said to name the precipitous conversion of apostasy from a standing-away into a falling, a falling that is neither isolated nor terminal but vertiginous and never-ending, as a "once" turns out to be an "always." And it is this repetition (as it is articulated in the Coleridgean economy of "once / always") that finally determines *apo-stasis* as a "state" of always falling. Recognized in the tangle of Coleridgean politics, irony does not afford an alternative to apostasy, a heading under which to explain Coleridge's "virtual consistency" or his "habitual method of disunity" (irony in lieu of apostasy). Instead, by dint of interrogating the very possibility of standing, irony interrupts romantic narratives of both his political consistency (the Coleridgean "He hath stood") and inconsistency (Hazlitt's articulation of Coleridge's "own specific levity" [7.117]). The question thus becomes, how long does Coleridge have to have stood for falling to count as such?

The question of Coleridge's "apostasy" continues to matter. It is the most telling example of what E.P. Thompson long ago recognized as "the intellectual complexity of [romantic] apostasy" ("Compendium of Cliché" 149), the "riddle" of which, as Alan Liu more recently affirmed, "has so haunted Romantic studies". And there is no shortage of possible solutions. In positions remarkably similar to those first articulated by Hazlitt and Coleridge, Thompson and Thomas McFarland maintain, respectively and unequivocally, that Coleridge "was, of course, an apostate" ("Compendium of Cliché" 149) and "that Coleridge was a committed Jacobin who then became an apostate Tory is, on the evidence, demonstrably not the case".

Of these was neither and was both at once: as Jerome Christensen (the most astute reader of the sinuousness of Coleridge's apostasy) has noted on several occasions, "Coleridge was always slightly away from a political position;...he was always technically an *apostate*" ("Once an Apostate" 464). And, in a more complex formulation: "At every point we examine him, even at the beginning, Coleridge is already falling away from every principled commitment" ("Guilty Thing" 772).

We will return to Christensen's reading as it bears on Coleridge's "metaphysics" of apostasy in the 1810s, but for the moment we might simply note that, presented in immediate juxtaposition to one another, these two brief citations reveal a crucial shift in Christensen's thinking on Coleridge: how did "always slightly away" turn into "already falling away"? As suggested above, irony can be said to name the conversion of a standing into a falling and thus to designate the disruption of any narrative of political consistency, however involuted. And Coleridge's word for irony, it turns out, is apostasy.

Before proceeding any further toward a reading of the tangled skein of Coleridge's "apostasies"—of the multeity of his apostasy—however, we would do well to sketch a trajectory of the inception, deployments, and appropriations of his youthful political squib, if only to situate both its ungovernable afterlife and Coleridge's peculiarly specular relation to it.

With the Peace of Amiens faltering and English support growing for a resumption of the war with France, Coleridge wrote a lengthy article in October, 1802, for the *Morning Post*, "Once a Jacobin Always a Jacobin," with the professed purpose of answering, once and for all, the question "What *is* a Jacobin?" and thereby provoking the English (with a decidedly Burkean indignation) into consolidating their own increasing anti-Jacobinism. While this piece is, as Erdman has noted, a "threshold-crossing essay" (insofar as it signals that Coleridge is backing away from the support he manifested for Napoleon during the overtures for peace), it is also, ironically, an essay that reveals the difficulties—if not the impossibility—of crossing or re-crossing any border marked "once / always."

For if Coleridge's purpose is to provide a suitable rationale for recantation to English Jacobins—staunch devotees of Liberty, such as he, still walking with awe and singing his stately songs—his own performance of crossing over repeatedly erodes the stable ground of consistency he would claim for himself as an enlightened anti-Jacobin of long-standing.

While the essay's polemic seems straightforward enough—to provide a detailed substantiation of Pitt's claim (recorded and embellished by Coleridge two years earlier) that "the mind once tainted with Jacobinism can never be wholly free from the taint"—it is complicated first by Coleridge's favorable (indeed, often sentimental) representation of Jacobinism and later by his disdainful mockery of Pitt's maxim as a presumptuous life-sentence passed "by those who would turn an error in speculative politics into a sort of sin against the Holy Ghost, which in some miraculous and inexplicable manner shuts out not only mercy but even repentance!". Admitting at the outset that "definite terms are unmanageable things", Coleridge nevertheless attempts to micromanage the term Jacobin here sinuously enough to "prove" the truth of what is in effect his own adage at the same time as he exculpates himself from its implications. No wonder, then, that it is "our duty to have clear, correct, and definite conceptions".

Though Coleridge reminds us at various moments that he never succumbed to the temptations of Jacobinism (and thus is ostensibly free of its indelible "taint"), both his passionate defence of a Jacobin as a sincere advocate of Liberty and his ridicule of the postulate "once / always," as applied to a speculative error, suggest otherwise.

The assertion "once a Jacobin always a Jacobin" requires, it turns out, not a counter-argument but merely a rejoinder—in this case, the blunt "we were never, at any period of our life, converts to the system of French politics" (1.372)—for, as Coleridge reminds us, the adage is not an argument but merely an assertion, and therefore cannot be disproved but only rebutted in like form.

So Coleridge does, with a signature pronouncement that he will repeat time and again over the years. The two declarations remain locked in a strenuous tug-of-war over the fulcrum of apostasy ("once / always" balanced against "never a convert"), until the "turn" and "conversion" implicit in Jacobinism itself are articulated (by Hazlitt, in 1816), after which the modality of the term "apostasy" shifts from a standing-apart to a falling-away in such a fashion that Coleridge can then "convert" politics into metaphysics—which, it would appear, is precisely what he was trying to do all along.

In the interim, Coleridge reprinted a lengthy section from "Once a Jacobin Always a Jacobin" in Nos 10 and 11 of *The*

Friend (October, 1809), as part of a disquisition on the "Errors of Party Spirit." While he proudly signals this incorporation of earlier material by pointing out to the reader that it was he who formulated "the first fair and philosophical statement and definition of Jacobinism and of Jacobin" in 1802 (*Friend* 2.144), Coleridge abjures the discriminating analysis of the varieties of English Jacobinism that would substantiate this claim, in favour of reprinting the essay's attempt to demystify the adage that continues to haunt him. "'*Once a Jacobin, always a Jacobin*'—O wherefore?" demands Coleridge:

> From what source are we to derive this strange Phaenomenon, that the Young and the Enthusiastic, who as our daily experience informs us, are deceived in their religious Antipathies, and grow wiser...; should, if once deceived in a question of abstract Politics, cling to the Error for ever and ever?

Coleridge's expostulations equating Jacobinism and heresy sound more hysterical than philosophical, and fail to address (let alone answer) the question of why one cannot shake it off, particularly when, in retrospect, the consequences of Jacobinism have proved to be such that "every good Man's heart sickens and his head turns giddy at the retrospect". There is no reason *per se*, but simply the incommutable sentence passed by the adage. The use of "giddy" at this juncture is telling: denominating a confused sensation or mental dizziness and suggesting a susceptibility to falling, "giddy" foreshadows the vertiginous valence that "apostasy" will acquire in the 1810s, and turns the "retrospect" from a looking-back into a turning-back.

Occurring as it does in the final sentence of the essay, "giddy" describes the verge from which to re-view Coleridge's theory of Jacobinism as well as the sensation attendant upon any attempt to unravel the temporal logic of the adage which he won't allow his readers to forget. How is one to survey the past when it is repeatedly conflated with and rolled into the present, as happens in the disconcerting temporal vise of "once / always"? Coleridge's formulation precludes the very retrospect that might free us from the snares of Jacobinism.

Leaving this critical question unanswered at the end of *The Friend* No 10, Coleridge abruptly begins No 11, "I was never, at any period of my life, a Convert to the System" (2.146). We have heard this before and will hear it again (1817-18). What is of note in this particular formulation of Coleridge's claim for political consistency is the allegorical emphasis on French Jacobinism not as a "speculative error" (a matter of belief, akin to an heretical opinion regarding the Holy Ghost) but as a "system" (a formal set of rules, modulated according to its own logic) and, more importantly, for the explicit characterization of Jacobin politics as a matter of conversion.

Before one can attempt to turn away from Jacobinism (before one can turn apostate), one must turn away from an anterior ideology and toward Jacobinism. Jacobinism is thus a product of an initial apostasy—indeed, of an initiating apostasy, once we consider (as Coleridge propels us to here) the taint of the "once / always" as pertaining not so much to the -ism of Jacobinism as to the conversion to it: once a convert always a convert. This shift in emphasis, from the temporality of Jacobinism to that of conversion, of apostasy, prefigures the ironization of apostasy that comes into play when Coleridge next rejuvenates the adage in the 1810s.

Coleridge's revivification in 1809 of the adage "once a Jacobin always a Jacobin" is representative not only of his insistence on restaging his own past but also his vulnerability regarding the past, both the status of his personal history and the operations of past tenses. Can the past (whether earlier political positions or antecedent conversions) be treated *as such* when organized under the heading "once / always"? The greater the lapse of time, the more susceptible Coleridge becomes to the curious, somehow binding temporality of his own adage.

This sense of the progressive time of the past is complicated for us, as it was for his contemporary readers, by the knowledge of Coleridge's susceptibility to charges of having been once—and thus still—a Jacobin. Robert Southey, Coleridge's accomplice in the pantisocratic scheme of 1794-95 (which, predicated as it was upon the communality of property, bluntly violates Coleridge's later claims always to have endorsed the rights pertaining to individual property), was quick to vent his irritation with Coleridge's insufferable "canting" and downright manipulation of the past in *The Friend*, writing to a correspondent, "It is worse than folly, for if he was not a Jacobine, in the common acceptation of the name, I wonder who the Devil was.

I am sure I was, am still, and ever more shall be". What is at stake in the objections of Southey and others to Coleridgean historicism is not simply the question of whether Coleridge was or was not a Jacobin according to the "common acceptation of the name," but whether, despite Coleridge's self-congratulatory claims to the contrary, the term itself can be governed. Never hesitating to assume for himself the merit of having been the first to have "explicitly defined and analyzed the nature of Jacobinism," Coleridge even goes to far in the *Biographia* as to claim that "I both rescued the word from remaining a mere term of abuse, and put on their guard many honest minds, who even in their heat of zeal against jacobinism, admitted or supported [its worst] principles" (1.217). Whether or not it was "fair and philosophical," Coleridge's 1802 analysis of the nomenclature of the term Jacobin repeatedly provides his "honest mind" with sufficient latitude in his oblique evasions of every accusation of ever having been one.

Beyond the barbed *j'accuse!* of the contemporary responses to Coleridge's performances of political versatility, the abiding significance of these repeated juxtapositions and conflations of the 1790s with the 1810s has more to do with the propriety and manageability of the terms themselves. Coleridge's concern at the outset of his 1802 essay—that "definite terms are unmanageable things," either bereft of any meaning whatsoever or hampered by too many—is all the more the case in the period between the composition of Chapter 10 of the *Biographia* (autumn 1815) and the re-publication of "Once a Jacobin Always a Jacobin" in the three-volume edition of *The Friend* (1818), and at no time more than the winter of 1816-17, when England was beset by a series of calamities (literary as well as political) which did not merely recall the tumultuousness of the 1790s but largely restaged them.

Chief amongst these was the pirated publication, in February, 1817, of Southey's jacobinical drama of 1794, *Wat Tyler*. The publication of this seemingly insignificant piece of juvenilia ignited a ferocious public debate regarding the status of English Jacobinism and apostasy, a debate which can be read as a critical referendum on the validity of Coleridge's adage and its ties to the modality of romantic apostasy.

Within a month of the appearance of *Wat Tyler*, Southey had been accused of sedition in the House of Commons not once but twice (by Henry Brougham and William Smith) and was further ridiculed by Hazlitt in the *Examiner* for disclaiming the "hypostatical union" between the dramatic poet of *Wat Tyler* and the critic of "On Parliamentary Reform," his vehement and nearly simultaneous attack in the *Quarterly Review* on the seditious liberties of the press (7.169). Soon thereafter, Southey defended himself in a letter to the *Courier*, prompting Coleridge to write a four-part vindication for the same paper, all the while Hazlitt and Hunt continued their merciless assault on both Southey's apostasy and his subsequent *apologia*, the *Letter to William Smith*.

Southey was moved to rebut Smith following Smith's designation of him as a malignant "renegado," and his indignation at being branded by this word in particular reveals the degree to which this climactic debate over revolutionary apostasy took shape as a struggle for control over several notoriously unmanageable terms—to wit, Jacobin, apostate, and now renegado—as well as over the problem of consistency, political or otherwise. More precisely, the furor provoked by *Wat Tyler* prompted Coleridge to re-examine the efficacy of his pet adage and finally to forge a way out of its previously binding atemporality. It catalysed his transformation of apostasy from a political dilemma into a metaphysical principle.

When revising *The Friend* in the spring of 1817, Coleridge introduced a footnote à propos his inclusion, yet again, of the extract from the self-consuming article of 1802 exculpating him from any charge of youthful Jacobinism. Reminding his readers that what followed was "the first philosophical appropriation of a precise import to the word Jacobin," Coleridge went on to note that "the whole Essay has a peculiar interest to myself at the present moment, (1 May 1817) from the recent notorious publication of Mr. Southey's juvenile Drama, the Wat Tyler, and the consequent assault on his character by an M.P. in his senatorial capacity" (*Friend* 1.221). Dating the present as precisely as he does, Coleridge brings his own writing of the moment (the four-part "Mr. Southey and Wat Tyler" of March-April 1817) into collision with the entirety of "Once a Jacobin Always a Jacobin."

The "present moment" designates not only the "now" of discourse but, of greater consequence, the time that will interrupt the vise-like grip of "once / always" on Coleridge's thinking about consistency and selfhood. As such, it operates as a fulcrum, the apex over which Coleridge lists as he begins to abjure the putative stasis of Jacobinism in formulating the apo-stasis and, finally, the falling of apostasy. The opportunity to defend Southey enabled Coleridge to shake off the binding decree of "once a Jacobin always a Jacobin" and formulate an economy of conversion in such a way that it would no longer be necessary for him to maintain the illusion that he had never been a Jacobin. Indeed, Coleridge's *apologia* ought to be considered not as a defence of but a eulogy on apostasy.

Taking exception to Smith's aspersions regarding the virulence and fury of the renegade, Coleridge presumed to explain in the *Courier* that "it is natural and necessary for a renegade ... to be more violent than another":

> He is ashamed of the errors he has committed, he regards those who delude others into such errors as the worst of men; and feeling the pangs of remorse, he seeks to make reparation for his sins, by preventing others from falling onto similar courses. He has been stung, knows the mischief of the poison, and cautions society.

It is in his capacity as defender of the faith, then, that the apostate emerges from Coleridge's defence as a member of a new clerisy—those select few who know just enough about the dangers of Jacobinism to warn others of the armed jacobin revolution that seemed imminent in 1816-17. This is the crux of what we might call Coleridge's construction of heroic apostasy, of apostasy in terms of clerisy, a position he maps out with even greater élan in the final article, where we are to consider the apostate not as a political opportunist but as "the Shield-Bearer of the Faith, the Crusher of Heresy":

> Had no other fragments of the works of the heretic Faustus been preserved but those in which he calls St. Augustine, Apostate and Deserter, yet these would have been amply sufficient to make it *certain* that Faustus himself had remained a Manichean. The very hatred attached to the name Apostate is the clearest proof that the most puissant and formidable enemies, are those who have themselves held the same doctrines, who are familiar therefore with all the sophisms which had ensnared them..., and who above all are able and eager to detail the fatal consequences of the error, with an authorised voice of warning, and the strong, persuasive eloquence of personal sympathy.

Apostates are the greatest defenders of the faith because they alone know the sophistical attractions of the error which they have renounced; they alone are qualified to prevent others from "falling" into the same trap.

The apostate's use of violent language establishes the authority of his voice in order that he may check others before they fall (as above) and, more critically, to demonstrate that his own conversion is complete, for the use "of qualified language respecting those who are deluding others into sin, as they deluded us, would prove the conversion to be insincere, or only half effected". Equivocal language would belie an incomplete or merely "half effected" conversion, leaving the would-be apostate either suspended over the abyss into which he might again fall, or at the very least in danger of a relapse.

Indeed, how can we know that the conversion is terminal? Though Coleridge represents conversion as a one-time affair (*once* I was a Jacobin, *now* I am not, with the clear implication that neither will I be one in the future; I will never again hold the opinions I held then), somehow guaranteed by the virulence of the apostate's language, the language of apostasy repeatedly shows itself—as we have seen—to be critically unstable. To infamize another as a renegade or apostate is to confess oneself, Coleridge explains, as continuing to retain the principles "which the other had *reneged* and *stood off from*—in modern phraseology disowned and *turned against*". The shift which Coleridge concedes to contemporary usage—that apostasy is not a simple matter of "standing off" but "turning against"—is significant: the introduction of turning destabilizes an operation which is otherwise to be understood as terminal and, furthermore, completed in the past.

If apostasy is not in fact a matter of standing but of turning, how are we to know if and when the turn has been completed? The versatility of the apostasy (not merely a standing away but a turning against) points out the *giddiness* of the transition from one state to another and alerts us to the implicit dangers of a lapse or, indeed, a relapse (as "the head turns giddy at the retrospect"). It furthermore implies the possibility of a "once / always" economy lurking in the "conversion" of apostasy—both as a turning that cannot arrest itself and, more vertiginously, as the turning of a standing into a falling.

Subsequent to his defence of Southey, Coleridge's considerations of apostasy abjure the term's contemporary political connotations in favour of more traditional theological implications (initially put in play above), as appropriated and reinvigorated by Coleridge in order that he might deploy apostasy as a standing away from the divine—a standing of little or no stasis, however, designating as it repeatedly does the fall from God. Thus in a fragmentary essay from 1820, "On Love, the Holy Spirit, and the Divine Will," "apostasis" names "the willing of a station ([stasis, standing]) *from* ([away, from God]) *merely* potentially", and in *Confessions of an Inquiring Spirit* (1824), it is the Second Class of Coleridge's "System of Credenda".

Following upon the First Class, designated stasis (the transcendent cause, or "whatever *verily* is"), the spiritual chaos of the fall from God (apostasis) results in the Third Class, "metastasis" (understood as a change of state), which is itself antecendent to the Fourth Class, "anastasis," or a rise in state (i.e. Redemption).

Given the multeity of significations overdetermining apostasis in Coleridge's writing, it should not come as any surprise that Coleridge and his critics have increasing trouble reining it in. Indeed, though Coleridge may not ever have presumed to have managed the term apostasy to the degree that he claims to have purified Jacobinism, it becomes for him yet another unmanageable term when, in conjunction with his re-reading of Schelling with T.H. Green in 1817-18 (crucial to much of his later thought, including the "System of Credenda" above), he would subsume it into the metaphysical operation of his emerging "Logosophia" as an initiating fall. Whether consequence or coincidence, it was in the immediate aftermath of the public spectacle of Southey's apostasy that Coleridge began to convert a political liability into a metaphysical necessity.

Hazlitt suggests something similar when, in castigating Coleridge for moving always "in an unaccountable diagonal between truth and falsehood," he notes the versatility with which Coleridge "slides out of a logical deduction with the help of metaphysics". Here and elsewhere, Hazlitt repeatedly draws our attention to Coleridge's sinuous logic in order to expose the "perverse obliquity" of his writing and its consequent inconsequentiality. Unaccountably oblique, Coleridge's apostasy is not, Hazlitt intimates, finally reconcilable with any static model of apostasy which would attempt to arrest the "always" that characterizes its falling away.

Christensen (Hazlitt and Coleridge's most sophisticated reader on this count), argues otherwise. Reading the "unaccountable diagonal" of Coleridge's thinking more recuperatively than Hazlitt, he argues that "Coleridge makes history by turning political vacillation into philosophical equivocation," then identifying as Coleridgean the strategy "that equivocates politics and political philosophy and that imaginatively converts the former into the latter" ("Once an

Apostate" 463, 464). Christensen's elaborate reading of Coleridgean sublimation would ground Coleridge through delineating apostasy as a principle, one with a concomitant "logic of equivocation proper to principles as principles", and thus arresting Coleridgean vacillation by insisting on the status of swaying as a principle.

Such a strong reading of apostasy as a strategic susceptibility to double signification, while both erasing and remarking the stigma with which Thompson and others would brand the apostate, furthermore "turns apostasy into a kind of power", namely the power of standing slightly away from both history and apostasy. Unequivocally an apostate, according to Christensen, "Coleridge was always slightly away from a political position; never a Jacobin revolutionary or a Burkean compromiser, he was always technically an *apostate*".

Fixing apostasy as the principle of standing *always* away, Christensen arrests Coleridge's fall from principle and ironically establishes the continuity of his career through empowering apostasy as a position resistant to power by virtue of being always away, always on the verge of falling out or in with power. Such a position is equivocal in the sense that it is susceptible of being assigned to either of the extremes between which it presumably wavers, an equivocation which, "*proper* to principles *as* principles" (emphasis mine), insists on the *apo-* of apostasy as both "off" and "against."

By virtue of Christensen's complicitous sublimation of politics into philosophy (and etymology), Coleridge can be said to be always off—off the mark and away from the principled position where both his supporters and detractors would locate him. And this includes Christensen, who of course cannot always control the numerous conversions to which his own reading is liable: if always away, may not Coleridge be said to be in all ways away (*now* as ever)?

As is the case with any significant consideration of Coleridgean apostasy, Christensen's is both guided and haunted by Hazlitt, whose own reading qualifies the salutary continuity of equivocation which Christensen constructs through attending to the variety of ways that Coleridge has of being away. Hazlitt is valuable as a critic of romantic apostasy because, beyond the vigilance and severity of his critique, his own writing practice can be said to succumb to the very falling it so ruthlessly exposes.

That is to say: what Christensen means by "Burke" (the identification of politics with the forcefulness of tropes) is what, for the purposes of reading Coleridge's apostasy, I mean by "Hazlitt." Though Thompson invokes Hazlitt as somehow exemplary of a committedly (empirical) political critique of Coleridge's apostasy, Hazlitt's writing is in fact distinctive for its contamination of the political with the literary, and therefore for the reminder it provides that there can be no stable ground of judgement regarding such a self-violating word as apostasy.

The ground of Hazlitt's critique repeatedly falls away under pressure from the ever-shifting modalities of Coleridge's apostasy. Indeed, Hazlitt's pointed deployment of Coleridge's adage on jacobinism against him provides a telling scenario of the complexity of an apostasy that can here be seen to contaminate Hazlitt as well as Coleridge. If, as Thompson puts it, apostasy is a matter of *falling back* in with the forms and sensibility of "traditional culture" ("Disenchantment" 155; emphasis mine), then, as we noted earlier, it is predicated upon a previous falling—a falling out with that culture prior to a falling back in.

It is not surprising that Hazlitt should make this point apposite Coleridge's own anti-jacobinical definitions of Jacobinism (which are themselves "not slightly infected with some of the worst symptoms of the madness against which they are raving" [EOT 1.370]), as he does in the second of his "Illustrations of *The Times* Newspaper" ("On Modern Apostates") in December 1816. Questioning the "liberal turn" that has of late been given to apostasy, Hazlitt clarifies the implications of Coleridge's notorious formulation:

Once a Jacobin and always a Jacobin, is a maxim, which, notwithstanding Mr. Coleridge's see-saw reasoning to the contrary, we hold to be true, even of him to this day. *Once an Apostate and always an Apostate*, we hold to be equally true; and the reason why the last is true, is that the first is so. A person who is what is called a Jacobin (and we apply this term in its vulgarest sense to the persons here meant) that is, who has shaken off certain well known prejudices with respect to kings or priests, or nobles, cannot so easily resume them again, whenever his pleasure or his convenience may prompt him to attempt it. And it is because he cannot resume them again in good earnest, that he endeavours to make up for his want of sincerity by violence, either by canting till he makes your soul sicken, like the author of *The Friend*, or by raving like a Bedlamite, as does the Editor of *The Times*.

According to Hazlitt's appropriation of Coleridge, Jacobinism is itself an apostatic position, characterized here as a shaking off of accepted prejudices. Furthermore, while the attempted resumption of these same prejudices is equated with the preliminary apostasy as a shaking off, it is not as simple as falling back. It is in fact the inability simply to fall back that prompts the violence of the apostate's condemnation of the jacobinism which he can now never entirely shake off—"He blusters and hectors, and makes a noise to hide his want of consistency.... He has ... no feeling of any thing but of hatred to the cause he has deserted".

The residue of what Hazlitt figures as "old jacobinical leaven," however, renders such blustering completely ineffectual: "You see the Jacobinical leaven working in every line that he writes, and making strange havoc with his present professions ... [as] the spectre of his former opinions glares perpetually near him, and provokes his frantic zeal". Recalling that "old leaven" is both that residue which remains behind, and that fermenting agent which enables a rising up, if the "logic" of the maxim "Once a jacobin and always a jacobin" is predicated upon leaven-as-residue, then that of "Once an apostate and always an apostate" relies on leaven-as-levity. The levity of apostasy names a falling up—especially as applied to the case of Coleridge's "own specific levity".

In his own reading of Hazlitt's diatribe (in a second examination of Coleridge's apostasy), Christensen overlooks the havoc wreaked by residual Jacobinism in suggesting that

Hazlitt unwittingly lets Coleridge off the hook: if Hazlitt shows that Coleridge is constrained by a compulsive rhetoric of reversal, Hazlitt himself is not free of the Coleridgean figure. By equating Jacobin and apostate under the act of "shaking off," he curiously vitiates the moral force of his indictment; he formalizes change into a pattern of mechanical repetition that is more exigent than any ethical posture or political programme. Hazlitt captures Coleridge within the restraints of his ironic equation only to open a trapdoor through which Coleridge escapes, leaving behind any responsibility, let alone culpability, for actions that are compulsive rather than wicked, paradigmatic rather than perverse. ("Guilty Thing" 772)

According to Christensen, Hazlitt's indictment loses its force when, in inscribing Jacobinism within apostasy as a pattern of repetition that is finally mechanical, it relieves Coleridge from any sort of responsibility for his actions and thereby sets him free. But perhaps that is exactly the "force" of Hazlitt's critique: if apostasy is unavoidable, then not only is Hazlitt subject to it himself (the real trapdoor here), but its never-ending economy (whether figured in terms of falling or of fermentation) gives it a far more radical agency than either Hazlitt or Christensen seems to realise.

Although Coleridge may "leave behind" any responsibility, he cannot, according to Hazlitt, so easily leave behind the jacobinical leaven that will (mechanically?) continue to rise up and implicate him.

While Coleridge may "escape" via a slide from logic to metaphysics (the performance of the sublimation that Christensen previously read), it does not follow that he will then be free from the "necessity of yielding to the slightest motive". As a "pattern of *mechanical* repetition," operating without the exercise of thought or volition, apostasy can not be stopped by the application of critical will—which as we will see, both Coleridge and Christensen (in a decidedly Coleridgean strategy) would bring to bear.

As with his previous diagnosis of Coleridge's apostasy, Christensen's reading here is valuable for its liberation of the charge of apostasy from the ethical overtones that so often determine it; what it doesn't do, however, is clarify or finally abide by the exigencies of repetitive falling it would articulate.

Whereas Christensen previously constructed Coleridge's apostasy in terms of the equivocation of his standing always slightly away, here, standing gives way to falling, but a falling which in no way compromises the "power" of Coleridge's apostasy. As Christensen continues:

Hazlitt's assertion, "*Once an Apostate and always an Apostate,*" is true but only if modified in a way that discharges it of its polemical force: "Once an apostate and *always already* an apostate" is the better, not to mention more fashionable, motto. At every point we examine him, even at the beginning, Coleridge is already falling away from every principled commitment—commitments which are, indeed, endowed with significance solely by that lapse and the critical reflection it allows.

Apostasy here is not merely a "lapse," nor even an "already falling," but an "always already" falling. The mechanics of this economy of falling seem to be already compromised, however, by Christensen's valorization of apostasy in terms of an attendant critical reflection. Indeed, Christensen's turn from the mechanical to the critical suggests that if Coleridge elides responsibility through escaping as he does out of a trapdoor, that exit is opened not by Hazlitt so much as by Christensen-as-Coleridge. If the trapdoor turns out to be metaphysically rather than ironically hinged, it can be seen to be held open by Christensen, who, in his apocryphal reading of Coleridge's apostasy, turns to Coleridge's notebooks to explicate what he terms a "metaphysics of apostasy".

In an important 1818 entry on Schelling's "two fundamental errors" with regard to the "establishment of Polarity in the Absolute," (in the *Einleitung zu seinem Entwurf eines Systems der Naturphilosophie*) Coleridge attempts, according to Christensen's reading, to construct "apostasis as the crucial articulation of a cosmogonic paradigm that would take account of the law of polarity and yet preserve the determinant, singular unity of an absolute". As cited by Christensen, the entry reads as follows:

> ...there must be the way downwards and the way upwards—but this is because there are two spheres,...the Plenitude and nature—the way downwards commencing with the Fall from God, Apostasy—the path of transit with the Chaos and the *descent* of the Spirit—the way upwards with the genesis of Light.—Thus in my Logosophia I have four great Divisions, I. That which is neither ascent or descent—for instead of a way, it's that "*from* which" and "to which," not a road at all, but at once the starting-post, and the Goal.—Call it then Stasis. II. Apostasy or the way downwards. III. Metastasis. IV. The way upwards. More neatly thus: I. Stasis II. Apostasy III. Metastasis IV. Anastasis.

Repeating Coleridge's immediate query, "Well but what is the use of all this?", Christensen clarifies:

> The use, clear from our neo-Hazlittian perspective, lies in the transformation of "*Once an Apostate and always an Apostate*" into a cosmogonic crux. Apostasy is the crucial, or rather, the *critical* stage of Coleridge's paradigm because it is the first break in the stasis that precedes all paradigms, the *standing away* that precipitates the creation. (773; emphasis mine)

While this makes a great deal of sense as a distillation of such a significant Coleridgean meditation, *our* neo-Hazlittian perspective suggests a somewhat different reading. Whereas he previously championed Hazlitt's maxim for its insight into the Coleridgean modality of an always already falling, Christensen now withdraws from the implication of always falling in this climactic deployment of apostasy as a "*standing* away." As an always falling, apostasy doesn't precipitate creation so much as chaos (according to the order of Coleridge's Logosophia), and it remains for metastasis to check this fall. Indeed, as the medial position which arrests the movement downward and re-orients its "path of transit," metastasis is far more crucial to the coherence of the Logosophia. Rhetorically, as a rapid transition from one point to another, metastasis enables Coleridge *and* Christensen to escape the precipitous state of always falling that is proper to apostasy *as* apostasy.

My point here is not to quibble with Christensen

regarding an arcanely apposite entry in Coleridge's notebooks but rather, in pointing out the way in which Christensen's reading falls away from its own most challenging insight (namely, the implications of thinking apostasy as a formalized "pattern of mechanical repetition"), to focus on the unpredictable yet seemingly unavoidable exigencies of apostasy from which the critical discourse on apostasy is not immune. While the escape into metaphysics (Coleridge's or Christensen's) depends on the sleight of falling back upon a strict etymological denotation, such a construction is explicitly at odds with the usage of apostasy that is everywhere apparent in Coleridge's notebook (in terms of "the Fall ... the *descent* ... [and] the way downwards") as a falling and a lapse.

Perhaps what is needed here is a different lexicon for apostasy, one more representative of the elusive operations of such a perverse *mot glissant*: slipping in this manner, apostasy revolts (in line with a second, Greek usage of *stasis* as faction and strife), and operates more like *catapipty* (*cata*-down; *pipto*-to fall), if not *apopipty* (to fall away; to fall and end up in a different place). Indeed, the word that the turn to (or is it against?) metaphysics really needs is *apocatapipty* (an apart-downward falling), a neologism so appropriate to the economy of Coleridgean apostasy that one would like to imagine his assent scribbled in the margins with a simple *stet*.

LABOUR, LEISURE, AND THE YEOMAN IN COLERIDGE'S WRITINGS

In the republican tradition, from Aristotle through James Harrington, leisure was essential to the cultivation of civic virtue; labour—associated with the oikos rather than the polis—was not. In the late eighteenth-century, however, some democratic republicans celebrated the yeoman, who cultivated civic virtue through both his leisure and his labour. As a union of ancient opposites, the yeoman was a compelling but politically unstable character in republican theory, as suggested in the work of Jefferson and Rousseau.

The same is true of the yeoman in Coleridge's and Wordsworth's early writings. Both writers began the 1790s convinced that in the yeoman one found the political realization of both labour and leisure. By mid-decade, Wordsworth no longer believed this, emphasizing instead the moral—rather than civic—value of landed property (the site of labour and leisure). Coleridge, too, came to question the significance of landed property, but not the significance of civic virtue; instead, he investigated new means to realizing that political condition, including a free press and a clerisy.

In his Politics, Aristotle described how the labour of slaves and women in the oikos enables citizens to have the leisure necessary to act with virtue in the polis. James Harrington, the most important of the seventeenth-century English republican philosophers, developed this same idea in his Oceana (1656). As J.G.A. Pocock argued in his seminal study of the modern republican tradition, The Machiavellian Moment, "the end of land [in Oceana] is not profit but leisure: the opportunity to act in the public realm or assembly, to display virtue". As Pocock and other historians have shown, Harrington's ideas formed the basis of an eighteenth-century "country republican" tradition, emphasizing the necessity of rural leisure for the ruling class to cultivate civic virtue.

Rural physical labour, too, was associated with virtue in the eighteenth century, though a moral rather than a political virtue, as those who labored were generally not yet recognized as political beings. Through the middle of the eighteenth century, republican theorists, at least, retained a highly elitist understanding of the nature of rule. This changed though with the new interest in democracy in the late eighteenth century. Republicans schooled in Harrington were faced with the question of increased participation in the commonwealth, and those that believed in democracy began to imagine how everyone—every free white man, that is—could cultivate the civic virtue necessary for participation in government.

Where Harrington's landed citizen would have relied upon a class of laborers to cultivate his property (just as Aristotle's citizens had), the democratic republicans of the eighteenth century described a citizen who not only held land but also worked that land himself. For these democratic republicans, rural labour, like rural leisure, came to signify political virtue, and the figure in which both politicized labour and leisure could be found was the yeoman farmer.

Highly compelling in this way, the yeoman was nevertheless a politically unstable figure, for the meanings of his leisure and of his labour could easily drift in opposite directions. Leisure, after all, had always been the province of the few, and it had time-honored associations with a conservative rural—that is, anti-urban and anti-commercial—elitism. In contrast, labour had long stood for the moral (though not political) worth of the humble working man. Its politicization in the late eighteenth century represented one of the most progressive developments in republican theory. Because of this unstable combination within the figure of the yeoman, commentators have often been perplexed by the politics ascribed to this figure by late-eighteenth-century writers: the debates that have centered upon the significance of Rousseau's yeoman, say, or Jefferson's, come immediately to mind. This essay examines the equally complex status of the yeoman in the political thought of Wordsworth and Coleridge in the 1790s.

While little criticism of Wordsworth and Coleridge has focused primarily on the yeoman in their writings, scholars have thoroughly established the republicanism of these two writers in the early 1790s. And, until recently, there was also consensus among scholars that this republicanism ended with the Terror and Wordsworth's and Coleridge's subsequent "apostasy," as E.P. Thompson put it. By and large, this remains the view of Coleridge: progressive democrat before the Terror, reactionary elitist after. But the same is not true of Wordsworth: the major criticism of the last two decades has argued either for the poet's early conservatism or his late progressivism. Focusing on the status of the yeoman in these two authors' 1790s writings, I reach the opposite conclusion in both cases: that when it comes to Wordsworth, Thompson's thesis basically still makes sense—but not actually when it comes to Coleridge. That is, while both Wordsworth and Coleridge began the decade committed to the yeoman and the republican principles he symbolized, by the decade's end only Coleridge did. For Wordsworth by the mid-nineties, the yeoman's leisure took on only moral (rather than political) significance. Coleridge, in contrast, continued to understand leisure in the political, republican sense: as the basis for civic reflection and action. By the end of the decade, however, Coleridge concluded that the overworked yeoman was incapable of converting what little free time he had into true civic virtue, and Coleridge therefore began to examine means other than propertied leisure for realizing one's political worth, such as a free press and (later) a clerisy.

This focus on the status of the yeoman throughout the 1790s writings of Wordsworth and Coleridge, then, reveals two things. One is that republican theory remained a vibrant tradition at the turn of the century in the hands of Coleridge, who sought to articulate new means, other than propertied leisure, for citizens to realise their political existence. Coleridge's work was consequently invaluable to nineteenth-century liberals such as Ralph Waldo Emerson, John Stuart Mill, and Matthew Arnold, who, while committed to newer liberal ideas like progress, individualism, and the extension of rights to more people, continued to value the same old civic virtues at the heart of the republican tradition. A second thing revealed by this focus on the yeoman is the evaporation by the mid-nineties of any constructive political programme in Wordsworth's writings, due to his new and exclusively moral understanding of leisure. Instead, Wordsworth's writings, while suggestive morally (to Mill and Arnold, not least), provided nineteenth-century liberals with nothing in political terms beyond a critique of their emerging liberalism, what I will call in conclusion a "country" rhetoric that was also heard in writers like Carlyle and Cobbett.

Wordsworth's and Coleridge's Yeoman in the Early 1790s

Wordsworth went to Switzerland in 1790 with an idealized understanding of the yeoman, partly from his youth among the "statesmen" as they were known in the Lake country (Johnston 22-25), partly from his reading of Rousseau's and Montesquieu's descriptions of the Swiss shepherds (Chard 96). Writing to his sister from Keswill on Lake Constance on September 6, 1790, Wordsworth expressed his disappointment with the Swiss citizens he had actually met but concluded that "it must be remembered that we have had little to do but with innkeepers, and those corrupted by perpetual intercourse with strangers [...]." "[H]ad we been able to speak the language [...] and had time to insinuate ourselves into their cottages," he surmised, "we should probably have had as much occasion to admire the simplicity of their lives as the beauties of their country" (Early Letters 35).

The Swiss shepherd was of course a popular idea among the revolutionary French, too, as this passage from the republican Bishop Grégoire suggests, delivered in a sermon which Wordsworth, on his second trip to France, most likely attended in Blois on March 3, 1792:

On the brow of the mountains of [...] the Alps one often still finds man in all his dignity, gifted with exquisite reason, manly virtue, and even crowned with broad understanding; [...] it is [...] there that at the head or the rear of his flocks he marches carrying a sword, a crook, and some books.

At the time, Wordsworth was finishing his Descriptive Sketches (1791-92) memorializing his earlier European tour, and his description of the shepherd-citizen follows Grégoire's closely. Wordsworth describes Rousseau's first man: "nature's child" disdainful of all above him except God and doing "all he wish'd and wish'd but what he ought". Then he describes the contemporary Swiss citizen, who retains "traces of primaeval Man":

The native dignity no forms debase,
The eye-sublime, and surly lion-grace.
The slave of none, of beasts alone the lord,
He marches with his flute, his book, and sword
[...] 530-533

The distinctive emphases of the yeoman ideal—represented by his implements of both labour and leisure—are both obvious here.

The idealized shepherd shows up again in Wordsworth's

unpublished 1793 letter to a different bishop, the Bishop Watson of Llandaff. Bishop Watson had protested the execution of Louis XVI in a January 1793 sermon, and, in response, Wordsworth wrote a vigorous (though never mailed) defence of the Jacobins in either February or June of the same year.

His letter emphasizes the same points Harrington did about the agrarian—including a deistic understanding of the republic within the cosmos, the nearly sacred importance of self-governance, and the indispensability of a rotating Parliament (Chard 83-91)—but Wordsworth's most passionate prose is dedicated to a defence of the people's ability to choose virtuous representatives (pace Watson's skepticism), his final proof being the Swiss shepherd. "[G]overnments formed on [a representative republican] plan," he argues, "proceed in a plain and open manner [...]. [A]nd, at the same time, as it would no longer be their interest to keep the mass of the nation in ignorance, a moderate portion of useful knowledge would be universally disseminated.

If your lordship has travelled in the democratic cantons of Switzerland you must have seen the herdsman with the staff in one hand and the book in the other" (Prose 39). Proof, in short, of the shepherd's civic virtue and his republican readiness for representative democracy can be found in both his honest labour and his reflective leisure, symbolized by his staff and book.

Thanks to his and Robert Southey's letters in the early 1790s about "pantisocracy," Coleridge's youthful commitment to the yeoman is even better known than Wordsworth's. Like Wordsworth, Coleridge had read the important French sources, particularly Rousseau (Holmes 62). Unlike Wordsworth, Coleridge had also read many popular reports about life in late-century America, most of which exaggerated the amount of leisure time enjoyed by independent farmers there.

The Girondist J.P. Brissot de Warville in his Travels in the United States (1794), for example, noted with some disappointment that while "[a] man in that country works scarcely two hours in a day for the support of himself and family[,] he passes most of his time in idleness, hunting or drinking" (qtd. in Eugenia 1072). (Coleridge would later cite Brissot at length on the duty of Spartan living in a February 1795 lecture [Lectures 45].)

The ample leisure of the yeoman was essential to Coleridge's and Southey's vision of pantisocracy, for they believed that during this leisure time the yeoman would be engaged in the civic reflections and actions required for effective self-governance, as Thomas Poole, their older friend and experienced Devonshire farmer, reported in a September 22, 1794 letter:

Twelve gentlemen of good education and liberal principles are to embark with twelve ladies in April next [...]. [Coleridge and Southey's] opinion was that they should settle in a delightful part of the new back settlements; that each man would labour two or three hours in a day, the produce of which labour would, they imagine, be more than sufficient to support the colony [...]. The produce of their industry is to be paid up in common for the use of all; and a good library is to be collected, and their leisure hours are to be spent in study, liberal discussions, and the education of their children [...].qtd. in Eugenia 1072

In Southey's vision of pantisocracy, leisure and labour are equal signs of the political worthiness of the enterprise: "When Coleridge and I are sawing down a tree we shall discuss metaphysics; criticise poetry when hunting a buffalo, and write sonnets whilst following the plow" (Southey 72).

Wordsworth's Yeoman and Coleridge's Republicanism in the Late 1790s

Crossing into the late 1790s, we now find a very different Wordsworth, at least if we remain focused on the status of the yeoman in his writing. For while Wordsworth continues to emphasize the importance of leisure to the yeoman, that leisure is no longer political (as signified once by the book and sword, for example) but moral, dedicated strictly to the cultivation of domestic affections. The point can be made most efficiently by citing two letters Wordsworth wrote to others (in 1801, actually) about Lyrical Ballads. In a January 14, 1801 letter to Charles James Fox, Wordsworth asks the leading Whig MP to turn his attention to the "rapid decay of the domestic affections among the lower orders of society" (Early Letters 260). Wordsworth traces this decay to the spread of manufactures throughout the country, heavy war taxes, and the new welfare state, including workhouses and soup-shops. "[T]he bonds of domestic feeling among the poor," he argues, "have been weakened, and in innumerable instances entirely destroyed". Wordsworth then explains to Fox that this great loss is what he hoped to capture in two poems in particular:

In the two poems, 'The Brothers' and 'Michael' I have attempted to draw a picture of the domestic affections as I know they exist amongst a class of men who are now almost confined to the north of England. They are small independent proprietors of land here called statesmen, men of respectable education who daily labour on their own little properties. The domestic affections will always be strong amongst men who live in a country not crowded with population, if these men are placed above property.

But if they are proprietors of small estates, which have descended to them from their ancestors, the power which these affections will acquire amongst such men is inconceivable by those who have only had an opportunity of observing hired labourers, farmers, and the manufacturing Poor. Their little tract of land serves as a kind of permanent rallying point for their domestic feelings [...]. This class of men is rapidly disappearing.

That Wordsworth was particularly interested in his poetic portrait of the yeoman or statesman is also apparent in a letter he wrote Thomas Poole later that year, April 9, to inquire if "Michael" in fact hit the mark:

I have attempted to give a picture of a man, of strong mind and lively sensibility, agitated by two of the most powerful affections of the human heart; the parental affection, and the love of property, landed property, including the feelings of inheritance, home, and personal and family independence.

This Poem has, I know, drawn tears from the eyes of more than one—persons well acquainted with the manners of the Statesmen, as they are called, of this country; and, moreover persons who never wept, in reading verse, before. This is a favourable augury for me. But nevertheless I am anxious to know the effect of this Poem upon you, on many accounts; because you are yourself the inheritor of an estate which has long been in possession of your family; and, above all, because you are so well acquainted, so familiarly conversant with the language, manners, and feeling of the middle order of people who dwell in this country.

Early Letters 266-67

In 1801 what matters about the yeoman to Wordsworth are his "affections," a domestic sensibility which includes "the feelings of [...] independence." Where independence in 1792-93 had meant the guarantee of civic virtue, symbolized in the book and sword, Wordsworth now views independence as a rare and valuable feeling whose loss is to be regretted on moral grounds but not political ones. Like a country republican, Wordsworth recognizes the threat of modernity to rural virtues; however, Wordsworth seems no longer interested in the once concomitant ideal of self-government, only in the private cultivation of domestic affections.

There would seem to be ample evidence in his late 1790s letters and poetry that Coleridge remained as preoccupied with the yeoman as Wordsworth. In the fall of 1796, in particular, when he was planning his new life as a farmer in Stowey, Coleridge becomes almost delirious about yeoman life. But in his lectures, if not in his day-to-day life, Coleridge was in fact rapidly moving beyond the yeoman ideal, imagining different ways in which a democratic republic could work.

I will conclude first by showing that even the pantisocratic Coleridge of the early 1790s recognized the limitations of the yeoman ideal and second by showing that by 1795-96 Coleridge was explaining ways all citizens—with or without land—could enjoy a politicized leisure, foreshadowing the more sophisticated republicanism found in The Friend (1809-10) and On the Constitution of Church and State (1829).

After meeting Southey in July 1794 at Cambridge and then heading west on a walking tour of Wales, Coleridge makes clear his boyish enthusiasm for pantisocracy in the letters to his new partner, opening his missives with "Health and Republicanism" and closing them with "Farewell, sturdy Republican" and "Fraternity & civic Remembrances" (Letters 1: 84-85). In a series of passionate letters to Southey in the fall, Coleridge reveals this interest in pantisocracy to be more about democratic republicanism than about a yeoman fantasy. In an October 21 letter, Coleridge questions Southey's decision to give restricted roles in the pantisocratic community to women and servants.

"I should assent to this innovation," Coleridge writes, and "I will most assuredly go with you to America on this Plan—but remember, Southey! this is not our Plan—nor can I defend it". Coleridge cites Southey's reasoning—"'Let them dine with us and be treated with as much equality as they would wish [...] but perform that part of labour for which their Education has fitted them'"—and then critically asks, "[i]s every Family to possess one of these Unequal Equals—these Helot Egalité-s? Or are the few, you have mentioned [...] to do for all of us 'that part of Labour which their Education has fitted them for'"? Coleridge himself cannot accept Southey's conservative roles for servants and women.

Coleridge's progressive view is that, provided with the proper leisure time, all men and women are capable of civic virtue. This is clear also in his suggestion in the same letter that the men assist in traditional woman's work in order to allow women time to develop themselves, too: "and what will that all be—? Washing with a Machine and cleaning the House. One Hour's addition to our daily Labour—and Pantisocracy in its most perfect Sense is practicable".

Coleridge repeats his democratic commitments in an October 23 letter: everyone in the community must "be incessantly meliorating their Tempers and elevating their understandings," and all must be educated, including the mothers lest the children be "tinged with the prejudices and errors of Society". In a November 3 letter Coleridge worries again about the status of servants. "Oxen and Horses," he writes, "possess not intellectual Appetites—nor the powers of acquiring them."

He continues:

We are therefore Justified in employing their Labour to our own Benefit [...]. But who shall dare to transfer this Reasoning from 'from Man to Brute' to 'from Man to man'! To be employed in the Toil of the Field while We are pursuing philosophical Studies—can Earldoms or Emperorships boast so huge an Inequality?

What Coleridge realized as early as 1794 is that the yeoman ideal was a perhaps unworkable combination of labour and leisure, one in which labour inevitably dominated the equation unless traditional elitist measures were taken to ensure the leisure of the few. And so, unlike Wordsworth or Southey, Coleridge began by 1794 to reject the yeoman ideal, and by 1795 he began to theorize different means by which a democratic polis might be realized. In some lectures given at the height of his opposition to the war against France in February and March 1795, later published in December as Conciones ad populum, Coleridge argues that it is everyone's duty to speak truth, "especially at these times, when to speak Truth is dangerous".

The reason for this, he writes, confirms the regulation of the Athenian lawgiver [Solon], which ordained, that it should be infamous for a Man, who had reached the years of discretion, not to have formed an opinion concerning the state of affairs in his country, and treasonable, having formed one, not to propagate it by every legal mean in his power.

Coleridge concludes with this call to action:

Are we men? Freemen? rational men? And shall we carry on this wild and priestly War against reason, against freedom, against human nature? If there be one among you, who departs from me without feeling it his immediate duty to petition or remonstrate against it, I envy that man neither his head or his heart! Nowhere in this 1795 pamphlet does Coleridge describe the ideal yeoman in rural isolation; everywhere he describes how free citizens must use their leisure time for political action.

How, though, are citizens to form political opinions if they do not have the leisure guaranteed by private property? The six Lectures on Revealed Religion of May and June 1795, based on Coleridge's extensive reading in republican sources at the time, begin to answer this question. In the second lecture, Coleridge explains how the ancient republican Jews received from God not only land (Lectures 125) but instruction (via the Levites), because their freeheld land was actually not enough to guarantee their civic virtue.

In an interesting anticipation of his argument in On the Constitution of Church and State, Coleridge argues that the priestly caste was necessary, for "before the Art of printing was discovered, when knowledge was vastly more difficult of attainment than it is at present, it became necessary that a number of men should be set apart whose business it might be to acquire such knowledge—that otherwise they could not be Teachers".

Coleridge by 1795 was no longer convinced of the tutorial power of freeheld property on its own and was instead much more interested in the free press as the best means to educating citizens for self-governance. His December 1795 pamphlet The Plot Discovered concluded with a celebration of the press in this regard (Lectures 312). Unlike Wordsworth, Coleridge was also willing to consider—though by no means enthusiastically—the republican potential of commerce. In the first number of his 1796 periodical The Watchman, for example, Coleridge sees the institution of large manufacturers as—in part—a positive development because newspapers are read aloud there to the workers.

And in the fourth number, Coleridge mirrors Jefferson, who around the same time also learned to see the value in the "comforts" brought to us by commerce as opposed to the "luxuries", in defending a certain kind of commerce, dedicated to making men free rather than corrupting them with false wants. "Whence arise our Vices?" Coleridge asks at the beginning of his essay "On the Slave Trade." "From imaginary

Wants" (Watchman 130). "[I]f each among us confined his wishes to the actual necessaries and real comforts of Life, we should preclude all the causes of Complaint and the motives to iniquity".

There are two conclusions, then, that can be drawn from this analysis of the status of the yeoman in Wordsworth's and Coleridge's 1790s writings. The first is that Coleridge remained deeply involved in republican theory through the 1790s and beyond, as seen in his commitment to two ideas: first, that all human beings are political creatures and, second, that the just state is necessarily "consecrated," as he wrote in On the Constitution of Church and State (1829), "to the potential divinity in every man, which is the ground and condition of his civil existence, that without which a man can be neither free nor obliged, and by which alone, therefore, he is capable of being a free subject—a citizen".

While some of his proposed measures for realizing this "divinity" within citizens were indeed cautious ("conservative" is too misleading a word), Coleridge never lost sight of this fundamentally republican and democratic truth. As a result, his creative articulations of different ways to realise humans politically—from the leisured agrarian to the free press to the national clerisy—were extremely influential among nineteenth-century liberals similarly concerned with the cultivation of civic virtue in a democracy, such as (to name his most famous readers in that century) Emerson in "Self-Reliance" (1841), Mill in Considerations on Representative Government, and Arnold in Culture and Anarchy.

The second point is equally important, though its significance is less clear. To value the yeoman's leisure for moral rather than political reasons, as the later Wordsworth did, does not provide one with a political programme, but it does provide one with a comfortable position from which to assail the progressive aspects of liberalism, such as the city or commerce or bourgeois individualism.

We lack an established term for this kind of anti-liberal rhetoric, and I would suggest "country," as this rhetoric echoes the language of the eighteenth-century country republicans.

However, unlike country republicanism, country rhetoric has no clear political programme, and can be used, as it was by major practitioners like Wordsworth, Cobbett, or Carlyle, for conservative as well as progressive purposes. It is the language of the "countryman," to adopt the word Raymond Williams uses to describe Cobbett, a language that precisely lambastes modern commerce for (as Cobbett put it in 1821) "reducing the community to two classes: Masters and Slaves" but only vaguely laments the loss of a world "[w]hen master and man were the terms, everyone was in his place, and all were free".

David Simpson's conclusions about Wordsworth could as easily apply to Cobbett and even Carlyle: "[his] views on civil society are much more coherent as an attack on urbanization than as a positive alternative in country life".

Chapter 12

The Poetry of Relationship: The Wordsworths and Coleridge

Richard Matlak's book, *The Poetry of Relationship,* is a difficult book for me to review. I found much to admire in this work, particularly the attention to the intertextual connections between William Wordsworth's poetry and both Dorothy Wordsworth's and Samuel Coleridge's writings. Matlak's often quite original close-textual readings and uncovering of intertextual echoes and allusions are alone worth the price of the book. However, I also cannot but address the theoretical assumptions of the work, especially its occasional dismissals of competing methodologies.

Before I do, I want to highlight the superb sections of the book and the ways that *The Poetry of Relationship* represents a valuable contribution to scholarship on the early life and work of both Coleridge and the Wordsworths. As I have said, Matlak is at his best when he is tracing the intertextuality of Wordsworth's poetry. His close readings of the *Ruined Cottage* and "Tintern Abbey", for example, are superb, for they clarify the ways that Wordsworth is countering the philosophical and formal ramifications of Coleridge's poetry, specifically and respectively the "Ancyent Marinere" and "Eolian Harp."

These sorts of close readings, which appear regularly throughout the book make *The Poetry of Relationship* an important companion to Paul Magnuson's intertextual readings in *Coleridge and Wordsworth: A Lyrical Dialogue.* Indeed, Matlak's book offers a different spin to Magnuson's approach by arguing for less a dialogic than what he terms a "forensic"—one might even say agonistic—relationship between the two poets. As Matlak explains,

In *Coleridge and Wordsworth: A Lyrical Dialogue,* Paul Magnuson argues for an opposing perspective on Wordsworth's vocational concerns; that Wordsworth would have feared his own tendency to absorb too much of Coleridge's work and style, especially in being attracted to Coleridge's meditative blank verse poems, "Eolian Harp," "This Lime-Tree Bower, [sic] and "Frost at Midnight." Wordsworth's fear of amalgamation with Coleridge's work thus caused him to misread Coleridge's meditative nature poems in the Bloomian sense so as to establish grounds for a belief in a myth of his poetic autogenesis. The reading provided here, however, finds the primary poet in Wordsworth, who would have to battle for his creative life against the remarkable gifts of originality and imitative prowess that Coleridge possessed.

In addition, Matlak makes a stronger case for Dorothy's influence on William's development of his poetic and philosophical principles, arguing for "the responsive nature of Dorothy's Journals to her brother's poetry and the resulting tension they provoke in his verse". Matlak also illuminates other influences on Wordsworth's poetry, particularly the debt Wordsworth owed to classical oration in the structuring of his "Tintern Abbey" and the importance of Erasmus Darwin's *Zoonomia* to Wordsworth's early ideas regarding the poet's relationship to nature.

In all of these cases, Matlak rests his interpretations on the undeniable proof that is close textual reading. Where he becomes less convincing is when he speculates about the psychobiographical meanings of Wordsworth's early poetry: "Descriptive Sketches" and an "Evening Walk" as commentaries on Annette Vallon's status as an eroticized surrogate for Dorothy and on Wordsworth's desire to leave Annette Vallon for Dorothy's sake; The Tale of Vaudracour and Julia as justification to Dorothy and Mary Hutchinson Wordsworth for William's affair with Annette Vallon; the "Adventures on Salisbury Plain" and the *Borderers* as commentaries on oedipal and incestuous fantasies; "Tintern Abbey" as William's effort to win back Dorothy's affections from Coleridge; the Lucy poems as fantasies about (and a secret desire for) the death of Dorothy; the spots of time, "Home at Grasmere" and Michael" as commentaries on specific events and relationships in Wordsworth's life.

These are just a few of the connections Matlak offers between Wordsworth's poetry and his psychobiography, and they make for some quite intriguing reading. However, I must admit that I was disappointed anytime Matlak chose to move from his rich textual analyses to these sorts of speculations.

What I find most disturbing about Matlak's analysis, however, is not its psychobiographical approach. For anyone who enjoys reading intimations of Wordsworth's immorality (on the unconscious level, of course), this book offers tantalizing and well-researched fare. What struck me, rather, were the occasional pot-shots at other theoretical approaches, particularly New Historicism and deconstruction, since these attacks seem to me to be just as easily re-directed to Matlak himself.

At one point, Matlak defends his own method by stating that "Dorothy Wordsworth being the referent [for the Lucy poems] opens wide rather than closes the possibility for interpretation", yet he follows this statement by closing down the very possibility of a deconstructive reading of the poems: "to read the Lucy poems most meaningfully, we cannot hypothesize that Lucy's absence means she is merely language or symbol", an approach that, he explains in a footnote, characterizes Susan Eilenberg's deconstructive reading of the poetry.

Matlak also adopts a dismissive view of Marjorie Levinson's New Historicist book, *Wordsworth's Great Period Poems*: "This now (in)famous argument has aroused spirited and even vituperous opposition, all impatient with its ploy of arguing for the importance of the text's meaningful 'silences' and even more so for its idiosyncratic selection of material that is predetermined to be relevant". This seems to me a strange critique since psychobiography is by necessity similarly limited by a selection of material that is predetermined to be relevant, given the tendency of biographies to impose narrative order to the heterogeneous chaos that is a person's day-to-day life. A psychobiography can make significant claims because of the vantage of the *ex post facto*: the determination of meaning in the retrospection of a pre-established narrative that represents the drama of a poet's life.

Besides the inherent limitations of psychobiography's narrative structure, there are the limitations that we all face as scholars—the need, at some point, to end and order one's interpretations, a limitation Matlak himself admits to: "I would wish to avoid accumulating all of the possible causes for Lucy's death that can be imagined, in other words, for 'overdetermining' the imaginative event, for that way critical anarchy lies; but *within the narrative developed herein*, with the support of corroborating evidence, patterns have been developing that ought to be acknowledged".

Given this sort of acknowledgment, I do not see how Matlak escapes the charge he himself levels at Levinson. In one footnote, Matlak responds to previous attacks by Brian Caraher and Mark Jones against the psychobiographical approach, including his own: "if the psychobiographical approach is fundamentally flawed, one would hope to see its readings convincingly critiqued". Strangely, Matlak does not feel the obligation to give New Historicism and deconstruction the same due.

Perhaps it is Alan Liu, Matlak's other imagined New Historicist combatant who offers up the best critique of *The Poetry of Relationship*. As Matlak argues in Part I of his study, "I will try to show that a clearer understanding of Wordsworth's biographical and psychological dilemmas provide a more satisfactory explanation for [the *Borderers'*] strange turns and improbabilities than do Liu's broader historical determinants". It seems to me that the superiority of Liu's study lies not so much in his approach as in his willingness to step back and question that approach at key points, specifically in his dialogic epilogue. Indeed, he illustrates in this epilogue the similar difficulties faced by both

New Historicist and psychobiographical criticism, specifically the problem of narrative retrospection:

Yet it is your very belief that we find disturbing. You have said that literature is historical in origin, and you have amassed historical context from whatever sources were available to you or that you had time to accomplish in order to make yourself credible. And on the whole, you believe that you have succeeded, that armies of context allow you to translate yourself from literature into history, from present into past, from yourself into someone other.

Yet consider the events in your own life in these past eight years—even the most joyful, frightening, or purposeful among them. Choose the most significant one—shall it be your marriage? your advancement in career?—and try to determine how that event reflects itself in your writing. Can you do so with certainty even in your own mind? Although there is much to recommend *The Poetry of Relationship*, I would have liked to have seen Matlak step back every so often and ask himself the same sorts of questions.

Bibliography

Life of Samuel Taylor Coleridge. Hall Caine. (Wipf & Stock Publishers, 2003).

Romanticism and Transcendence: Wordsworth, Coleridge, and the Religious Imagination. J. Robert Barth. (Univ of Missouri Press, 2003).

The Cambridge Companion to Coleridge. Lucy Newlyn. (Cambridge University Press, 2002).

Poetry Realized in Nature: Samuel Taylor Coleridge and Early Nineteenth-Century Science. Trevor H. Levere. (Cambridge University Press, 2002).

Coleridge, Schiller and Aesthetic Education. Michael John Kooy. (Palgrave Macmillan, 2002).

The Symbolic Imagination: Coleridge and the Romantic Tradition. J. Robert Barth. (Fordham University Press, 2001).

The Gang: Coleridge, the Hutchinsons, and the Wordsworths in 1802. John Worthen. (Yale Univ Press, 2001).

The Challenge of Coleridge: Ethics and Interpretation in Romanticism and Modern Philosophy. David P. Haney. (Pennsylvania State Univ Press, 2001).

S.T. Coleridge: Interviews and Recollections. Ed. Seamus Perry. (Palgrave Macmillan, 2000).

Yeats, Coleridge and the Romantic Sage. Matthew Gibson. (Palgrave Macmillan, 2000).

Coleridge and Wordsworth: The Crucible of Friendship. Tom Mayberry & Richard Holmes. (Sutton Publishing, 2000).

Coleridge: Early Visions, 1772-1804. Richard Holmes. (Pantheon Books, 1999).

Coleridge and the Psychology of Romanticism: Feeling and Thought. David Vallins. (Palgrave Macmillan, 1999).

Romantic Aversions: Aftermaths of Classicism in Wordsworth and Coleridge. J. Douglas Kneale. (McGill-Queens University Press, 1999).

Samuel Taylor Coleridge. Stephen Bygrave. (Univ Press of Mississippi, 1998).

The Completion of Kubla Khan. Julio Delatorre. (Nova Classics, 1997).

The Life of Samuel Taylor Coleridge: A Critical Biography. Rosemary Ashton. (Blackwell, 1996).

Coleridge, Wordsworth, and Romantic Autobiography: Reading Strategies of Self-Representation. Sheila M. Kearns. (Fairleigh Dickinson Univ Press, 1995).

Strange Power of Speech: Wordsworth, Coleridge, and Literary Possession. Susan Eilenberg. (Oxford Univ Press, 1992).

Coleridge's Figurative Language. Tim Fulford. (Palgrave Macmillan, 1991).

His Brother's Keeper: Psychobiography of Samuel Taylor Coleridge. Stephen M. Weissman. (International Universities Press, 1990).

Unruly Times: Wordsworth and Coleridge in Their Time. A. S. Byatt. (Hogarth Press, 1990).

Wordsworth and Coleridge: The Making of the Major Lyrics, 1802-1804. Gene W. Ruoff. (Rutgers University Press, 1989).

Coleridge and Wordsworth: A Lyrical Dialogue. Paul Magnuson. (Princeton Univ Press, 1988).

The Politics of Imagination in Coleridge's Critical Thought. Nigel Leask. (Palgrave Macmillan, 1988).

The Bondage of Love: A Life of Mrs. Samuel Taylor Coleridge. Molly Lefebure. (W.W. Norton & Company, 1987).

Coleridge's Defense of the Human. Anya Taylor. (Ohio State Univ Press, 1986).

The Interpretation of Belief: Coleridge, Schleiermacher, and Romanticism. David Jasper. (St. Martin's Press, 1986).

Samuel Taylor Coleridge (Modern Critical Views). Ed. Harold Bloom. (Chelsea House Publishing, 1986).

The Hamlet Vocation of Coleridge and Wordsworth. Martin Greenberg. (University of Iowa Press, 1986).

The Design of Biographia Literaria. Catherine M. Wallace. (Unwin Hyman, 1983).

Romantic Weather: The Climates of Coleridge and Baudelaire. Arden Reed. (University Press of New England, 1983).

Coleridge's Blessed Machine of Language. Jerome Christensen. (Cornell Univ Press, 1981).

Perturbed Spirit: The Life and Personality of Samuel Taylor Coleridge. Oswald Doughty. (Fairleigh Dickinson Univ Press, 1981).

Romanticism and the Forms of Ruin: Wordsworth, Coleridge and Modalities of Fragmentation. Thomas McFarland. (Princeton Univ Press, 1981).

Coleridge the Visionary. John B. Beer. (Greenwood Publishing, 1978).

Coleridge and the Literature of Sensibility. George Dekker. (Barnes & Noble, 1978).

Coleridge, the Damaged Archangel. Norman Fruman. (George Braziller, 1971).

Twentieth Century Interpretations of the Rime of the Ancient Mariner: A Collection of Critical Essays. James D. Boulger. (Prentice Hall, 1969).

Patterns of Consciousness; An Essay on Coleridge. Richard Haven. (Univ. of Massachusetts Press, 1969).

Twentieth Century Interpretations of Coleridge: A Collection of Critical Essay. Ed. Kathleen Coburn. (Prentice Hall, 1967).

Samuel Taylor Coleridge. Virginia L. Radley. (Twayne Publishing, 1966).

Coleridge, Opium and Kubla Khan. Elisabeth Schneider. (University of Chicago Press, 1953).

Coleridge: The Sublime Somnambulist. John Charpentier. (Dodd, Mead & Co, 1929).

Samuel Taylor Coleridge. Hugh I. Fausset. (Jonathon Cape, 1926).

